THE **Who**

Concert Memories From the Classic Years ## 1964 to 1976

Edoardo Genzolini

Jeremy Goodwin, editor and contributor

SCHIFFER PUBLISHING

4880 Lower Valley Road · Atglen, PA 19310

Also from the publisher
Swing Street: The Rise and Fall of New York's 52nd Street Jazz Scene: An Illustrated Tribute,
    1930–1950 (ISBN: 978-0-7643-5973-6)
The Blues: A Visual History, 100 Years of Music That Changed the World (ISBN: 978-0-7643-5975-0)
The Atlanta Rhythm Section: The Authorized History (ISBN: 978-0-7643-5564-6)

Cover image credits
Front cover: photos by Mike Barich–the Barich Archive, Piero Togni, Frank Zinn–Richard
    Martin Frost archive
Jacket: photos by Chris Bradford and Rick FitzRandolph
Endsheets: photos by Pete Minall, Paul Sommer, and Shawn Crowley

Originally published as *The Who, a Million Little Memories: Ricordi di Una Rock 'n' Roll Band*
    by Lit Edizioni, Rome © 2018 Lit Edizioni
Expanded and translated from the Italian by Edoardo Genzolini

Library of Congress Control Number: 2021942719

Designed by Christopher Bower
Cover design by Molly Shields
Type set in Dystopian/Cambria

ISBN: 978-0-7643-6402-0
Printed in India

Published by Schiffer Publishing, Ltd.
4880 Lower Valley Road
Atglen, PA 19310
Phone: (610) 593-1777; Fax: (610) 593-2002
Email: Info@schifferbooks.com
Web: www.schifferbooks.com

For our complete selection of fine books on this and related subjects, please visit our website at www.
schifferbooks.com. You may also write for a free catalog.

Schiffer Publishing's titles are available at special discounts for bulk purchases for sales promotions
or premiums. Special editions, including personalized covers, corporate imprints, and excerpts, can be
created in large quantities for special needs. For more information, contact the publisher.

We are always looking for people to write books on new and related subjects. If you have an idea for a
book, please contact us at proposals@schifferbooks.com.

Dedication

To my family: my mum and dad Afra and Marco, my brother Leonardo,
my grandparents Ambra and General Gianni, and my uncle Ferdinando.
To every Mod without a Vespa.
To every Mod without a gang.

Reel No. _____

it speaks for itself

☐ Single Track   ☐ Dual Track   ☐ Binaural

Track	Speed		Subject		Date	Footage	Reco Ti

Winterland, San Francisco, California. Saturday, February 24, 1968. © Jim Marshall Photography LLC

Epigraph

I remember pleading with the universe to please let me not forget this. Closing my eyes to hope that the visual memories would become indelible. And they have.

—Mark d'Ercole

Contents

Preface

The origins of this book are difficult to pin down. Its first conception is now lost to time, gone with the vibrations of the music that a boy from Italy started hearing around the age of thirteen. I fell in love with the Who after seeing their performance in the *Woodstock* film. *Tommy* became the redemption of the teenager I was in the first few years of the 2000s, one with many insecurities and no music that I could relate to. The Who became that music I wanted to hear because there was nothing else around that talked to my young and troubled self so insightfully.

This book was not something initially planned; it was a necessary consequence of the way I experienced the Who.

Basically, the idea of this book was generated by the rising tension between my visceral passion and hunger for the Who's music and the frustration I felt in not finding any books about them that could really satisfy it. This work is the reflection of what my thirteen-year-old self would have loved to have read about the Who from someone else; not a chronicle with uniform, one-dimensional perspectives or a tome employing a top-down approach based on information from secondhand sources, but the story of the band from the same perspective that I was seeing them: that of an audience member and listener with a direct eye and ear to their live performances, their societal stage.

The take in articles and books on the Who back then was often one from a music business point of view, with its museum-like affection and focus on how many tickets were sold in record time to fill huge stadiums, or how the band sustained the cost of all those smashed guitars, drum kits, and hotel rooms. All well and good, but what about the music? What about the teenagers and young adults whose lives were forever changed? There simply wasn't enough about the music itself or the social context in which it evolved. I felt there was a whole dimension of the band's experience and its effect on people around the world that was missing, a pulsating, living dimension to the Who that had yet to be fully unleashed and expressed emotionally.

I discovered this pulsating feeling in others, too, residing in the surprisingly clear memories of people who were once my same age, albeit forty or more years before, people deeply touched by the Who's music, enlightened by a brief conversation with Pete Townshend, or whose luck was to have once or repeatedly been swept up and flung around by the band's intensity onstage.

I wondered back then how someone might talk about the Who without referring to its audience. After all, it seemed to me that the two were one.

Wasn't Pete himself imagining through his *Lifehouse* project a new rock and roll force that would arise from interactions between the band and its audience? The Who had given so much to their audience that it just had to still be there to tap. And it was. I felt intuitively that the Who's audience must have been keeping unexpressed its most precious secrets about the band, remembrances that only they could tell, stories that would surely help throw off the fossilization of Time's shackles wrought too often from false or exaggerated myths and legends.

The research I started soon proved my assertion correct: I was told stories (many of them, and so personal!) that clarified and fleshed out myths and legends about the Who, and I was sent photos of each member of the Who, of rare and sometimes unprecedented quality, together forming a more human and intimate picture than could be found in most public archives.

I started this work—a compilation of many people's perspectives—intending to reflect and reproduce the same complexity and wonder that made these people's experiences so life changing.

Except, it does not quite happen that way. Nothing can be as complex or as rich as life itself.

But I could at least offer a glimpse of what had been, what was still there, and what will always be until the song is over.

At thirteen, I could not have foreseen that my passion for the Who would have propelled me to put this work together some fifteen years later, nor that it would be published in 2021. But somehow I always knew that '21 was gonna be a good year.

Acknowledgments

This book was made possible thanks to a variety of people from all over the world. It simply couldn't have been made at a better time than this. The material I have had access to, and the variety and great number of people I have connected with, has been possible mainly thanks to the multiple ways we have to connect with each other from long distances—at no cost. Before now, I cannot see any way an Italian Who fan like me could have had access to this amount of original negatives, reel-to-reel recordings, cassettes, films, and the people who owned them, scattered around America, England, and Europe, without traveling all over the world for years. That is why what I learned from this experience is not to demonize the new tools we have nowadays to communicate, and through which we see always different representations of reality. We *can* control what to see, and we must realize that the vast quantity of information we are exposed to is not something that is there to confuse us, but to give us the chance to witness the complexity of what is around us. In this respect, those who call me a nostalgic, given the subject of this book, couldn't be more wrong.

Anyway, I do not believe the potential of algorithms can be more effective than synchronicity, and this is why I now want to thank a person with whom I was *necessarily* meant to meet: Jeremy Goodwin. His moral and material support was uncountable. He patiently and thoroughly (and passionately, I hope!) worked on the editing of my text, enriching it with information and anecdotes that only an attentive *connoisseur* of Pete Townshend and the Who like him could provide. Jeremy is an academic neurologist from London, based in America, and comes from the same circles that influenced Pete Townshend's creative output. The meeting between Jeremy and me was so meaningful that I cannot help but call him, other than a valuable ally, a faithful friend.

I want to thank my parents, Afra and Marco, for the spiritual, moral, and material support and resources they have always given me, out of the deepest love possible, to help me realize who I wanted to be and to help me become who I am now. Thanks also to my brother Leonardo, and his alter ego "Tuisku," endowed and eclectic musician and sensitive, respectful life companion. Sorry for forcing you to play Who songs on the bass, when I was sixteen, still a guitarist, and you were thirteen. I was working on my troubled ego at the expense of others. But that's also what brothers are for!

I want to thank Chiara. I thought I had already known beauty, but then along you came. You are a really true artist and a fortune teller: all the dreams you had about this book have come true. The adventures you joined me in to rescue, from all across Italy, packages containing invaluable treasures, always shipped from America with the wrong zip code, really deserve a book on its own.

Thanks to those who were around me when my passion for the Who really burst out: to Andrea Venturi, the only person at the time with whom I could share the enthusiasm of seeing *Woodstock* or *Monterey Pop*. I would freak out for the Who, while he for Jimi Hendrix. At the time, 2006–07, we still didn't have internet at home, and we would die to spend some money to connect at some shabby internet café just to see ten minutes of performances of both artists. Those were just glorious days.

Thanks also to Laura Barchi, whom I really don't see too often any longer, but our friendship at the time is among the things I remember most fondly of those years. Our days were made of Who (and Lou Reed's) music blasted from your dad's office's speakers, and everything was just pure and easy.

Thanks to Leon Benz, who works now in Germany and whom I miss dearly. You were the first friend who encouraged me to write and who made what I was doing feel important and worthwhile.

To the cinema PostModernissimo, especially Ivan Frenguelli and Jacopo Fiore, two precious cinema adventurers, inspiring minds and audaciously creative beings. Jacopo is the best drummer in the world too. And without Ivan's scanner, you couldn't have enjoyed the mind-blowing quality of some of the pictures featured in this book!

Thanks to the Soul Sailor and our band—Mara, Todd, Manu. We played small venues, but they felt like arenas; we had pretty decent lifestyles but felt like it was the wildest rock and roll; we had little success but felt like the Beatles.

Thanks to my brotherly friend Sebastiano, who simply has always been there.

Thanks to my beloved cat Nemo, who sat on my lap most of the times while I was writing this book and researching photos. His purrs undoubtedly contributed to set my writing to the right vibrations.

Thanks to everyone who spontaneously wanted or accepted to take part of this project, and whose textual or photographic contribution (or both) is displayed inside

this book; those who sent me their material, which unfortunately, for different reasons, hasn't made the final editing; those who helped behind the scenes: Craig Abaya, Genero Alberto, Alexander Turnbull Library (Wellington, New Zealand), Linda Allen, Jeanne Andersen, Mike Barich, Dermot Bassett, Ellen Berman, Tim Bernardis, Leonard Bisgrove, Chris Bradford, Paul Brewer, John B. Brown, Max Browne, Peter Buckley, Janice Burnham, Brian Cady, Bruce Campbell, Janice Cantelon, Michael Chaiken, Chris Charlesworth, Olivier Coiffard, Glenn Coleman, Albert Cooke, Joseph Crachiola, Shawn Crowley, Christine Currie, Sam Cutler, John Darsey, John Denk, Mark d'Ercole, Alan DeRocher, Sepp Donahouer, Russ Dugoni, Frank Dunlop, John Ellis, Jon Erdahl, Steven J. Epstein, Giampiero Evangelista and Edoardo Evangelista, Michael W. Ewanus, George B. Feist, Five Sided Circle, Virginia Flavia Dolce, Ivan Frenguelli, Richard Martin Frost, Jack Garrett, Joe Giorgianni, Jeremy Goodwin, Kim Gottlieb-Walker, Larry Gross, Donald Groves, Jim Gustafson, Nick Hairs, Dawn Hall, Ian Hallam, Carrie Anne Hart (the Barich Archive), John Hellier, Stewart Hellman, Tom Henneberry, Aaron M. Hodgett, Ruth Hoffman, Chris Hogg, Bob Hollis, "Irish Jack," Mike Jahn, Kevin Jarvis, Elza Jensen, Nicola Joss, Robert Kavc, Alex Kipfer, David St. John, Allan Lazarus, Joe Leatherman, John "Spider" LeQuesne, Les Who en France, Robert Lipson, Phil Lorenzo, Thom Lukas, Olle Lundin, John Lustig and the Illinois State Museum, Brian Lux, Jonathan Lyerly, Tony Mann, Sally Mann Romano, Jim Marshall Photography LLC, Nancy Mathon, Bob McNab, Kay Mattos, Pierrot Mercier, David Miller, Pete Minall, Scott Morgan, Russell Nardi, Gerry Nass, Ngā Taonga Sound & Vision, Linda Orbeck Beaumont, Wendy Orbeck Crowley, Liz Pacini, Rich Pacini, Tony Palmer, Craig Patterson, Michele Patucca, Sunny Paul Photographer, Jonathan Pearl, John Peden, Jack Perno, Guy Perry, Al Pethel, Paul Petraitis, Craig Petty, Gary Piazza, Henry Pile, Jerry Pompili, Cheryl Prati, Howard Pratt, Alessandro Prepi Sot, Princeton University Library, Paco Prior, Dennis Quinn, Steve Richards, Rick Rieckhoff, Brad Rodgers, Bill Scarnati, Nick Schram, Jon Scott / JSGraphics, Dave Seabury, Charlotte Von Segesser, Barry Smith, Paul Sommer, Frank Stapleton, Marc Starcke, Jim Stark, Georgiana Steele-Waller, Ursula Stewart, Studio Legale Minelli (Perugia, Italy), Mark Suall, Pat Thomas, John Tilson, Piero Togni, Ann Marie Vasta, USS Mullinnix DD944 Association, John Visnaskas, Beatrice Vivani, Will Vogt, Kevin Walsh, Joshua White, Doug Wilcoxen, Charlie Wilson, and Larry Yelen.

Last, but not least, thanks to the Who. Keith: there is a reason why I can listen to Who songs only up to 1978.

John: Do I have to explain why I play the bass?

Thank you, Roger: you have sung my youth better than anyone else.

And thank you, Pete: you taught me to see that this is me, and I will be.

Chiara's Dream

I can't exactly remember when—it was probably around the end of October 2019, but I dreamed about Pete and the other boys. I found myself in London, at the end of the 1960s.

It felt strange being there, among the cigarette smoke and the city chaos. I started wandering around, when I suddenly saw Roger leaning against a club's entrance. He was in the flower of his youth. He took one hand out of his burgundy-red jacket and waved at me, smiling. He invited me to follow him into the club, as if he had been waiting for me for a long time. After walking a flight of stairs, Roger opened a door. We walked in and I was in shock. In that room, which looked like a studio, there was Pete too.

But wait . . . all of a sudden, they were getting older. They looked old. What happened? I tried to hide my puzzlement and reached over to Pete to introduce myself. He is a really nice guy, I thought.

He asked me how old I was. "Twenty-one," I replied. He lowered his head, staring at the floor, and with a wry smile on his face, he said, "Isn't it strange that people still get born?"

After a little chat, I started to feel myself at ease with the two guys, so I invited them to sit down somewhere. I had to tell them something really important. They accepted.

They sat on a green couch and I started gathering my thoughts. Pete in particular was looking very curious to know what I was so urgent to tell them.

I started telling them about Edoardo's book on the Who. I told them about the great deal of effort Edoardo took to make it, and the people he had met and contacted that he invited to participate. I wanted Pete and Roger to know how Edoardo loved the Who at the point he created this polyphony of stories and memories from people from all over the world, and I started to tell them some I remembered reading in the book.

I could not believe my eyes. I suddenly realized that while I was talking, Pete and Roger were getting younger . . . their look was changing, and they started to look again like they were twenty-three or twenty-four.

"It is incredible," I thought. "Edoardo has given Pete and Roger a second youth."

I was so incredibly happy.

It was time to say goodbye to the guys, and they thanked me for my company and especially for giving them the news of this book.

When I turned around to walk out of the room, I felt even more surprised to realize Pete and Roger were not alone: Keith had appeared out of nowhere and was sitting cross-legged on a desk.

There was John, too, dressed in a black suit and white tie, kind and charming as only he could be, lighting a cigarette and showing me the way to the door, out of that studio and out of that dream.

Chiara Marinangeli, 2019

CHAPTER 1

Introduction

"In 'My Generation,' you wrote,
'I hope I die before I get old'
—do you in fact mean it?"

"Yes."

It feels almost unnatural to associate *that* sharp answer with *that* guy, the one looking as if he would rather be anywhere but sitting on a stool in a TV studio with the piercing eyes of Auntie (the BBC) upon him. Not just the BBC cameraman or the interviewer and the studio audience, but the countrywide audience who'd be either won over or lost in a moment if he approached the series of questions betraying the interviewer's ignorance as something other than that to be gently corrected, when sarcasm would have been so much easier. What would Joseph K. in Kafka's *The Trial* have answered if he were in that specific setting? You could almost see the mind of Townshend fighting within himself over whether to educate that smug older man, walk out in disgust, or simply strangle him right there on the spot.

That day, January 5, 1966, Peter Dennis Blandford Townshend was just twenty, his almost paradoxical youth betraying an ill-concealed shyness disguised as effrontery, and maybe for the first time he was becoming aware of the generational declaration of war—his generation's—toward the English establishment that he had essentially summarily dismissed as dead and gone or at least to be avoided with that now-historic musically lyrical line.

That night, Pete was the guest on *A Whole Scene Going*, invited as the frontman of "England's hottest new group,"[1] the Who. Since then, over fifty years of counterculture and counter-countercultural evolution has been unfolding and clashing, such that today, upon seeing that interview for the first time, someone might think that Pete Townshend was just acting tough, and that his stage act was merely a "put-on," an eminence front intended to rouse scandal and shake up the prudish middle class, or . . . simply to make money. In fact, that episode hardly stood alone: the year before, providing an answer to a similar question about his personal professional ambitions, Pete replied, "To die young."[2] Likewise, on the night of August 13, 1968, following the first of three nights' performances in a row at the Fillmore West in San Francisco, Townshend explained to *Rolling Stone* magazine's director Jann Wenner that he used to work with the thought that the Who were merely going to last but another two minutes: "If the tax man didn't get us, then our own personality clashes would."[3]

Such an assertion left no doubt about the self-destructive attitude of the Who, that their music and theatrical stage act were meant to violently amplify and thus elucidate the chaotic sounds of their time, creating and then destroying their art in the process. This and subsequent interviews for *Rolling Stone* would become known as Townshend's "State of the Generation" address. He became one of the most interviewed stars in music history.

Of course, Townshend was heavily influenced by Gustav Metzger, whose autodestructive art movement rose to prominence shortly after World War II. Inherent within the philosophy of Metzger is the tension created by promoting a form of art and philosophy that depends on the wheels of commercialism to promote an anticommercialism message. Welcome to the world of conflict and resolution that lies at the heart of the Who's success. Part of the credit for that should go to such aesthetic influences raining on Pete during his time as a student at Ealing Art School, a revolutionary institution in its own right. Pete's schoolmate and photographer Tom Wright remembers Ealing Art School as

exciting—for everyone. The battle cry at Ealing was "Art is more than just a dusty bowl of fruit." The challenge was to do something mind-blowing, build a following, make changes for the better by making waves. At Ealing, there were always the "what ifs": What if

you did a series of paintings that self-destructed at the exhibition? What if you made up a language; . . The idea was to go out and do something worthwhile—like change the world.[4]

Metzger aside, modernity and its sounds were the Who's main source of inspiration, more so than the skiffle of Lonnie Donegan or the rock and roll of Johnny Kidd, mentioned by the band as some of their early benchmarks.

In this sense, the band's expressivity is strictly connected to war semantics. The violence expressed by the band onstage was no affectation; rather, it became a collective catharsis aimed at resolving the trauma caused by World War II. Rivers of feedback from huge Vox amplifiers sounded like machine guns firing, while the destruction of the drums almost reminded one of London's buildings crashing under Nazi-dropped bombs. Yet, the destruction of equipment and instruments implied something much more than that. Musically, it became an expedient to pull away the hypocritical or at best delusional veil that the escapist and popular ballroom music of the day had cast over the English culture of the 1950s and 1960s. In this regard, Townshend said during a *Rolling Stone* interview in January 1968 that in the context of a wounded social fabric like England's, violence onstage was a necessity: "The audience wanted aggressive music."[5] It is noteworthy that destruction is an antonym of generation.

And from an aesthetic point of view, as Mark d'Ercole pointed out, the iconoclastic attitude of the Who made each concert a *unicum*—a unique and non-re-creatable event in which the band, by smashing up all of its gear, precluded an encore. Everything that needed to be said had already been stated. Nothing was held back for a staged "surprise" reappearance.

In this regard, Pete told director Tony Palmer in 1968:

Our performances and our music have got much more to do with art and life than people imagine. . . . I think the most important music development we've made in pop is free-form music. Complete abandon in music, completely uncontrolled music which does exactly what it wants. We don't allow our instruments to stop us doing what we want; we don't even allow our physical health to stop us doing what we want. Ours is a group with built-in hate. We smash our instruments, tear our clothes, and wreck everything. The expense doesn't worry us, because that would be something which would get between us and our music. If I stood on stage worrying about the price of the guitar, then I'm not really playing music. I'm getting involved in material values. So, I don't have a love affair with a guitar; I don't polish it after every performance; I play the fucking thing.[6]

Last, and from a social perspective, we can assess how the Who became spokesmen for a generation of youth, or at least a vocal portion of them, a generation rebelling against that of their parents' era, one scorned for having adapted passively to the order of the day while marginalizing those who believed that there must be something more. And as with America's Flower Power generation of the mid- to late 1960s, high-profile, newsworthy movements in England were in truth a minority if loud and visual. In England, there were the Rockers who had evolved from the 1950s Teddy Boys, a still mostly young, postwar, working-class English youth hooked into American rock and roll music such as Gene Vincent and Eddie Cochran. But by the 1960s they had switched their blue suede shoes for leather jackets and powerful motorcycles, where they became relatively antifashion, holding a strong distaste for drugs. On the other hand, there were the Mods (originally modernists from the late 1950s who had been fascinated with American jazz and all things Italian, such as cafés, art films, and clothing), who only later gravitated to the music of the Kinks, the Small Faces, and the Who, albeit when the Who was in its early incarnation as the High Numbers, managed by publicist Peter Meaden. The Mod movement started as an élite generated around some tailors' shops in Soho, becoming an all-encompassing counterculture of youth. The identity of the Mods as commonly thought of in the early to mid-1960s was based musically on American R&B, soul, "Tamla"—otherwise known as Tamla-Motown (the British term and record label for Detroit's Motown sound), and blue beat, only later to include London-based rock. Aesthetically, it stood on the use of Vespa and Lambretta scooters with lots of mirrors, parka coats, American zoot suit jackets, or smart Italian clothing such as flashy tailored suits, short-collared shirts with thin ties, expensive shoes, and tidily cut, fairly short hair. Women wore shorter skirts, polo-neck sweaters, tights, and white or black patent leather shoes.

Pete becomes fascinated with the Mods:

It was a great show of solidarity, and you felt that you belonged to something. It was the first gesture of youth. We made the establishment uptight, we made the rockers uptight, we made our parents uptight and our employers uptight because although they didn't like the way we dressed, they couldn't accuse us of not being smart. We had short hair and were clean and tidy. And being aware of this uniform, we gravitated to the like sort of people. You would only talk to the girl who dressed in this way because you knew she would have the same tastes as you and would automatically be in the same age group. This was when I first became aware of the force of rock as a reflection of what was going on in the streets. It was the only real bridge between real events and getting events into perspective. . . . But we, the Who, were never in any danger of getting obsessed with the mod image, because we were not so much a part of it as a mirror. When we were on stage we reflected the mood of the kids and caught their frustration and aggression.[7]

Much later, in 1972, Pete would point out that

it was an artificial situation. I was at art college and the rest of the guys were at work, and we were more rockers, really. Trying to be like the Stones, long hair, and Beatle jackets.[8]

Producer Kit Lambert remembered the Mods as

a French student uprising—don't talk, just seize power! Don't worry that you haven't any concrete ideas of change, they will come in time. . . . Aggression without target.[9]

Originally, directors Kit Lambert and Chris Stamp (brother to the more famous Terence) were looking for a band on the rise to stardom, about which a movie could be made that would revolutionize pop filmmaking. Despite that goal, their impact with the Who as a vehicle was totally unexpected and quite devastating.

As Kit Lambert stated some years later:

The Who have always been very popular on stage. This is because they have a direct sexual impact. They ask a question: Do you want to or don't you? And they don't really give the public a chance of saying no. It is a sort of rape. I suppose that's what happened to me when I first discovered them.[10]

The encounter between Lambert and Pete Townshend must have been, to say the least, an example of destiny and synchronicity. It was as if each saw in the other the embodiment of his own ideals via the projection of music. Furthermore, they were both raised in a posh-enough environment through which a classical musical imprinting would be more likely to "take," but also one likely to foster a stand against the bland and hypocritical pretenses of the middle-class milieu. As Kit Lambert remembered:

My father, who was a classical composer, brought me up to mistrust musical snobbery of any kind. The music he was writing when he was nineteen and twenty was full of jazz idioms, which were considered unthinkable by the musical élite. When his music was played at the Albert Hall, people were shocked. They couldn't understand how someone of his talent could hang around with such as Louis Armstrong rather than with the classical musicians and the whole Establishment BBC crowd of Queen's Hall followers.[11]

Lambert and Stamp provided the Who the chance to throw off the shackles of the Mod image imposed by Meaden to finally start a management team that would give the band expressive freedom. Pete Townshend immediately recognized Kit Lambert as his mentor, a figure who would encourage him to compose what would become the Who's and some of modern music's greatest works.

Like Townshend, Lambert agreed that "none of the Who were actual Mods—they didn't look right. Mods were supposed to be pretty in a rough way, and the Who certainly weren't that."[12] Keith Moon recalls, "I remember when we first started through, how we tried to create a great 'Mod' image, . . . John and I weren't at all the build for it—I'm a bit too podgy—but we got away with it."[13]

The Who did not embody the Mod ethos as much as their contemporaries, the Small Faces and the Kinks, who were genuine Mods. The Who were, nonetheless, its best and among its most sensitive expositors. The Who celebrated and epitomized the fragility of a movement based on the suppression of a significant generational existential discomfort; in a nutshell, as Pete Meaden would later elaborate, it was a movement based on "clean living under difficult circumstances."[14] Mods essentially elected the Who as their spokespeople because they were "in a way, doing the sort of thing that most of their audience would do if only they had the courage," reported *Record Mirror* in 1965.[15]

Roger would deepen this concept by saying to Maureen O'Grady, "We put across for them our own feelings of violence, toughness, and coolness."[16]

By perpetually making changes to their distinctive traits, the Who developed an ability to adapt to changes in its audience that in turn allowed the band to evolve without departing too much from its roots. They were just as much at home elucidating the emotional turmoil of teenagers in songs such as "I Can't Explain" and "My Generation" as they were screaming the need for individual recognition in *Tommy* and, later, in *Quadrophenia*, each topic tackled being but a tile in a much-bigger mosaic.

Serving as a backdrop to their work was the necessity of self-determination, the drive of the group or even a single person to carry out a revolution that evolves from a social movement to something more spiritual and introspective. This same process is evident in the discography of the band, a spectrum of songs that range from generational anthems to more-introspective and more-existential musical compositions.

In such a picture, the synthesis between the individual dimension of the Who's songs and the collective and generational expectations of its audience allowed the band's fans to identify with Pete Townshend's bewilderments and obsessions. Thus, the sense of frustration over an uneasy look led the guitarist and composer in time to be elected senior spokesperson for the Mods. Similarly, his attempt to process his violated childhood became a generational "parabola" through *Tommy*, following which Townshend's unhappy experience at Woodstock became food for thought for his never-quite-realized *Lifehouse* project. Through *Lifehouse* he envisaged a more interconnected world in which the founding hippie ideals of aggregation and spiritual connection degenerated into preventive control handled by power—something that in Townshend's mind takes the form of a Grid, a restricting net that fed everybody with ready-made experiences from which the people would ultimately need rescuing in order to regain control over their lives. This is why it is said that Townshend's vision was prescient, years ahead of the internet or World Wide Web.[17]

From 2014 to 2016, the band celebrated fifty years in music with what was believed to be their last world tour. Yet, a new North American tour with a symphonic orchestra in tow took place in 2019. And in 2020, another UK tour was planned, halted only by the COVID-19 coronavirus pandemic. This, along with autobiographies from Townshend and Daltrey plus two novels from Pete over the years, far exceeded their own expectation of minimal longevity and in fact violated their most famous statement from "My Generation": "I hope I die before I get old." In 2020, both the surviving members of the Who are well into their midseventies, and the 2019 UK, Ireland, and North American tour promoted *WHO*, their first album in thirteen years, following *Endless Wire*, which came out in 2006. The *WHO* album's reception surpassed even the best expectations, to the point where it competed for the first #1 Who album spot in the UK charts in nearly fifty years (after *Who's Next* in 1971).

After Keith Moon's death in 1978 and John Entwistle's passing in 2002, the band found itself rearranging their whole repertoire while trying to enrich its live sound or at least to adequately compensate for the loss of harmonics and chemically explosive energy needed to fill the enormous gap left by the loss of one of music's truly great rhythm sections. This derives from the fact that although the Who could be seen musically as a power "trio," they were in fact very different from any three-piece lineup utilizing drums, bass, and guitar. This was evident at their concerts, where the canonical roles each musician was expected to respect were in fact betrayed. They did something different. That's how John Entwistle transcended the playing of the bass guitar from its primarily rhythmic role into a lead solo instrument. Likewise, Keith Moon was incapable of being restricted to the role of timekeeper or metronome, playing his battery of drums as if with eight maniacal arms in a nearly ferocious assault on the music, leaving only Townshend to hold down the rhythmic line, if brilliantly so, while having to *force* his way in to play solos.

Although such an unusual scheme became one of the undeniable trademarks of the Who, on the other hand, it fed Townshend's frustration at having to stem the outpouring of sound coming from an unbridled rhythm section, thus limiting his own expressivity with the guitar. This subject became evident in a *Rolling Stone* interview by Stephen Rodrick published on November 25, 2019, which created a lot of controversy around Townshend's statement of "gratefulness" that Keith and John were no longer around.[18] His later apology was articulate, appropriate, short, and to the point. He declared that his assertion was a very dry English way of expressing his awe for his two missing friends and fellow musicians. This was particularly so with respect to John Entwistle's musical ability, original sound, and style of play, which employed a sonic range and complexity of harmonics that used to leave Pete, the guitarist, relatively little room for creativity. And yet—out of necessity perhaps—Townshend became arguably the best rhythm guitarist of his time, one whose range of styles could be minimalist or grandiose but always musically very interesting if you listen beyond the amplitude of his thunderous crash chords. He owes much of that development to the Who's unorthodox rhythm section of bass guitar and drums, which

threatened to displace him into the role of mere spectator. His rhythm guitar style has evolved in complexity beyond his contemporaries, such that in 2015 he was publicly recognized with the Stevie Ray Vaughan Guitar Award for his contribution to music while helping those in social and medical need. Pete was introduced and lauded to the audience by Bruce Springsteen as "the greatest rhythm guitarist of all time!" This should not surprise anyone, though: photographer and friend Tom Wright recognized Pete's unique style way back in 1962, when the guitarist was just seventeen:

> This wasn't someone who just played scales. Pete played the right note at the right time, notes that not only went along with whatever was playing on the record player, but that made the record stronger and better. Meaningful. Records that I'd been listening to for years took on new layers of significance, thanks to Pete.[19]

It is difficult, if not impossible, to see what has happened in music from the 1970s up to now without taking the Who's influence into consideration. It is almost impossible, also, not to acknowledge what the band has done to and for rock music, demolishing by subtraction its standard grammar elaborating on and adding an unprecedented music lexicon. This makes the band one of the most representative examples of that twentieth-century aesthetic process of deconstruction of language and demolition of traditional canons. Seen in such a context, the creative nature of their music is always related to destructive elements and acts in the rock body of that time like a virus, forcing it to face its contradictions.

> Rock is AIMED at young people, it hopes to tell them about themselves, it hopes to gather up the excitement of being young and frustrated and glorify it. It doesn't usually mean that because the hunter gets his prey he becomes hunted himself, but you have heard of Karma? They'll get you in the end. Rock is self-destructive by its very nature.[20]

This is what Pete Townshend wrote in *Melody Maker* on December 12, 1970, in his "Pete Townshend Page," where he proved to be one of rock's major theorists. His statement reflects the evolution of the classical canons of rock and roll as carried out by the Who, both in sound and conceptual terms, stripped of its function of divertissement for the masses. Rock and roll is taken very seriously by Townshend, who recognized very early on its function as a driver of social change and generational emancipation. The Who used rock and roll to reflect the identity of each generation—a process that reached its peak during their live concerts, where, as if in an intense and somehow personal consciousness-raising experience between band and audience, a new level of self-awareness was reached.

One particular episode defined this concept well. On August 13, 1971, the Who returned to the United States a year after playing their last performance of *Tommy* (July 1970). *Who's Next* was released the following day, on August 14, and that night the band performed at the Hara Arena in Dayton, Ohio. Halfway through the concert, Townshend addressed the rowdy audience in an almost prophetic tone antithetical to his *Lifehouse* project's message of redemption through music, and perhaps influenced by the myth vs. reality of Woodstock and the mood surrounding the tragedy of the Rolling Stones' concert at Altamont, California, at the end of 1969:

> Rock and roll is all that counts. I'm telling you, in ten years you'll know, 'cause ten years has passed we know. This song is about our last ten years . . . it's about you, it's about us, mainly it's about rock and roll. It's a song called "Won't Get Fooled Again."[21]

The story of the Who seems like a constant effort to find new stylistic and compositional solutions only to be ultimately deconstructed in favor of something new again. The band's forays into new declensions for rock and roll, a frail genre of music if outwardly loud and somewhat brash, is easily disillusioned by its definition reflecting the frail and disillusioned attitude of the Who itself. This is what emerges from the picture of that time as offered by *Creem* magazine:

> The Beatles have split, The Stones have pissed off and the majority of British rock groups are splitting and reforming like so many confused amoebae "with no direction home." Yet, The Who are still in there, plugging away, growing up but never selling out.[22]

At that time in 1971, *Who's Next* was released. The Who was at the peak of its musical trajectory and *still* did not expect stability in its future. A state of tension persisted, be it latent and held back in quieter moments or exploding outward at others, the latter usually unexpectedly. The members of the Who were extremely physical and particularly gifted in outwardly displaying raw instinct. They had a particularly expressive talent for transforming impulse into sound. This is typical of those who have long endured emotive and existentially threatening exposure to the travails of life in such a way that it leads them to look up and down, left and right, right from the razor's edge, as they march further on. Each of the band members is a story that, as a band, started with strict contractual obligations marked by restrictive debt and internal tension. All four musicians were completely different from one another, yet tightly and chemically bonded. It is a career that was built

upon the strain that lies within the timing of being held back and being released for maximum effect, something felt and seen every time Pete Townshend's arm windmills, hesitating just briefly before crashing out the chords from his Rickenbacker guitar.

It is exactly that same movement these pages try to replicate, not by analyzing the Who's entire career but by focusing particularly on the period from 1967 to 1974; just as that windmill action and crash chord can provoke a shock wave through the audience, this book represents the most exciting time of the band's story—the period of maximum R&B, a growth that, as everyone knows, comes before the fall.

What you will find inside these pages are memories from those who knew the Who and those whose lives were touched by the Who. The purpose of this research is to give voice to a collective consciousness that will inevitably be lost in time. These tales, anecdotes, pictures, and set lists aim to freeze the sound of that collective voice, a sound and meaning that the Who's music seems to have always tried to reproduce. And that, especially during those seven tumultuous years, became louder and louder, and, for a while at least, it never really seemed to quieten down.

CHAPTER 2

1964-66

Anyway Anyhow Anywhere

John Hellier

The High Numbers: Shandon Hall Dance Club, Essex, on Friday, October 2, 1964

They were just an unknown group at the time. I'd never heard of them previously. I used to go to the Shandon Irish Club most weeks to watch whoever was playing. I remember them being young and fresh faced, and, unusually, having short hair. Long hair was fashionable with groups (the Pretty Things, the Rolling Stones, etc.). The other band playing that night was a local band called Scrooge and the Misers, who went on to make a couple of singles in 1966 under the name of the Attraction. I can't remember who headlined. The High Numbers were playing pretty much a Motown set, with a few exceptions, for example, "You Can't Sit Down," and a couple of James Brown songs, "I Don't Mind" (ended up on the first Who album) and "Just You and Me Babe." Even as early as then, Moonie was an eye-opener!

David St. John

The High Numbers: Waterfront Club, Cliff Hotel, Southampton, on Saturday, October 31, 1964

I started out as a rock and roll singer back in 1958 in my hometown of Southampton, England, but at the tender age of ten! Music came into my life as the new wave of American mid-1950s records hit the UK and changed many young lives. The exciting sounds of Bill Haley, Elvis Presley, Buddy Holly, Little Richard, Jerry Lee Lewis, Gene Vincent, and many more amazing USA artists could be heard at high volume on jukeboxes in the new wave of coffee bars across the country. We played the 45s and LPs on our own record players, as each year brought a taste of American culture to our drab postwar years.

As a young lad, I used to sit in coffee bars and ask the teenagers to play my favorite hits, and I sang along with them so quickly knew many lyrics. This led me to singing at Teen Dance Nights on the Royal Pier Ballroom near Southampton Docks and other local ballrooms in the area, but I was under the legal age of twelve for public appearances. The school found out, so at the age of ten—I had to retire! I kept on singing in pubs and clubs and pubs for a few years, but only with the backing of a piano player and a drummer, but also made music with a few friends. The skiffle boom had also inspired many youngsters, and I had a cheap guitar, learnt a few chords as my pals knocked out the music on tea-chest bass (broom handle attached to string on a tea-chest from the Docks), plus washboard and basic drum kits.

The 1960s swept in, but the music was mainly watered-down USA singers—all very clean-cut, wholesome types, as the old rock and roll stars had faded out. However, in 1962–63, an amazing new sound came along in the shape of the Beatles, who were a tightly knit group that had a great grounding in the tough clubs of Hamburg, Germany. Their first records were pop hits, but their stage act was a great mix of rock and roll classics plus new sounds of early 1960s R&B like the Miracles, the Marvelettes, and many obscure artists. I was lucky enough to have seen them at live concerts in 1963, and this inspired me to make serious efforts to form my own group. At the same time, the Rolling Stones emerged with more-exciting R&B sounds, including Chuck Berry numbers that many new groups were including, and my first band took off in 1964, by the name of the Abdo-Men. One of our first bookings was at the Waterfront Club, near the River Itchen that runs out to sea past the Docks, [which] was a very popular R&B club owned by Ron Pope. His son Roger was the drummer for the Soul Agents, who became Rod Stewart's backing group, before he went on to play with the Elton John Band, Hall & Oates, and many more. Other new groups popped up, like the Animals, the Kinks, the Yardbirds, and many bands who played the usual mix of rock and roll and R&B in those early years. As we all know, another bunch of young lads had formed their own group up in West London around that time, by the name of the Detours. They changed this to the High Numbers and were booked in at the Waterfront, as were many new bands that traveled some 80 miles down the old roads to Southampton, which had several venues catering to the new sounds.

I was lead singer with the Abdo-Men, plus playing blues harmonica and maracas (perfect for the Bo Diddley numbers!), and we turned up at the Waterfront Club, which was a long, narrow annex built onto the Cliff Hotel, which had rooms and bars. The stage was rather small, with low ceiling tiles just a few inches above our heads, but we noticed some of them were smashed in, much to the annoyance of the manager, Ron. He explained that a new bunch of Cockney lads had played the night before, and that the guitarist ("big-nosed bugger") seemed to be angry with the cramped stage and kept bashing his guitar through the roof tiles! I never forget his words as he said, "I'll never have those bastards back here again!"

We all know what happened in a few months.

Irish Jack

"The Who's last night at the Goldhawk": Goldhawk Social Club, Shepherd's Bush, London, on Friday, December 3, 1965

The Who had branched out: with three hit singles, playing northern English cities, even Sweden, as well as a trip to Paris. Under the new management of Kit Lambert and Chris Stamp, who had formed the company New Action, the Who decided to do a "thank-you" gig for all their Mod followers at the Goldhawk Social Club. This would have been December 1965—my little red book says Friday, December 3. For about the first time ever in the history of the Goldhawk Social Club—apart from appearances by Adam Faith, Sane Fenton, and Screaming Lord Sutch—a ferocious queue lined the street outside. I had gone with Kit Lambert, and that had given me the required buzz, making me feel like I was his assistant or one of the band's brothers—funny that the only one who had a brother was Pete. The atmosphere had spilled out onto the street, charged no doubt by the length of the queue. The last time the Who had played the Goldhawk, their reward was no more than £50, shared between four of them. Now they were on something like four times that amount!

Inside, the air hummed in anticipation as everyone waited for the Who to take the stage. They hadn't actually been to the Goldhawk for a good few months, and there was a noticeable absence, considering their regular Friday night appearance. What was immediately apparent, however, was how much the band's stature had grown in the time they had been away. They appeared to be a lot more organized and had increased the staff by the acquisition of two new roadies. Now they had a professional edge to things.

Down in the crowd, the main topic of conversation—apart from the latest price on pills—was the Who's new lighting rig. They were one of the first bands to have a lighting system and a production engineer in Mike Shaw, who traveled around on a scooter. Mike had been an old school friend of Chris Stamp's and worked in theater lighting in Bristol. So I suppose that by today's high-tech standards, the Who's music hall color changes would have looked somewhat prehistoric. Yet, for the time, pretty innovative.

I was standing on the steps of the stairs that led to the bar. With me were other Mods, Goldhawk regulars like myself who would have known the band as well: Martin Gaish and his brother Lee, Peter Campbell, Tommy Shelley, Joey Bitton from the White City estate, Jez Clifford, and Alan Bull. Below us, the crowd was jammed tight like sardines.

Glad Rag Ball, Empire Pool, Wembley, London. Friday, November 19, 1965. *Copyright: Jeroen Ras*

Up at the main door they had long posted the "House full" sign, and this gesture had been met by a wave of four-lettered derision from those in the queue who claimed they were club members and had a right to be admitted.

The band was coming to the end of a pulsating set, the excitement climbing as the crowd sensed some kind of final assault. Roger Daltrey had already thanked the Goldhawk Mods for their royal support, all of which had been greeted by hearty cheering and much stomping of feet on the Goldhawk's timber floors. As the applause died away, the Who suddenly launched into "The Ox." "The Ox" is the last track on the *My Generation* album (third to last on the American issue), and I suppose it's best described as a pile driver of an instrumental. You don't need any lyrics with "The Ox": it rumbles like a wild beast run amok in a busy High Street.

The Who had got about halfway through it when, from out of the corner of my eye, I noticed what looked like a mobile ruck going on at the far side of the dance floor. I turned to look back at the others, and yes, they had seen it too. There appeared to be fifteen people involved, maybe twenty, as the ruck pushed its way across the floor. It reminded me of a rugby pack powering its way over a goal line. Only this wasn't a bunch of guys looking for a rugby ball: this was a bloody army of Mods trying to kick some guy across the Goldhawk dance floor. It left a bad feeling in the pit of my stomach. My friends and I exchanged glances, disbelieving that anyone could take such a kicking. Confusion reigned as people stepped away from the fight. If you could call that "a fight"! The guy was using one of his arms to protect his head; this left the rest of his body wide open to more flying boots. In the melee of bodies it was difficult to tell whether he was

actually trying to roll his way out of trouble or if he was being shunted along like a rag doll by the force of the kicking. He didn't look like a Mod or indeed a Rocker. He was one of those nonstyle types who drifted in and out of clubs without a clue. His kind usually ended up in fights because they always gave the wrong answers and never belonged to either side. I noticed how one of his arms now hung limp like it needed maybe a splint! I'd seen a few rucks in my time, but this was something else. And what was so remarkable was that most bands, either of their own free will or upon instruction from the management, would have stopped playing at the first hint of trouble. In fact, the Goldhawk Social Club entertainments committee, run by a bevy of elderly gentlemen, were pretty strict about bands stopping the minute any bit of trouble broke out. But the Who didn't stop! They looked like part of the disturbance. Possessed! Moon went berserk like he had sixteen pairs of hands, as his sticks flashed around the kit. And instead of actually stopping the number to restore some calm, the Who, in a kind of chemical reaction to what was going on down on the dance floor, went into overdrive.

I mean, "The Ox" in overdrive.

Everybody was stunned by this. It was shocking and, yes, irresponsible and so cool. . . . I felt sorry for the poor guy in the rumble, but the truth is that like everyone else, I just couldn't take my eyes off the Who. Townshend rammed the neck of his guitar clean through the cloth face of a Marshall speaker cabinet. The feedback coming out was eerie. Moon was now up off his stool, hitting crap out of his drum kit. Daltrey had smashed his tambourine to pieces off a mic stand and was now pushing the head of the stand through a speaker. The whole hullabaloo was anchored by John Entwistle, who

Glad Rag Ball, Empire Pool, Wembley, London. Friday, November 19, 1965. *Copyright: Jeroen Ras*

stood motionless in a corner of the stage, like a well-dressed city gent playing clarinet on a deserted beach 1,000 miles away. And yet, there was a subscribed sinister about his remoteness. Almost as if he approved of the mayhem but considered himself too cool to get involved.

Chaos abounded on the stage. Meanwhile, down on the floor, a handful of bouncers led by Dennis Townsend and Big Basil Kew were trying to stop what they considered "a fight." Other bouncers, especially hired for the evening, converged around the sides of the stage. They assumed their positions in their regimental monkey suits and, mouths agape, hung on to the side curtains like the building should be preserved. Their panic drill begged the question "What were the Who?" Were they a four-man wrecking crew hired to demolish the Goldhawk stage, or a group of musicians with the hippest act in London?

Whether or not the Who actually got to the end of "The Ox," I can't be sure, but the feedback coming from the speakers was harsh, and my eardrums sang when low impedance whistled from mangled microphones. The band had stormed off the stage, leaving their instruments and gear lying in a broken heap. Bits of equipment still plugged in at the mains continued to emit amplified moans, like the system was trying to die.

I had left my position on the stairs and now stood next to one of the fire exits. Ted Woolgar, the club secretary, had opened this door to allow a draft of cool, welcome air. From where I was now positioned, I could see the Who coming out of the tiny dressing room next to the stage. They were still dressed in their stage clothes, drenched in sweat, as they fought their way through the thick, back-slapping crowd.

They were getting closer to me, and when they came up, I could see they were completely wired. Wired not from pills, so much, as the human experience.

Next thing I noticed was one the local hard men, Norman Foreman, and a couple of his cronies escorting Roger Daltrey out through the crowd. And—Jesus!—he had a fucking shooter, this fella Foreman. It was the first time I had ever seen a handgun, and by now the hairs were standing up on the back of my neck. Cuz this guy Norman Foreman was a notorious villain and well known throughout Shepherd's Bush as the number one man to avoid. And there he was, large as life, offering his personal protection to the lead singer of the Who. It seemed so fitting.

I actually came to speak to Townshend as he came by. He was looking straight at me but don't think he even *saw* me, if you know what I mean. And I think that everyone of us Goldhawk Mods must have realized, somewhere in that breathtaking time lock, that the Who had come of age.

I remained standing by the fire exit, still unsure if I should follow the band out into the side alley—something I would normally do—but a force I cannot explain was stopping me, holding me back.

Knowing them was stopping me. Because that night, the Who became untouchable.

They had stepped into a danger zone no friend, or fan, could follow.

And they had served their friends and left the old Goldhawk Social Club—for good!

CHAPTER 3

1967

They Tried, Tried, Tried . . .

Famine, Frustration

In the beginning of 1967, the Who found themselves encumbered with debt, tangled up in a financial impasse dating back to their 1964 management shift from Pete Meaden to Kit Lambert and Chris Stamp. Lambert in particular held a rather freewheeling, creative, and entrepreneurial notion of record producer that was a little simplistic:

> Do it, go ahead and do it; if you have the ideas and the luck, then it's not difficult. . . . I believe anyone can get into production if they have the right ideas. After all, it's not like making a movie, which costs a lot of money. Anyone in any job can surely save enough money to hire a studio for three hours, find themselves a good group, and try out their ideas.[1]

On one hand, that devil-may-care attitude allowed the band to publicly reexpress its artistic identity, starting with a name shift back from the High Numbers to the Who, "because we wanted it on big posters, so that it would stand out among the other attractions."[2]

On the other hand, Lambert and Stamp's lack of experience and their naivety in management led the band to pay for some ill-considered moves. Starting in 1964, when the two managers signed a one-year production contract with Shel Talmy, the famed producer of America's Decca Records and its English subsidiary, Brunswick Records, they agreed to a series of unfavorable contractual obligations that cost the band dearly, a glaring example being the Who's first hit single, "I Can't Explain."

In 1965 the single, having initially grossed around £35,000, failed to make the Who and its managers any money. The record stores took £10,000; Decca Records, £16,000; the "taxman," £5,000, with Townshend and his publisher receiving only £2,000 in composer royalties, and with the members of the band as musicians being paid only £250 apiece. Lambert and Stamp failed to break even. Many weeks would pass before Lambert and Stamp were able to convince Shel Talmy and Decca to raise the group's royalties from 2.5 to 4 percent both in England and Europe.[3] In a later interview, Daltrey said:

When we got our first hit, "I Can't Explain," we started earning what was then pretty good money, say £300 at night. But after the first year we were £60,000 in debt. The next year, after working our balls off, we were still £40,000 down. And the biggest choke of all came the year after that, when we found we were back up to £60,000 again. Every accountant's meeting was ridiculous. We always owed so much money that we ended up rolling around the office laughing ourselves silly.[4]

As Kit Lambert remembers:

When we started managing the Who, we had a capital of £5,000—which was the savings I'd made from working in movies. And it looked very rough at one time; I mean the £5,000 vanished in four or five months, and we were down to practically nothing; shillings. It really was very close to the nail, and several times during the two years after that people came and took the furniture away. . . . It's very depressing when you're managing a group and you're supposed to be making money, and you arrive and there's a big furniture van on the steps of your office and a big bloke's carrying out your desk.[5]

Things only got worse from that point on, when the Who, trying to get rid of Talmy, temporarily shifted from Brunswick Records to Robert Stigwood's Reaction Records, the label that put out "Substitute" as the follow-up single to "My Generation." Talmy had planned on releasing "Circles" as the follow-up. And to make matters worse, the B side of "Substitute" was a different recording of "Circles," renamed "Instant Party." Talmy was furious. To counteract its potential sales, Talmy rush-released the song "A Legal Matter" as a single on the Brunswick label, with "Circles" as the B side. Furthermore, outraged by the Who's audacity, he filed and won a lawsuit against the band for copyright infringement. As a result, the single was withdrawn, only to be reissued a week later, the B side now featuring "Waltz for a Pig," a song recorded by the Graham Bond Organization but labeled "The Who Orchestra." Some felt the title to be a dig at their former producer. The feud between band and producer was to persist for years, during which time the Who was prevented access to the original master tapes of "My Generation," needed to remix and rerelease it. It finally came out as such, but only in 2002, when a court ruled in Talmy's favor. He did the remixing, not the Who.

The next single, "I'm a Boy," would come out after six months of silence, with the Who finally succeeding in getting rid of Shel Talmy and thus regaining creative freedom, but it was at the expense of allocating him 5 percent on all Who recordings for the next five years.

The Who thus entered 1967 particularly shattered from experiences that had almost split them up, and tensions that ran deep. The *A Quick One / Happy Jack* album was the most collective work of the band to date, possible only because Chris Stamp managed to get a publishing deal with Essex Music that provided a cash advance of £500 to each member of the group, providing that each one wrote two songs.[6]

MORE MUSIC!

The year 1967 started with the risky and premature decision by Lambert and Stamp to launch their own record label, Track Records, which would feature the Who, the Jimi Hendrix Experience, the Crazy World of Arthur Brown, Marsha Hunt, and the Merseybeats. "Pictures of Lily" was the Who's first song on that label. It was initially intended by Townshend as an ironic comment on the commercialization of sex by show business but would go down in history as an ode to masturbation, depicting a teenager's hormonal chaos calmed by pictures of the vaudeville actress Lillie Langtry.[7] "Lily," just like "Substitute" and "I'm a Boy," represented a new compositive season for Townshend, with less aggressive sounds, and songs that strayed from the more serious statements made by "My Generation" and "Anyway Anyhow Anywhere" but still stood for iconic portraits of teenage lifestyle during the second half of the 1960s.[8]

A particularly lucky season, yet one not completely free from frustration, 1967 introduced a new texture to the social fabric of England and America, providing the potential for new musical approaches that were open to or were the product of experimentation, a process often fueled by psychedelic drugs. A new lysergic society was in place, but still, the only reaction by the Who to that prolific atmosphere, at least initially, was represented by their recording of the Stones' "Under My Thumb" and "The Last Time" as a show of solidarity toward Mick Jagger and Keith Richards, both of whom had been arrested for possession of amphetamines. Meanwhile, Hendrix ventured into unexplored musical territories with his "Blues Impressionism" and "Psychedelic Soul," something Pete himself would later define[9] as visionary lyrics that aimed to open up higher levels of consciousness. The Who, meanwhile, were still dealing with the teenage angst and pop art themes that they wanted to blend with newer and more expressive formulae:

I just don't know where we've got to. I suppose in one way we've got what we set out to get a long time ago—

fame and acknowledgement. But now it's all sort of closing in on us and we feel more or less trapped. We thought we could evolve our own kind of music. Well, we have evolved it. But ever since we got into the charts, everything we're doing is in the pop context. And pop was the very thing we tried to break away from.[10]

Miles and Miles

As if it was the last thing that they would ever do, the Who set out for America:

Even in those days, success in this country and on the Continent simply wasn't enough. You either crashed in on the multi-million dollar American industry, or died.[11]

What other bands would see as a simple transatlantic visit to promote their music became for the Who something like the ultimate "conquest of a new frontier." The Who, after all, unlike its contemporaries, was used to taking an intense attitude toward any given opportunity simply to separate itself from the pack and to get noticed beyond the shores of England. Perhaps as a result of this, and compared to some bands, the Who took longer to win over America.

As *The Observer* reported:

The foursome which launched the Liverpool Sound swept along on Beatlemania—a popularity initially so powerful that it even broke Sooty's traditional hold on the fancy soap and tea-towel market. John, Paul, George and Ringo were the lovable schoolboys, naughty but nice, whose songs were sung on every coach that headed for Margate or Blackpool. Pete, Roger, John, and Keith, on the other hand, surged with violence. They bred their own cult, which needed to be seen to be understood; and that is the likeliest explanation why it took them longer than the groups which were little more than reflections of The Beatles to break into the American market.[12]

The Who would travel to the States four times in 1967, starting with New York, where the band appeared on Murray the K's show. Intended as a hit-and-run visit, it would turn out to be a strenuous weeklong series of concerts from March 25 to April 2, and the first of a long run of challenges in America. "Happy Jack" came out as single in the States on March 18, but it was portrayed with nowhere near the intensity for which the band was known or would later explode onstage before American audiences. Murray the K's "Music in Fifth Dimension" took place at the RKO Radio Theater in New York, and its program foresaw five "concerts" a day, for nine days, starting at 10:15 a.m., each "concert" being but two songs, usually "I Can't Explain" and "My

Generation"—which for the Who meant destruction of at least one guitar at the end of each performance. Up to that time, the bedlam at the end of each concert had become the hallmark of the Who live, and while on the one hand it made a definitive impression on Murray the K's audience, on the other hand it became another nail in the band's financial coffin. Pete explains:

There was a time when the band was paying for my guitars. Not during the first three years, but after a while it became part of the act, and I demanded that the band pay for them or else I was going to stop. Then I had to be a bit more careful, I had to make guitars last a bit longer. I started using Stratocasters which take about an hour to break, and I used to repair them and stick them together again. We used to occasionally refret guitars and sometimes I'd break the same guitar three or four times before it would become unplayable.[13]

The Who's second visit to America involved mainly the West Coast, where they quickly became known as of one of the most sensational live acts around. The Who made their first appearance at the Fillmore Auditorium on June 16 and 17, in San Francisco, California's lysergic "mecca."

The Fillmore, as well as its second incarnation, known as the Fillmore West—inside the old Carousel Ballroom building, and its East Coast version, the Fillmore East, marked the golden age of the 1960s counterculture by hosting the performances of the most-eminent and most-representative American and English musicians of the time. The Fillmore Auditorium is remembered by Pete as the first venue the Who really enjoyed playing, for its professional PA and, perhaps most of all, the attitude of its manager, Bill Graham.[14] He was ahead of the whole music scene in San Francisco and held an especially affectionate attitude toward the Who, such that they would be invited to play in multiple venues there every time the band came to the States.

In this respect, during an interview at Wellington airport in New Zealand's capital on January 31, 1968, when Pete was asked for his impression of the most sophisticated audience he had played to, he replied:

In San Francisco. If you've ever been to San Francisco you know that the atmosphere and the people are very English oriented, and they have just a politeness and a respect . . . something you [usually] get from good audiences in England.[15]

Pete also told Jann Wenner of *Rolling Stone*: "Nowhere in the world compares with San Francisco in what's in the air, . . . the vibes that this place gives off are fantastic."[16]

If those two dates on June 16 and 17 mark an important time in the Who's history, the concert after them would definitively establish the Who as a musical force in America. On June 18, 1967, the band landed at the Peninsular Airport to appear on the last day of the Monterey Pop Festival along with Blues Project, Big Brother & the Holding Company, Group with No Name, Buffalo Springfield, the Grateful Dead, the Jimi Hendrix Experience, and the Mamas & the Papas.

What had been an unfolding as a quiet happening for two days was eventually "atom-bombed" by the Who, a concert that climaxed with a smashing finale of rarely seen violence onstage, leaving the dozy audience and musicians dumbstruck—especially Jimi Hendrix. Jimi was also with Track Records, the same label as the Who, and he was fully aware of their stage presence. At Monterey, before either of them would perform, Hendrix envisaged what it would have meant to let the Who go on first. Both Jimi and Pete shared with one another a mutually fond respect: Pete had started playing Fender Stratocasters after seeing them played by Jimi, and Hendrix's concern about playing before the Who at Monterey was a clear sign of deference, if not fear. As a matter of fact, since none of them wanted to follow the other onstage that night, the decision was left to the flip of a coin by John Phillips of the Mamas & the Papas. The Who won the toss and chose to go on first, but Jimi promised to "pull out all the stops," which he certainly delivered, smashing his own guitar yet also sensuously setting it on fire. It was a performance that would make history.

Nevertheless, the Who's American tour that followed Monterey represented their real first time in the States. Through this nine-week, coast-to-coast tour, from July 13 to September 15, ironically supporting Herman's Hermits and special guest stars the Blues Magoos, the Who familiarized itself for the first time with the broad range and color of America's cultural fabric.

Photographer Tom Wright joined in. Eight years prior, in 1959, he had to move from the States to follow his father to London. There, Tom first attended the American school and then photography courses at Ealing Art College, where he met Pete, who was studying graphic design. The two spent glorious times together after classes at Tom's place on Sunnyside Road, in which circumstances Pete was turned on to American blues and pot. Eventually Tom got busted and was subsequently forced to immediately return to America, leaving the flat with all his belongings, among which was a guitar and a ton of records. Pete still relates the birth of the Detours, the Who's first identity, to that guitar and those blues records. Years later, in 1967, Pete and Tom reunited on July 31 in Florida, for the Bayfront Center concert.

Tom followed the rest of the tour with his camera, taking some of the best shots of the band, most of which are featured in the great memoir *Roadwork: Rock & Roll Turned Inside Out*.[17]

The band's visits to auditoriums and ballrooms across the US made them realize that, as Keith Moon phrased it to the *Record Mirror*, "America is like the Marquee Club in London, only ten million times larger."[18] He was referring to the benefit of relatively unknown bands gaining public attention and recognition in America by playing as many dates as possible, relying almost exclusively on word of mouth.

On this third visit to the States, the Who became aware of just how much their popularity had grown despite the rather slow process and tepid record sales. In this "ten million times larger than the Marquee Club" setting, the band realized just how much they were gaining a reputation as one of the British avant-garde bands, unlike in England, where they were still seen as a mere pop group.

The Who's Fan Club secretary Sue Dunlop recalls that when the four came home from that tour they spent the whole afternoon in her office drinking twenty-six cups of tea between them, surprised at how much better it was than American tea, a stew horrendously brewed from mere tea bags in individual cups.[19] It would be one of the few relaxing moments for the band before finding itself once again submerged by greater debt than it had accrued even before setting off to America. Pete recalls that

it wasn't just financial trouble, what actually happened was that we got so into debt, because we weren't making big money in America like most other bands. When we went to the States, thinking we were going to make our fortune, we actually came back, I think, close to 600,000 dollars in debt.[20]

Also,

We hired a bus for one tour; that seemed like a fundamentally good-sense thing to do. It cost us about nine-thousand dollars or something. There were incredible sort of money things going on. We tipped the bus driver a hundred, and he tore it up; because everybody really thought that we were earning like millions and millions and millions of dollars. . . . Of course, that's just one side of it. The other side of it was the equipment. I used to break a guitar every performance—if not two sometimes—and they would always cost around $150. . . . And Keith used to go through a lot of drum kits. . . . Just a set of skins for a drum set is about $300.[21]

While John would say later that

on the first tour in 1967, when we were backing Herman's Hermits, we played thirty concerts and earned $40,000— and I still had to borrow $100 to get home. It was heart-breaking . . . Really, we were being milked dry by the Americans. Why, I even remember one concert where the fellow actually fined us for playing too long.[22]

By this time, the equipment-breaking ritual had helped draw in the American public, but it personified something that the band could no longer continue: "Now, the audience feels cheated unless they see X hundred dollars worth of equipment broken up under their eyes."[23]

Not knowing what else to do, Pete decided to release "I Can See for Miles" as a single. This song had been written the year before and was being kept as an ace up the sleeve for whenever the band might have found itself in trouble. Although now hailed as one of that era's great songs, much to Pete's surprise the single did not go down quite as well as he had expected, especially in Britain:

That was the real heartbreaker for me. It was the number we'd been saving, thinking that if The Who ever got into trouble that would be the one that would pull us out. The Who did a marvelous performance on it, in my opinion Kit did an incredible production, and we got a marvelous pressing of it. It reached number seventeen in the charts and the day I saw it was about to go down without reaching any higher, I spat on the British record buyer. To me, this was the ultimate Who record and yet it didn't sell.[24]

Feeling almost betrayed by their motherland, the Who decided to work on a new stage act through a small series of concerts in English theaters to then set off for their fourth time to the States, on which they projected all of their hopes for the future. In America, "I Can See for Miles" had reached #7 in the charts, becoming their most successful single there. In this respect, when the Who would return to San Francisco on February 22, 1968, at the Fillmore Auditorium, Pete would introduce "I Can See for Miles" as

our last record, which we don't play on the stage 'cept here. The reason we don't play it onstage is because . . . outside of here we played it in England mostly and Australia. . . . And it wasn't a hit in England for real, it was kind of a hit, but it wasn't the kind of hit it was here. It's a number called "I Can See for Miles."[25] (*See page 76 for information on the recording this dialogue is from*).

At the end of 1967, the Who played the Cow Palace in San Francisco, the Village Theater in New York (before it became the Fillmore East on March 1968), the Hollywood Bowl, and a few high schools such as Southfield, Kansas:

The most fantastic thing happened in Kansas City. There were 500 kids at the airport. They all had our records and were making the point of "We remember you when . . ."[26]

The Who Sell Out

Returning once again to England on December 3, 1967, the Who released the album that they had started recording ten months prior. *The Who Sell Out* initially was to be called *Who's Lily?*, featuring the "Pictures of Lily" single meant to be released before the Who's departure to the States. The "plot" of the album eventually took a significant twist, and the idea was dropped. The idea for an album beginning with the *Batman* theme, which had already been included in the 1966 EP single *Ready Steady Who*, provided the band with the inspiration to write a humorous musical jingle for Jaguar:

The number was a really powerful and loose thing, something like "The Ox" from our first album, with Keith thrashing away like hell and us all pumping out "Jag-u-a-r," like the *Batman* theme tune.[27]

That song led to the composition of other new jingles about Coca Cola, Top Gear, and Rotosound Strings (the bass guitar strings that John had a hand in developing), which would together make a theme-based project centered on commercial advertisements.

In the middle of the recording sessions, however, Pete conceptualized something that would change the album completely, making it the first concept album of the Who and one of the most original pop works ever conceived. At midnight, Monday, August 14, 1967, the approval of the Marine Broadcasting Offences Act abolished unlicensed musical broadcasting by pirate radio stations, such as Radio Caroline 999 and Radio Luxembourg, typically emanating from ships at sea. Their demise epitomized the death of a phenomenon that, in opposition to the more conservative and corporate BBC, had helped rock music spread rapidly across England. The Who's third album, *The Who Sell Out*, was therefore intended as a tribute to and an act of love for those radio stations that had contributed so much to taking early songs such as "I Can't Explain" into the homes of hundreds of thousands of teenagers:

> You don't realize how good something like the pirates are until they've gone, so to give the album that ethereal flavor of a pirate radio station we incorporated some "groovy" jingles. And so, *The Who Sell Out*.[28]

Not all jingles written for the vinyl album made the final track list, though, although they would eventually end up on the CD reissues many years later. Some of the definitive tracks even caused a delay in *The Who Sell Out*'s release date—from November to December—since some of the firms mentioned on the album were late in sending in their written permission to Track Records. For example, "Odorono," a song about

> a girl who's worried about B.O. For some reason Odorono didn't like being referred to in connection with sweat. . . . What I did was ring them up and tell them that as we were doing a very pro thing for their deodorant, maybe they should pay us something. They didn't take the suggestion at all kindly.[29]

On the other hand,

> Heinz didn't mind a bit. When we told them that the album sleeve showed Roger Daltrey sitting in a hipbath full of their product, they sent us another crate for free.[30]

The Who Sell Out was also the result of a thorough attempt to find a balance between conservation of topics dear to the Who and the embrace of the psychedelia of that year, for which *The Who Sell Out* became one of the best proponents via "Armenia City in the Sky" and "I Can See for Miles." It is also an album composed between miles and miles of concert touring with the Herman's Hermits and multiple studios in London, Nashville, and Chicago.

The album was eventually released in America on January 6, 1968. Apart from being banned by Radio WMCA, whose program director Joe Bogart defined it as "disgusting!"[31] *The Who Sell Out* was praised by critics, especially those writing for *Rolling Stone* magazine. Good reviews by the newborn magazine represented, however, a momentary proverbial "calm before the storm," a force that would again crash down on the Who later that year in 1968:

> Strictly on basis of musical merit, The Who finally made their name on this side of the Atlantic, where they had long been the hapless victims of a thoroughly uninterested record company and no air exposure. Partially through the energy of two cross country tours of small concerts and one-night gigs, they brought off two top single hits: "Happy Jack" and "I Can See For Miles." Anyone who has *Happy Jack* and their subsequent album, *The Who Sell Out*, knows of their totally original sound, their refreshing attitude, their fine instrumental work, and excellent song writing.[32]

© Pete Minall

CHAPTER 4

1967

Anyway Anyhow Anywhere

Nick Hairs

"Rag Rave," Granby Halls, Leicester, on Monday, March 13, 1967

On Monday, March 13 1967, I attended my very first Who gig: the Rag Rave at the Granby Halls, Leicester, England. The term "Rag Rave" is or was used by students to raise money for charities. Rag meaning to persuade with force—not violence! Anyway, this gig was pivotal for me, being the first time I saw the Who. Yes, I was excited.

How I got so close to the stage, I have no idea. But I do remember one of the roadies saying it was cool as long as I didn't move about.

The band was everything I expected it to be, and to be stood so close was just a dream come true. To see Pete Townshend from a few feet away was just awesome.

Craig Patterson

Fillmore Auditorium, San Francisco, California, on Friday, June 16, 1967

The psychedelic purple-and-orange poster in the record store's window announced "From England—The Who," June 16 and 17 at Bill Graham's Fillmore Auditorium in San Francisco. The boys and I shelled out three bucks apiece for our tickets and drove up to San Francisco in high anticipation on Friday 16. We had all digested the Who's latest album, *Happy Jack*, and read about their high-powered stage act, but we really didn't know exactly what to expect from them.

Rag Rave, Granby Halls, Leicester, UK.
Both photos by Nick Hairs

The Fifth Dimension Club, Ann Arbor, Michigan.
Wednesday, June 14, 1967.

Fillmore Auditorium, San Francisco, California. Friday, June 16, 1967. *All photos by Craig Patterson*

We got to the Fillmore about an hour and a half before showtime, and there were only about half a dozen people in line ahead of us. We were stoked! When the doors opened, we ran inside to grab the best seats. Because none of us had seen the band live before and hadn't seen full pictures of them onstage, we quickly debated as to which side of the stage to sit on for the best view of Peter Townshend. We chose the *wrong* side to sit on, as it turned out, but it really didn't make much of a difference. The Fillmore Auditorium was fairly small and the stage wasn't all that big, so we had a great view anyway.

The Loading Zone, a Berkeley-based R&B outfit, opened the evening. The Santana Blues Band (whose name was left off the poster and were evidently a last-minute addition to the bill) played second. Even back then you could tell that Carlos Santana was going to be successful. His band that night was more bluesy than Latin infused, and they soon became members of Bill Graham's stable of bands (which already included Big Brother and the Holding Company and the Quicksilver Messenger Service).

There was a hush from the crowd (along with some scattered cheers) as the Who walked onstage. Diminutive Roger Daltrey had a shawl on over some Carnaby Street finery, and Pete wore a multicolored robe and lavender running shoes. The whole band exhibited a real splash of color, something that the two opening acts lacked. Pete and John were using two Vox Super Beatle amplifiers each, and

Keith Moon's Ludwig gold sparkle double-bass drum set had black block letters with "THE" on the left one and "WHO" on the right. (Note: two nights later at the Monterey Pop Festival, Keith's left bass drum head was blank, since he had gored it on a mic stand at the Fillmore the night before and destroyed "THE").

The band tore into their opening number, "I Can't Explain" (my favorite Who song at the time . . . and for a long time afterward). I stood up and clicked off three pictures of Roger and Pete, as I had a good angle on them, with my trusty Kodak Instamatic camera (complete with flashcubes).

Unfortunately, I had only three shots left on that roll, and I hadn't brought a spare roll with me, a decision I would regret forever.

Their live version of "A Quick One" was absolutely *savage* compared with the version on the *Happy Jack* LP, as was the song "Happy Jack" itself. The house PA system was a good one, and the Who's harmonies were full and sweet. We had of course read about the "My Generation" finale, with the smoke bombs and destruction of instruments, but there's nothing like witnessing it up close and personal live. Fantastic.

We left the show energized and with great anticipation of seeing them again in Monterey two nights later.

"They're sharp, sarcastic, cynical but never weighted down by their own self-importance" (Jon Landau, *Crawdaddy*, August 1967).

Craig Patterson

Monterey International Pop Festival, Monterey Fairgrounds, California, on Friday–Sunday, June 16–18, 1967

So, two days after seeing the Who at The Fillmore, me and the boys found ourselves aboard a Greyhound bus on our way to the Monterey Pop Festival, 100 miles away. The event had started Friday, and the Sunday night show would feature "the first West Coast appearance" of the Who (wrong!). There were other festival attendees aboard our bus, and we spent much of the two-hour trip comparing notes with them regarding the bands slated to appear at that night's show. We learned that the order of the bands' appearances had not been consistent with the order that was originally published. However, since the Who had played in San Francisco for the past two nights and therefore were immune to any major set time changes, we had no doubt that they would play on that night as scheduled. The early start time of 7:30 p.m. was good news for us, as the last bus from Monterey back to the Bay Area left at 10:30 p.m., and we HAD to be on it! This would come to be a matter of some concern before the day was over.

Iconic columnist Ralph J. Gleason wrote in the *San Francisco Chronicle*, on June 11, 1967, that "the first annual Monterey International Pop Festival is bringing to the Fairgrounds Arena the greatest aggregation of popular song stars assembled in any one place for a weekend event . . ." and "the roster of performers includes some of the greatest names in today's popular music, some newcomers and some performers from other lands (Ravi Shankar)."

While we strolled through the fairgrounds with the Flower Children, we were definitely NOT hippies. We were observers, not members of their ilk. We were there for the *music*, not necessarily the *vibes*. With Ravi Shankar's music sounding all through the fairgrounds, we passed most of the afternoon checking out the booths of artisans, painters, weavers, poster displays, pictures, and photographs. The mellowness of the scene was augmented by the frequent whiff of marijuana smoke. The few police that were minding the fairgrounds were very hands off and therefore practically invisible to the wandering guests.

Sunday evening's music started off with the Blues Project. Good band, featuring the perennially cool Al Kooper. Then Big Brother and the Holding Company came onstage for their second appearance of the festival. Their version of "Ball and Chain" from that night is the one that wound up in the *Monterey Pop* film by D. A. Pennebaker and helped make Janis Joplin's career. Next was a motley collection of studio musicians put together by record mogul Lou Adler (who was on the Monterey Pop executive committee) called

the Group with No Name. This was a horrible mistake. The pacing of the night came to a *grinding* halt when they started to play their unrecognizable but, more importantly, *unhip* songs. Audience members were asked to submit ideas to help "the band find a name." Suggestions poured in. "Lou Adler's Lonely Hearts Club Band" was a good one, but I preferred "the Lead Balloon" or my own "the Band without a Clue." These clowns burned up at least twenty minutes of showtime, and we began watching the clock, hoping that the Who would come on soon, as it was becoming obvious that we weren't going to be around for all of the scheduled acts.

Buffalo Springfield played next. A favorite of ours, but without Neil Young they were fairly flat and unexciting. Even with David Crosby from the Byrds guesting with them, they played a forgettable set. Of course, our anxiety over the swift passage of time and the uncertainty of whether we'd be able to see the Who probably had something to do with our objectivity. We were definitely stressing at this point. Then, as the Springfield filed offstage, emcee Tommy Smothers announced that the next band on would be "the Whos" [*sic*]. YES!

Fillmore Auditorium dressing room, San Francisco, California. Saturday, June 17, 1967. All photos by Frank Zinn, Richard Martin Frost Archive

My buddy Allan Lazarus was sitting with me as the Who hit the stage and broke into their set opener, "Substitute." He recalls:

First time I saw them. We had floor seats about midway. First impression of the Who was that they were very bright and much different than the other acts. The Who were colorful, moved around on stage a lot, and I had never seen the drums and guitar played like that. That is the chief image and essentially the same for every Who date. Struck me as a ferocious band where something could always happen. Attacked their songs, and as I found out in later concerts, they were always in some sort of control. Even Moon. A madman, but he always hit his marks. You knew that Moon would never want to be anywhere else in the world than on stage, behind the drums. The glee and happiness in his face was evident, especially up close. The destruction at the end was startling, even as it was expected. Then we ran for the bus. Always regret that we missed the rest of the show.

The best part? We got to see all of that and STILL caught our bus home!

Ann Elizabeth Carroll

Monterey International Pop Festival, Monterey Fairgrounds, California, on Friday–Sunday, June 16–18, 1967

I grew up on the East Coast, New England, but when I turned twelve I moved with my family to Oakland, Berkeley, Bay Area. That would be in 1961. Berkeley was always a place that I really liked. It was more political than San Francisco, and that is why I felt more comfortable there. While San Francisco and Haight-Ashbury had a new, kind of hippieish newspaper called *The Oracle*, Berkeley had its own paper called the *Berkeley Barb*, and it was very left wing, very political. That was really the difference between the two areas. I remember I was probably just fifteen, maybe younger, when I became interested in the civil rights movement, the Berkeley free-speech movement. And that's how Berkeley stayed—it didn't get the "flowers in your hair" thing. We were less easy to be taken advantage of, I think. I didn't like Haight-Ashbury that much; I would go to San Francisco just for the concerts and for seeing friends. I'm sure people would have thought of me as a hippie, even though I always felt like I wanted to be more bohemian, drinking black coffee, reading poetry, and the literary thing. I think I was a bit precocious.

A huge event that really got the 1960s started was the Beatles. I saw them twice in San Francisco, in 1964, when I was fifteen, and again in 1965, at sixteen.

I remember that in summer 1965 you could feel something was in the air—it seemed like a really special time. We knew we were on a special time; there was just so much going on everywhere. I went to my first concert at the Fillmore Auditorium in summer or fall of 1966: I saw the Grateful Dead and a black woman, the blues singer Big Mama Thornton. That was an amazing thing. From then, even though I was still in high school, I spent most of my time hitchhiking over to Berkeley and just being around that kind of environment.

I remember in spring of 1967, before Monterey, the word had gotten out that the summer was going to be pretty weird, because a lot of young kids were going to be flooding to San Francisco; this was going to be *our* thing. I remember there was an event in the Golden Gate Park; it was called the Human Be-In, and that was one time when we were just surprised how many like-minded people were there. I remember also we were so amazed to have the chance to buy the amazing albums that were coming out then. Before that, we always bought the 45 discs. We were young, we were around seventeen, and we would just take these albums and stare at the cover art forever.

Everything seemed to be opening up; it was all happening at the same time.

Later that year I kept going to different concerts. I really liked the Avalon Ballroom; it just seemed more family oriented than the Fillmore. I got to see there all these amazing groups that were coming out, like all of a sudden. It seemed like everything blossomed almost overnight. It had been building for a few years, but then it blossomed. At that time in San Francisco there was Winterland, there was the Fillmore Auditorium, there was the Avalon, the Carousel Ballroom, which later became Fillmore West. I had returned at the Fillmore Auditorium in the spring of 1967, before Monterey. I remember one thing in particular: there was a big basket of apples one passed at the other, and then we went up the stairs and there was the ballroom. They were really old ballrooms, relatively small. I think we only paid like $2 or something to see three groups. Bill Graham used to have auditions for different bands on Tuesday nights at his Fillmore and it cost like $1, so we went there a lot. One time I was there, and guess who was auditioning? It was Santana. I remember the first time I saw the Jefferson Airplane; they were one of my very favorite groups; they were just amazing. Marty Balin had just the most gorgeous voice in the world; they were just remarkable. You could see Big Brother and Janis Joplin in these obscure little places. This was before Monterey, and they weren't famous yet. They were well known in the Bay Area and other spots, but they weren't big stars. All that really changed with Monterey.

I graduated from high school just a couple of weeks before Monterey Pop Festival. Some friends of ours had been talking about it, so I decided to go. I went with a friend, hitchhiking down from the Bay Area. Back then, girls for the most part didn't have cars, so we either went with some guy's friends, or we hitchhiked. We had tickets; I can't remember the price—I think they were like $5 or $6. I was going to meet a young man I had met the summer before, a surfer guy from Santa Barbara. Monterey is such a beautiful area: the weather was ideal; there were all these gorgeous dressed-up people, wearing all kinds of either old-timey dresses like from the 1800, or Indian dresses. It was almost like a dream. Everything was so gorgeous, and everyone was so nice and gentle and well behaved. We were still like the well-brought-up kids. It was just magical, and everyone was just so good about sharing everything: we brought food to share, etc. I had seen lots of these groups before, but it was just all of them in one place for three days, and there were some that I hadn't got to see before, like the Buffalo Springfield. I'm pretty sure the Byrds were there, along with all the L.A. people we weren't familiar with that much. It was well organized. People who didn't have the tickets to go inside the venue were in the fairgrounds, and they could still hear the music, so everything was sort of free for everyone. They had the Monterey police that was keeping an eye on things, because I think they were sort of worried how we might all be acting, but it turned out that they thought we were fine, we thought they were fine, everything was so cohesive.

I was sitting toward the back during the festival. I remember wandering around outside the actual venue and seeing Brian Jones. He was very close to me. He was just so beautiful, and he had a gorgeous blonde girlfriend; they were almost like a mirage floated by! And there wasn't any bodyguard, and no one was bothering the famous people; they were part of the party and we were too. Nobody was going up and doing silly things asking for autographs. It was all before the movement, before the Summer of Love. I don't even know if the word "hippie" had been invented yet. When the media got involved, it suddenly got blown out of proportion and really began to bring it all down. But for a short period it was just so wonderful.

I think the most spectacular thing was Jimi Hendrix, because none of us knew about him. He had been living over in London, and we hadn't heard anything about him, so when he came out it was like, "Who is this amazing man and what is he doing?!"

I saw Big Brother there for my second time. I think they played twice. You could just see how happy Janis was. Everything was brand new for her too. It was before the bubble burst for her. I remember how Janis was dressed: compared to how she got when she became famous, she wasn't the super-flamboyant Janis; she was one of the crowd.

I had never heard of Ravi Shankar before; he played for a long, long time. It seemed like he went on for hours actually!

I saw the Who there for the first time. I liked them; I always liked their music a lot. I got to know the Who right about the time the Beatles had their music and all the British groups were coming in. I liked them a lot. I had seen them on a couple of television shows; one was called *Shindig!* and the other was called *Hullabaloo*, so I was really aware of them. Once I saw them in concert, I really liked them, but I think they were almost too intense for me and for what was happening at Monterey! The Who obviously hadn't been around the San Francisco Bay Area scene; they just didn't seem appropriate for that time. I'm not saying their music wasn't good, but they were just too violent; they didn't seem to go with the atmosphere of that weekend.

I remember leaving with my boyfriend, and we thought that was really, really special.

Right after Monterey, I went back to New England for about a month, just to see the people I had grown up with. Kids back there didn't know anything that had been going on in San Francisco until they met me! I was telling them things about what had been going on, the Bay Area, Monterey . . . I had my long, straight hair, my kind of hippieish clothes, and they had not seen anything like me! I guess I was kind of the first "alternative" counterculture person they ever met, actually! I guess they were impressed, because I came in with all these stories.

When I got back to the Bay Area, everything had changed in that month that I had been gone, and really not for the better. All of this had been building up over the years, from the time the Beatles first appeared on the scene and then just sort of exploded. I think the best part of it was Monterey—it was the pinnacle, probably the best time. Afterward, things were still fine and cool; we would go to the ballrooms, but I think things had just lost their innocence.

Then, we had the assassinations of Martin Luther King and then of Bobby Kennedy: I was nineteen when they got shot, and it was so devastating. It is hard to explain how devastating that was, because we were so hopeful, especially with Bobby Kennedy. It just changed the whole landscape of everything, especially for people probably around my age. Then came Altamont. As good as Monterey was, Altamont was just bad; it had a bad omen kind of feeling. That new shiny effect was rubbing off, plus we were growing up a little bit too. I started all of this when I was just sixteen, and by the time Altamont had happened I was twenty, going on twenty-one. Earlier on, we truly thought we were going to change the world.

Tom Henneberry

Monterey International Pop Festival, Monterey Fairgrounds, California, on Friday–Sunday, June 16–18, 1967

I was between high school and college and had been working at a newspaper in San Francisco for about a year when I had an opportunity to see the Beatles on their first visit to San Francisco in August 1964. It was within a year of President Kennedy's assassination when the Beatles arrived on our shores and helped lift America out of its collective gloom. God, it all happened so quickly.

There's a picture with my friend Pat and me at the Beatles' press conference before the show. You can see Brian Epstein, Derek Taylor, and some of the other Beatles' principals in the upper left-hand corner. It was quite a heady event! To be able to stand in front of the stage at the Cow Palace, in front of the first row, was an unforgettable experience in Beatlemania, even though the band was all but drowned out by screaming fans and an explosion of flashbulbs.

Then my life took some bad turns in 1965. I had to take a compulsory physical for the military and was worried about being drafted (with the Vietnam War raging at the time). I had just broken up with my girlfriend, which had been a long-term high school relationship, and I had quit the newspaper. Then a friend who I had worked with there who was in Greece sent me a couple of postcards and suggested that I join him in Europe, and I thought, "This is the time; I'm going to do it." After applying for a passport and booking a flight to Luxembourg, I soon was off to begin seven months of eye-opening experiences.

Meeting Dan at the airport, we were off traveling together during January and February in France and Spain. But my heart was set on London, and when we went our separate ways in late February, I was off for England and spent most of the next six months there, with a side trip to Liverpool to see where it all began for the Beatles at the Cavern Club. I lived in London and I got to see the Stones, Yardbirds, and the Animals on *Ready Steady Go!* live on TV, and Spencer Davis, Manfred Mann, and the Small Faces at the reigning club at the time, the Marquee in the Soho district of London. It was the time to be in London, with Carnaby Street and the Mod movement in full flower and the British Invasion bands such as the Beatles, the Rolling Stones, the Who, the Yardbirds, the Kinks, the Hollies, the Animals, and other beat bands beginning to make waves in America. The movement even earned a "Swinging London" cover story in *Time* magazine—a huge acknowledgment of the scene taking place there. It was the mecca of popular music at the time, as San Francisco would be the following year.

I remember hearing the Who singing "Substitute" on a jukebox in a restaurant and was immediately caught up in their compelling sound. My introduction to the Who was "My Generation," which I heard on a pirate radio station, either Radio Caroline or Radio Luxembourg, and from that moment on, I became an instant Who fan, and as far as a live act, they eclipsed the Beatles and the Stones as the most exciting.

My focus on the Who was between 1967 and 1971, during which time I saw them six times, beginning with their incendiary performance at the Monterey Pop Festival, sandwiched between the Grateful Dead and Jimi Hendrix on the night of June 18, 1967.

Since I was in England most of 1966, I missed out on a lot of what was going on in San Francisco. Bill Graham was putting on unbelievable shows at both Winterland and Fillmore Auditorium. When I got home, the first show I saw was the original Santana Blues Band at the Matrix—a club co-owned by the Jefferson Airplane's Marty Balin—in September of 1966, followed by the great Otis Redding at the Fillmore in December.

I attended many, many shows in 1968, but none better than two memorable performances from the Who—one in February at Winterland with Cannonball Adderley and the Nice, and one at Fillmore West with James Cotton. These were groundbreaking outings for the band, and to my mind they never played or sounded better, thanks to Bill Graham's exacting standards for balancing sound. This cemented the Who's reputation for being the greatest live band on the planet—at least in my mind. Then I saw them again in 1969 with the Woody Herman Jazz Band, again at Fillmore West, in 1970 at the Berkeley Community Theater, and in 1971 at the San Francisco Civic Auditorium.

This was during the band's creative height, when they delivered *The Who Sell Out* (1968), *Tommy* (1969), *Live at Leeds* (1970), *Who's Next* (1971), *The Who by Numbers* (1975), and, finally, *Who Are You* (1978). With the passing of Keith Moon, the band was set back for several years, mostly coasting through the 1980s with live albums and greatest-hits packages. It would take years to regain a foothold in the fiercely competitive world of rock.

The thing that I most remember about those Graham years is that the sound was always perfectly balanced. It was unbelievable. When I walked out after the Who shows at Berkeley Community Theater and the Civic Auditorium in San Francisco, my ears were ringing for a couple of days afterward. Graham was remarkable in that way, and I'll always be indebted to him for taking care of the fans.

The outdoors concerts—the Days on the Green in Oakland in the 1970s—were more about drinking, socializing, and less to do with music. I liked the smaller venues where you really could appreciate the music, and that's what I was there for. The only exception was the Monterey Pop Festival.

The experience at Monterey was like none ever before or since. The parade of bands would mostly go on to greater heights, and some, like the Who and Jimi Hendrix, to superstardom. It was a truly magical and enchanting event—the vibe peaceful and loving. The Magic Mountain Festival a week before set the stage for Monterey with the Doors, Jefferson Airplane, etc. But the Monterey Pop Festival was immortalized in the documentary by D. A. Pennebaker.

Watching the Who break into the opening chords of "Substitute," I knew that they had to make a huge and hopefully lasting impression on the audience, because Hendrix was waiting in the wings to cut them down to size. Their set, which included "Summertime Blues," "Happy Jack," and "Pictures of Lily," was filled with unsuppressed aggression—a kind of take-no-prisoner attitude. The finale, "My Generation," in which Townshend destroyed his guitar and Keith Moon kicked over his drum kit, galvanized the audience and set the stage for Hendrix's finale on "Wild Thing," in which he saddled his guitar, humped it, and then poured lighter fluid on it, igniting his axe as festivalgoers sat astonished at what they were witnessing.

For two guys from San Francisco, it was an eye-opening, jaw-dropping experience. Pat and I celebrated with some face painting, which became symbolic of the event some fifty-two years ago. It was the first and last event of its kind.

Other than the glorious parade of nonstop bands, the communal spirit and love vibe suffused the entire weekend. Eric Burdon was inspired to memorialize it with his hit "San Franciscan Nights," a Top 10 record in August 1967, and with his reflection on the signal event "Monterey," another hit in December. Although the Beatles and the Stones were no-shows, Brian Jones attended the festival as a spectator, and George Harrison and his wife, Pattie, visited the Haight-Ashbury in August, the Monterey International Pop Festival was quickly a memory, but the music scene in San Francisco was reaching new heights, with virtually every major band passing through in the coming years on their way to greatness: Cream; Hendrix; the Doors; Paul Butterfield Blues Band; Led Zeppelin; Creedence Clearwater Revival; Jethro Tull; Santana; Crosby, Stills & Nash; Jeff Beck; Rod Stewart, to name just a few. San Francisco was the music mecca from which the Monterey Pop Festival sprung, and would be celebrated for years to come. Pat and I agreed that this was a momentous event in our rock music lives, and one we would never forget.

The Who's trailblazing performance there catapulted them into the consciousness of every American fan and paved the way for their jaw-dropping rock opera *Tommy*, from which they never looked back.

Tom Henneberry (*left*) at Monterey International Pop Festival. *Photo by Tom Henneberry*

Joe Giorgianni

War Memorial Auditorium, Rochester, New York, on Wednesday, August 30, 1967

It was the summer of 1967. As a fifteen year old growing up in upstate New York, I was too young and too far removed to be much affected by the hippie movement taking place.

Minneapolis Auditorium, Minneapolis, Minnesota. Sunday, August 20, 1967.
Photo by Mike Barich, the Barich Archive

Boy Scouts and baseball had lost their allure—through the magic of TV, transistor radios, and a 45 record player, I now had rock and roll. Some of the "cooler" guys at school were forming bands. I talked with my friend Mike Ingalsbe, and we decided we should do that too. Didn't look too hard—if the Rolling Stones could do it, we surely could. Mike could sing, and our friend Johnny Butto had a guitar, a Gibson Firebird. His cousin Ricky had a nice set of Ludwig drums, just like Ringo. Guess I would have to be the bass player.

After enough pestering, my mother decided I could buy a bass. When we got to the music store, she suggested I might be happier playing a "regular" guitar. I was all for that if she would buy me the Fender Mustang that was hanging there. Too much money. I ended up with an inexpensive off-brand white bass guitar, a Sekova.

A few weeks later we were practicing at Ricky's house. Probably after listening to us for a short time, his parents decided we might want to play some baseball outside. Stuffed with Fritos and soda, off we went. Passing through the garage, I heard a song on the radio that really caught my ear—"Happy Jack." "That bass is really loud," I thought, "and those drums sure are different." There is just something about this song I like, more so than anything else I had ever heard.

Fast forward—summer is almost over. I'm at our summer home on Lake Sunnyside with my three younger brothers. Mom and Dad are at work. Mike Ingalsbe calls. "Want to go to a concert?" I'd never been to a real concert before. "It's in Rochester. Herman's Hermits and also the Who." Hey, I like Herman's Hermits. "Mrs. Brown, You've Got a Lovely Daughter" and all that. And the Who. They did "Happy Jack." I also heard they smash things up. Heard they smashed a car onstage or something. Sounds good.

I call my mother. Tell her Mrs. Ingalsbe is going to drive. Be back the same night. She says OK.

August 30 arrives, and we're off to Rochester. It's a lot farther than I think. It's a lot farther than Mrs. Ingalsbe thinks too. We get into a driving rainstorm, and Mrs. Ingalsbe pulls over to the side of the New York Thruway. Can't blame her; she is an old lady. Probably all of thirty-five.

Finally arrive in Rochester, kind of a rundown town, a bigger version of my own Glens Falls. Gloomy, gray, and wet. We find the War Memorial Auditorium. There is a casket company nearby. Maybe this isn't such a great idea. Maybe I wish I was home with my brothers, eating popcorn or something.

We go in and find our seats. I'm sitting next to Andy Rogers, another guy that had joined our band. We had auditioned him, and since he was better than the rest of us combined, we let him join. He is a genius. Started college at like fifteen or something. Built his own amplifier, a Heathkit. I like when he kicks it; makes a really neat crashing sound. He's also got a few screws loose. He's at my house and throws his Fender Mustang down my cellar stairs. How can he do that to a beautiful guitar? I like the idea, though.

Sitting in the same row are John McDonnell, Chris O'Hanlon, and other members of their band, the Loners. These guys really know how to play. Up near the ceiling of the auditorium, there is a walkway and a guy with a flashlight. A bomb, maybe? These were funny times.

The first band comes on—the Blues Magoos. I had liked their single "We Ain't Got Nothing Yet." I must have liked them, as I ended up buying their album later, and I didn't have much money for albums back then, only singles. The guitarist has a coat on with colored panels that light up.

They now start setting up for the next band, the Who. They are nailing the drummer's bass drums to the floor! And is that a BUSHEL of drumsticks? Some guy comes running on the stage, wearing a cape and acting like Batman, who was very popular at the time. This guy is crazy! The band comes on. Of course, I have to check out the bass player. Looks like he has a Fender Bassman or Showman amp, and he's playing a white Fender bass with a chrome pick guard. When the light hits it just right, it's blinding. And the guitar

Minneapolis Auditorium, Minneapolis, Minnesota. Sunday, August 20, 1967.
Photo by Mike Barich, the Barich Archive

player, does his guitar have two necks? My eyes aren't that good, and I just can't tell. I do recall "Happy Jack" being played and also "Barbara Ann." Definitely "My Generation." I remark to Andy that it is a Count Five song. He looks at me like I'm crazy. If I'd checked their album a little more closely, I would have seen that "My Generation" and "Out in the Streets" were credited to a guy named Townshend. I remember smoke and

destruction. A few months later, when my brothers and I were watching the Smothers Brothers, they announced that the Who were going to be on. I told my brothers to watch— you're really going to like this. They did.

I slightly remember Herman's Hermits. They did "Mrs. Brown," and the guitarist played it on his guitar, rather than a banjo.

After the show, Mrs. Ingalsbe picked us up and we started the drive back. Mike was teaching me how to sing "Happy Jack." "Lap, lap, lap." We realized we would never make it home at a reasonable hour, and had to stay at a motel.

The Who. I can barely remember what I had this morning for breakfast, but some of the memories of that show and others stay with me. Tough to remember my kids' birthdays, but every August 2 I recall where I was in 1971.

My life had changed.

Minneapolis Auditorium, Minneapolis, Minnesota. Sunday, August 20, 1967. *All photos by Mike Barich, the Barich Archive*

At the Holiday Inn after the concert at the War Memorial Auditorium in Rochester, New York. Wednesday, August 30, 1967.
All photos by Sunny Paul

Keith with Peppy Castro of the Herman's Hermits. Holiday Inn after the concert at the War Memorial Auditorium in Rochester, New York. Wednesday, August 30, 1967. *Photo by Sunny Paul*

Bob Pridden and Pete leaving the Holiday Inn after the concert at the War Memorial Auditorium in Rochester, New York. Wednesday, August 30, 1967. *Photo by Sunny Paul*

Music Hall, Cleveland, Ohio.
Thursday, August 31, 1967. *All
photos by Robert Kavc*

Kim Gottlieb-Walker, www.Lenswoman.com

The following two photos are the only images of the first time John Entwistle smashed his bass on stage, at Anaheim Convention Center, on September 8, 1967.

The only known photos of John smashing his bass. Anaheim Convention Center, California. Friday, September 8, 1967. *Both photos © Kim Gottlieb-Walker, www.lenswoman.com*

Cow Palace, San Francisco, California. Saturday, November 18, 1967. *Both photos by Frank Zinn. Richard Martin Frost archive*

Cow Palace, San Francisco, California. Saturday, November 18, 1967. *Courtesy of Craig Patterson*

Cow Palace's dressing room, San Francisco, California. Saturday, November 18, 1967. *Courtesy of Craig Patterson*

Southfield High School Gymnasium, Michigan. Wednesday, November 22, 1967. *All photos by John B. Brown*

Russell P. Nardi

I own a guitar body that was supposed to be Pete Townshend's that he smashed at a high school performance. It was given to me by my older brother's friend, Jerry Warzywak, who was at the show and was supposed to interview the Who after the show. When he went to the room they were supposed to do the interview in, they were gone already, but on the table was this guitar body. This may have been a prop guitar used at various performances. It may have traveled with the band, even if Pete didn't use it for that particular show (he played a Gibson ES 335), and was just left behind in Southfield. As you can see, it looks like it was repaired a few times! I think the telltale thing to look for is the triple pickups—the third one in this body was added along with the control knob for it.

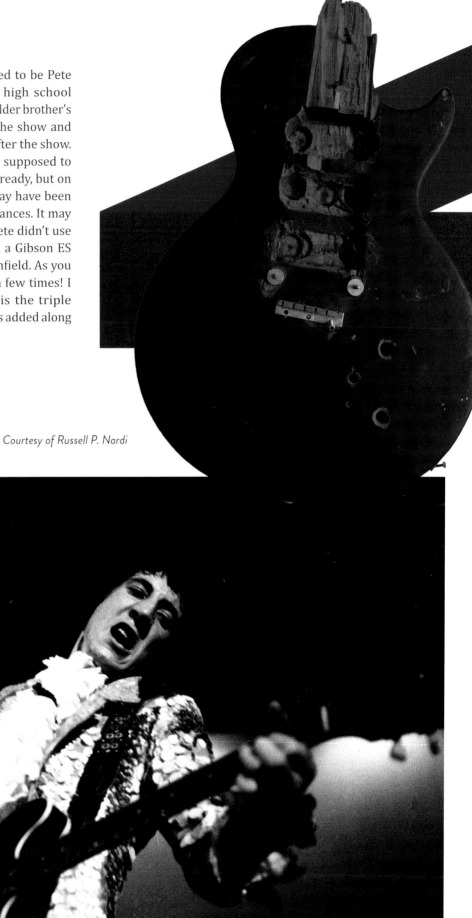

Courtesy of Russell P. Nardi

Village Theater, New York. Saturday, November 25, 1967. *Photo by Charlotte von Segesser*

CHAPTER 5

1968

A Young Man Blues

The year 1968 represented a turning point for many of the rapidly developing political and social movements of the time. It was the same for music. On April 4, Martin Luther King was assassinated. And with his passing, at least temporarily so, the pride and hope of the entire Black American community died with him, gutted and dismayed after only briefly glimpsing the realization of his dream of social equality. In May of that year, this time in Europe, and particularly in Paris and Rome, students revolted against the establishment, particularly against an education system they considered archaic, repressive, and authoritarian. And less than three months later, on August 20, Soviet tanks invaded Czechoslovakia, putting an end to the Prague Spring and thus ruling out the possibility of liberal socialism under Prime Minister Dubcek. The Soviets replaced it with their far-darker and more draconian rule of communism.

Art inevitably absorbs the turmoil of such swift social fracture and transformation, changing its face to new and often very original expressions of creativity. In the realm of popular music, the Beatles composed their Esperanto known as *The White Album*, while Jimi Hendrix expanded the boundaries of rock with *Electric Ladyland*. At the same time, also in England, Cream sang and played its musical swan song with their *Wheels of Fire* album before performing its farewell concert at the Royal Albert Hall. In San Francisco, Jefferson Airplane translated violent student protests against Vietnam into music with *Crown of Creation*, also performing a rooftop concert in New York, filmed by Jean-Luc Godard, D. A. Pennebaker, and Richard Leacock,[1] one year after the Grateful Dead played on the roof of the Chelsea Hotel on August 10, 1967, and months ahead of the Beatles' version in early 1969. For the Who, however, 1968 was a time of relative artistic stasis, a critical gap in the band's unique timeline of creativity, although in retrospect it was really a necessary "breather" and then a catalyst for their soon-to-come superstardom.

Rare Winterland and Fillmore Recordings

On a rare recording from February 23, 1968, at Winterland in San Francisco, Pete introduced the song "I'm a Boy" as "a song off a feature album that is going to be called 'The Who Greatest Flops.' It's a song which is probably the best we've recorded. We recorded it a couple of times and we're going to put all the different versions we dig the most in the album." On a later date, August 15, 1968, at the Fillmore West in San Francisco, Keith introduced "I'm a Boy" as "a song off our *Greatest Flops* LP." (*see page 76 for more information on these recordings*).

The Missing Sellout

After "I Can See for Miles," we launched a string of singles that were all total disasters and this really brought us down. It was at this point that I said The Who would never make another single. When this happens a group generally splits up. If a group goes along without accelerating its talents it is inevitable that you either split up or go into cabaret. But we say it can't be that simple. Why should we split up? The group were in a quandary.[2]

The Who spent 1968 in a near-constant effort to recover from the unexpected flop of their single "I Can See for Miles" and from the lack of expected success of the *Who Sell Out* album, reaching only #13 in England and #48 in the US. Furthermore, the then-somewhat-demoralized band had to survive near-suffocating pressure brought about by regular new material releases imposed by contracts with the US's Decca and the UK's Track Records companies. They simply didn't sell well, and the persistence that year of directionless artistic expression and frustration over contractual requirements almost broke the band up. Townshend summed up the situation adroitly by saying that he "might have to be less serious about art, and more pragmatic about how to sell records in millions."[3]

The band released three songs, none of which reached higher than #20 in the charts. Both "Call Me Lightning" and "Magic Bus" were songs that had been demoed by Pete back in the days of "My Generation," the former being rejected in early 1968 by Track Records for not fitting in with the current sound of the Who, but which was nonetheless released by Decca in the US, where it subsequently flopped. Three months later, in June 1968, "Call Me Lightning" appeared in the UK as the B side of "Dogs"—an ironic "tribute" to the White City dog races in West London. Other songs were recorded but not released until 1974 on the album of "rejects" titled *Odds & Sods*.[4] "Glow Girl" and "Faith in Something Bigger" were two such songs with a vaguely spiritual vibe, with "Little Billy" having been commissioned by the American Cancer Society as a jingle to discourage young people from smoking.

"Dr. Jekyll & Mr. Hyde," one of the few Who songs written by John Entwistle, was initially meant to be part of an album of horror songs for kids, a project that never came to fruition.[5] It eventually ended up as the B side of "Call Me Lightning," as released in America, and then the B side of "Magic Bus," as subsequently released in England that year.

Before the big "castles made of sand" projects, *Lifehouse* and *Rock Is Dead—Long Live Rock*, meant for release in 1971 and 1972, were washed away for being too ambitious in concept and too difficult to record at that period in time, the Who experienced other musical failures that year: *The Who's Greatest Flops* and *Who's for Tennis?*

The first one featured early singles that had either been overlooked or had long been unavailable in America, and the second was an album that had been due out in June 1968, contracted to be released in time for the Wimbledon championships.[6] The year didn't start well.

Later, with no new material to release in 1968, Decca impatiently put out *Magic Bus: The Who on Tour*—the record label's final solution to the failed contractual obligations of a band now four albums behind schedule. One year later, at a radio interview just before the Who's famous appearance at the Fillmore East on May 16, 1969, Pete Townshend referred to the album *Magic Bus* as "disappointing and disgusting," a work reflecting the typically utilitarian attitude of a record label toward a band.

In 1972, Pete remembered *Magic Bus* as

a culmination of all the most terrible things American record companies ever get up to, mere exploitation. . . . They just wanted to exploit The Who while The Who were big—though we weren't that big then, really—and make a few bucks, because who knows what may happen tomorrow? Plus, the fact that they made it look like a live album.[7]

Meanwhile, in England, the Who's problems above were echoed by Track Records' release of *Direct Hits*, a compilation album of early songs previously unavailable because of the courtroom battles with Shel Talmy, a matter that had now settled.

Ain't No Cure For the Summertime Blues

During 1968, however, a general evolution of awareness was taking place in the English music scene, maintaining its distance from West Coast psychedelia and the escapism atmosphere of the previous year, clearly an attempt to get back to basics. A much more down-to-earth trend appeared, but not necessarily one less inspired. Keith said to *Record Mirror*:

> Pop has now turned full circle. At one time it got very complicated but it's getting back to the basics . . . as opposed to the great orchestrations. Pop is young, but it isn't immature.[8]

At this time, along with the Beatles' *White Album*, even the Rolling Stones seemed to be following a similar backward path to their roots. *Beggars Banquet* was plain and simple rock and roll. Around that time, Led Zeppelin burst upon the scene too, with a massively visceral brand of rock infused with the blues. The Who embraced such austerity too, albeit mostly onstage. And it was onstage that their own viscera exploded. While suffering their seemingly never-ending recording studio débacle and probably struggling with the songwriting process they wanted to leave behind, the Who suddenly ignited onstage, perhaps out of anger, and they did so far more influentially than even before. Robert Plant—as David Bowie had before him, Alice Cooper, and others all recall the Who's ferocity onstage with absolute awe, sometimes singling out Daltrey's singing or Moon's maniacal playing in near disbelief.

Some of those changes onstage were due to the great amount of time that the band spent on the road. And some of that time spent on the road was due to those changes having fired up its creativity. It was a loud and energetic feed-forward cycle. After a visit in Oceania with the Small Faces and Paul Jones, from January 19 to February 1, the band flew back to America for their first tour as concert headliners in that country. The first leg kicked off February 21 at the Civic Auditorium in San Jose, California, ending on April 7 at the CNE Coliseum in Toronto, Canada. Townshend, Daltrey, Moon, and Entwistle played at some of the most prestigious venues around and became the highest-paid act to perform at the Fillmore Auditorium.

The Who even conquered Detroit, playing the Grande Ballroom, the first component of the British Invasion to pass through there, if in reality more a second invasion along with such groups as Cream, Pink Floyd, and the Jeff Beck Group.

Photographer Tom Wright traveled with the band for the second time and, in his memoir *Roadwork*, called the Grande Ballroom gig "the best show they had ever put on, for the explosive formula The Who and the Grande audience managed to create."[9]

The band then played what was once known as the Village Theater, now renamed the Fillmore East, thanks to it having been taken over by Bill Graham, who ran the Fillmore Auditorium, Fillmore West, and Winterland venues in San Francisco.

The Who were invited to play that new rock "mecca" on April 5 and 6, only a month after its opening and one day after the murder of Martin Luther King. Despite the tense context, however, the Who's performances would be remembered as monumental.

The Who's "musical austerity" could be seen and heard onstage through the addition of rock and roll covers such as "Easy Going Guy (My Way)" and "C'mon Everybody" by Eddie Cochran, who also wrote and originally recorded "Summertime Blues"; Alain Toussaint's "Fortune Teller"; Mose Allison's "Young Man Blues"; and "Shakin' All Over" by Johnny Kidd & the Pirates. The Who introduced "Daddy Rolling Stone" into their set list, a rare B side of "Anyway Anyhow Anywhere" that had originally been released by them in 1965 in England on Brunswick Records. The song was played at the Fillmore West on August 15, during the second leg of their North American tour that started on June 28 at the Shrine Exposition Hall in Los Angeles, ending at the Hi-Corbett Fields in Tucson, Arizona, on August 30.

The focus on live performances contributed heavily to the Who's internal change in direction and artistic creativity, an internal change perhaps most clearly displayed by the outward appearance of Daltrey and Townshend. Gone was the pop art clothing of 1967 and early 1968. Pete looked less flamboyant live than he had previously. He donned totally different stage clothes, wearing mainly a t-shirt, white or black trousers, and English "Monkey Boots," later changed to Doctor Martens' that were very popular in Britain at the time (years later to be very successfully marketed as "Doc Martens" in the United States). Yet, it was Daltrey who manifested the most-significant changes. Before 1968, he was "just" a singer serving a power trio, but that year he started to build his own character and finally open up as a frontman performer, an intuitively expert interpreter of Pete Townshend's multilayered songs. He became a real fashion icon, starting to grow his hair and to dress up like no other front man before him, with pink velvet trousers, white silk shirts, and shiny vests, etc. He suddenly became, as photographer Thom Lukas would say, "great in camera lenses."[10] He was becoming a superstar in his own right. Yet, even here the differences between Daltrey and Townshend added to other internal band tensions that would ultimately fuel their musical intensity, chemistry, and visually captivating performances onstage. They became louder, more serious, and far more intense. There was no one else like them. No one.

Pete also switched from Fender guitars to using the Gibson SG Special, a guitar with which he would become most closely associated:

> I got fed up with Fenders, because they were too clean, but I liked them because they were tough. In guitar smashing days, the Fender would last two or three shows and ten minutes if I wanted to smash it up. . . . So, I went to the manager and said I really need an alternative to this and he said I think you'd like the newest SG. . . . They're made out of really light wood, it's a light guitar.[11]

It is important to remark here that the band's growth as a hugely influential musical entity, which early record sales and recording techniques only partially represented, was expressed mostly through their energy onstage. Live recordings from 1968 are a demonstration of how Townshend wanted the Who to break away from the two-and-a-half-minute "pop group" identity in order to take on a much-higher level of musical experimentation. From the long "Relax" jam played at the Fillmore East on April 6—lasting over eleven minutes—to the thirty-three-minute jam of "My Generation" from the same night; the nineteen minutes of "Magic Bus" played at the Jaguar Club of St. Charles, Illinois, on August 10; and the sixteen-minute-long version of "Young Man Blues" performed at Fillmore West on August 14. Something had changed and for the better.

And just after the first of those historic three nights—August 13, 14, and 15—at the Fillmore West, *Rolling Stone* magazine's director Jann Wenner joined Pete at Jefferson Airplane's mansion on 2400 Fulton Street for the guitarist's first "*Rolling Stone* Interview."

Wenner was so amazed by Townshend's eloquence and ability to wade through the "swampy" concepts behind the Who's next album that he decided to print the whole conversation, spread over two issues, published on September 14 and 28. That night, Pete proved to be one of the few authoritative intellectuals on rock music and life, as evidenced by his articulation of unusually deeply contemplated perspectives. Among the many topics that he tackled was the nature of studio recording. He even brought up Walter Benjamin's theory that every form of art, once reproduced, is fated to lose its aura:[12]

> A lot of people, I'm convinced, that buy records don't realize what happens when a group records on an eight-track machine. . . . They record it in eights at different locations and this ceases to become music to me.[13]

Referring to this theory, he mentioned a song called "Now I'm a Farmer" that he had written for the Who's new album, saying that "it wasn't music, it wasn't a happening, it wasn't an event, it wasn't a musical situation, it wasn't a beginning and it wasn't an end. It was just roughly parallel musical statements."[14]

The last part of the conversation between Pete and Jann Wenner focused on rock music, its criteria, and its possible developments. Pete used Bob Dylan's and the Rolling Stones' recent releases as examples of where rock music would probably go. His impressive assertions would prove to be prescient:

> Dylan's thing about writing the lyric and then picking the guitar up and just pumping out the song as it comes out, is a direct guide to what will happen in music. People are going to want music to be more realistic, more honest. . . . Music is going to swing, is going to be simple, is going to be impulsive. . . . It's going to be the case that the Stones are going to groove along. A lot of other groups are going to groove along and make good music, in a transitional period, but they're going to be part of the transition and the transition is going to be very delicate. It's going to be, believe it or not, into a kind of a broad, unified thing. Rock and roll is going to embody itself. . . . There's going to be no visible change, the structure of the music will change. I don't think the way the people perform is going to change. The lyrics won't change or anything, but rock and roll is going to change.[15]

Not only is this interview known as Pete's best and most characteristic self-portrait; it is known as his most sensible declaration of intent around the work that would change the Who forever:

> We still worshipped the two-and-a-half-minute rock single, but worshipping it and playing it are two different things. Musically, The Who were totally capable of making records like these but by now we were doing things that just couldn't be captured on the pop single. We needed a bigger vehicle and this led us to *Tommy*.[16]

CHAPTER 6

1968

Anyway Anyhow Anywhere

Jeremy Goodwin

Impressions of a Rock Star: Meeting Pete for the First Time, Gold Albums in the Toilet, and Jerry Garcia's Message to Pete Townshend Just before He Died

My father, Denis Goodwin, was one of Britain's top comedy writers. He partnered with Bob Monkhouse for thirteen years, writing for themselves on radio and television, Jack Benny, Bob Hope, Dean Martin, the Two Ronnies, and Peter Sellers. When I was six, my parents' marriage fell apart, and my mother, Barbara, married her hairstylist, Dallas Amos. He spent five years working with Vidal Sassoon, but now, in his own right, he was a hairdresser to the celebrité: actors such as Lawrence Olivier and Michael Caine, and musicians such as the Who, Eric Clapton, and Cat Stevens. And later, a bunch of the Arsenal Football Team, and a number of top runway models. He did all the haircuts for the Who's *Quadrophenia* album and story booklet and was the first hairstylist to cut Eric Clapton's hair short.

When I first met Pete Townshend in 1968, he was already old, going on twenty-four. I was ten. I saw him standing in the doorway at the Meher Baba Centre, London, on Wardour Street. And Dallas said to me, "See that man in the doorway? He's the best rock guitarist in the world," and I said, "Really? Who is he?" Well, I had never heard of him. However, when I went to school the next day, I proudly told my friends who liked avant-garde music, "I've met the world's best guitarist!," and they said, "Who's that?," to which I responded proudly, "Pete Townshend. He's in the Who." They laughed at me and said, "Oh, Jimi Hendrix would blow him off the stage any day!" I shrank in size, defeated, wishing that the ground would swallow me up. I was so embarrassed because I didn't really know who Pete Townshend was, let alone Jimi Hendrix, and went home that day very upset with my stepdad, to whom I cried, "Why'd you lie to me? My friends said that Jimi Hendrix is the best!" Dallas just said, "Oh, Jeremy, you'll learn as you get older that everybody has their own opinion." That didn't make me feel any better though.

One day, a few years later when I was at Pete's house in Twickenham, I got into his home studio and started playing the drums—well, trying to, but clearly not very well. It was the year that his daughter Emma was born. I was probably thirteen or fourteen. He asked me, not unkindly, to stop playing the drums because I was keeping the baby awake (a bit rich, given his penchant for playing music so loud). He told me that I could keep the drumsticks though, and I still have them. So, I decided to explore somewhere else. I remember going downstairs, where, in addition to on another wall, he had many of his gold and platinum albums lining the toilet walls and ceiling, which I thought very funny. He told me that he had tried to play the first *Live at Leeds* gold album awarded him, and it turned out to be a 1951 Brenda Lee record.

Another time, looking through his records in the living room during a joint birthday party with Dallas (their birthdays are but a day apart), I was surprised to find no albums by the Rolling Stones, Led Zeppelin, the Who, or Jimi Hendrix, nothing like that. Maybe there were a few albums by Joni Mitchell, Leonard Cohen, Bob Dylan, Nina Simone, Stevie Wonder, and Randy Newman, but it was mostly classical music, blues, and jazz. The records were next to his Revox reel-to-reel tape player. I asked him about the collection because I was surprised, and he said, "Oh, I don't listen to things that we or our friends produce, only a bit here and there. I like to listen to classical or jazz; they help provide me new ways to interpret and expand rock music. Listening to one's own stuff is boring. It's work. I prefer something different when home." Now *that* I found cool.

Pete's an interesting man. He's read a lot of philosophy; he's intelligent and really quite funny, unless you are on the wrong end of his biting sense of humor. Clearly, I am not the only one to think so.

One of the last times I saw Pete was backstage with our mutual friend Geoff Gilbert at the Shoreline Amphitheatre, in the San Francisco Bay Area, circa 2000. I was about forty-two. A woman called Annabelle asked if she could interrupt us very briefly. She introduced herself as Jerry Garcia's daughter and said that she was thrilled to be there and was very impressed with the show, especially since it was her first time seeing the Who. She was about thirty-two years old. Pete looked surprised, given that he and her father were friends, and the Who had played on the same bill with the Grateful Dead a number of times. Annabelle explained that her father had wanted to protect her ears because the Who, as he had repeatedly told her, were simply too loud. Pete thought that quite amusing. Jerry Garcia had died only five or six years before, so Pete told Annabelle how much he missed her dad. Apparently, they used to sit up all night talking after their shows. Annabelle explained that her father had taken her hand just before he died and said, "If you ever meet Pete Townshend, please tell him that Jerry Garcia said that 'he's the nicest fucking asshole I've ever met,'" and he said it with great affection too. She had worried that Pete would be offended, but he smiled so warmly, thanked her rather emotionally, and gave her a hug. Annabelle thanked him for letting her speak openly and told him that she was so relieved to have passed on the message.

I don't remember much after that. That was enough. And I like Jerry Garcia.

Peter Buckley

Sydney Stadium, Australia, on Monday, January 22, 1968

January 1968 in Sydney was in the middle of summer, and summers in Sydney are notoriously hot, dry, and sweaty. The "Big Show" tour in Australia, which hit Sydney with the Who, Small Faces, Paul Jones, and the Aussie group the Questions, fronted by the big-voiced and later to be legendary Doug Parkinson, was eagerly anticipated. I walked a long distance from the city to the concert at Sydney Stadium, an uncomfortable, crowded venue, and the show atmosphere was building and building until the Who came on, and then it was utter musical chaos. Screaming girls, and musical theatrics of every kind onstage, culminating in the mechanical revolving stage breaking down, so the Who were facing in one direction and the crowd rushed from the other sides so that they still had a view of the band. The stadium was always known as "the old tin shed," and it was uncomfortably hot and not the best venue for loud bands. The acoustics were woeful, and it was a case of full-on ear-jamming noise made bearable by the unbelievable gymnastics of Pete Townshend and Keith Moon onstage. Guitar smashing, drums flying everywhere, smoke, and a not-to-be-forgotten Armageddon-like finale where you were left wondering whether a small atomic explosion had just gone off. Following that concert, I definitely wanted to be in a band, like every other young, postschool lad, and got busy on that project not long after.

Sally Mann Romano

An Evening with Keith and John

My memories of the Who do not center on their appearance at Woodstock, although I was there with Jefferson Airplane, who performed immediately after the Who. Before either band's performance, however, late in the evening on the Saturday the Airplane had been originally scheduled to perform, I became ill with a high fever and had to be flown back to our hotel via helicopter, which was arranged by the Airplane's manager, Bill Thompson, and Bill Graham. Even so, I did have some "interesting" experiences with the Who before Woodstock, particularly Keith Moon and John Entwistle, and while the memories are a bit dim after almost fifty years, there is one particular night that I will never forget.

In 1968 I was living in Hollywood, working, when the spirit moved me—meaning rarely—as an actress and model, and fortunate enough to have been close with John Mayall, Frank Zappa, Phil Spector, and some of the other more colorful characters of the day, relationships that had made me persona grata at many of the clubs on the Sunset Strip. As

Centennial Hall, Adelaide, Australia. Saturday, January 27, 1968.
Photo by Barry Smith

The Who in concert at the Wellington Town Hall. *Dominion Post* (newspaper): photographic negatives and prints of the *Evening Post* and *Dominion* newspapers. *Ref: EP/1968/0473/2-F, Alexander Turnbull Library, Wellington, New Zealand*

you know, it was an amazing time musically, and my social life revolved to a significant extent around the Whiskey à Go Go, the Trip (until it closed), the Troubador, and the other nightclubs where the most incredible bands could be heard, seen—and, most importantly, met—on a nightly basis. I'm almost certain that I was first introduced to Keith and John at the Whiskey—I recall being in Elmer Valentine's VIP booth with them, along with the standard copious amounts of champagne and other potent potables, while we watched whatever exceptional band may have been playing that night. At some point during the evening's festivities, it was decided that we should continue our celebration, of what I have no idea, back at the Who's hotel. Unlike most English and American bands at the time, the Who did not stay at the Landmark or any of the more popular hotels on or near Sunset, but, as best as I recall, had broken tradition and taken things up a notch by booking suites at the much more upscale Beverly Wilshire.

In my most vivid memory of that night, Keith was driving a Porsche 911, and the three of us crammed into the front seat of the car as we sped off from the Whiskey in a cloud of cigarette smoke and exhaust. Somehow, we made our way down Wilshire Boulevard at an obnoxious rate of speed, without getting killed or caught, and were preparing to turn left off the main street into the driveway at the entrance of the hotel. We caught a red light at the left turn, and after waiting impatiently for all of about ten seconds or so, Keith became exasperated that the light was not turning green at his command, and simply jumped out of the car, exhorting John and I to do the same. He abandoned the incredibly expensive Porsche outright, leaving the coveted car *running in the empty intersection*, where it stood out like the proverbial sore thumb, and the three of us ran across the street on foot without a backward glance, although, I have to admit, I remember being completely astounded at the whole devil-may-care aspect of it. The fate of the Porsche, obviously a rental and thus imminently replaceable or interchangeable in Keith's eyes, is unknown to me, and I'm sure to Keith and John as well. I feel certain they never gave it another thought—after all, that's what road managers are for.

I later reconnected with John after I had moved to San Francisco with James Gurley of Big Brother & the Holding Company. My great friend, Karen Seltenrich, mother of Gareth Kantner (son of Paul), who was featured on the cover of the infamous so-called "Groupies and Other Women of Rock" *Rolling Stone* issue, in which I also appeared, hitchhiked (!) down south to see them in San Jose. We thought nothing of standing on the shoulder of US 101 in *full-length, white satin, Jean Harlow–esque gowns* and the

Keith (standing away from his drum kit for the intro of "A Quick One") about to hand Kevin Jarvis's Fender Esquire to Pete. Kevin is seen on the right-hand side going back to his seat. *Courtesy of Craig Patterson*

odd feather boa or two, but as foolhardy as this may have been, we got there in one piece, and, as reckless acts go, it came in a distant second to Keith's leaving a Porsche 911 running on Wilshire Boulevard.
©2017 Sally Mann Romano

Kevin Jarvis

Civic Auditorium, San Jose, California, on Wednesday, February 21, 1968

Kevin Jarvis and Pete Townshend. Is it a story of unrequited love, teenage foolishness, one of those chains of events where one unusual happenstance leads to another and another, or is it really a story about the life of a guitar, an Esquire? To me, that is the real story. Pete and I were an accident.

Why I grabbed the guitar and took it to the concert just because my friend Craig said, "Bring it along," I will never understand myself. Craig asked me to bring the guitar along to wave at Pete in between songs, to get his attention so that Dave Pityer (our companion and photographer for the evening) could take a picture of Pete. We did this as Pete was doing his lengthy intro to "A Quick One," and Pete saw it and said, "Ah, yes ... smash!" The crowd *loved* it and called for me to *give* Pete the guitar, and I blindly complied. Pete thanked me, saying, "It's always nice to have gifts ..." Then he continued on with the show, leaving me standing there. I go back to my seat and realize "*Fuck, my guitar.*"

Personally, I don't think it tells well. Misunderstanding what was going on versus a loving fan's gift doesn't draw the listener in. I can't believe I talked the security guard into letting me up into backstage. I can't believe I stood there just behind the curtain next to Entwistle the whole

Pete with members of the band Sagittarius, opening for the Who. Backstage of Civic Auditorium, San Jose, California. Wednesday, February 21, 1968. *Frank Zinn, Richard Martin Frost archive*

rest of the show and nobody booted me. I can't believe watching a demon-eyed Keith Moon telling John to break it. John shaking his head "no" ever so slightly.

Keith fills the snare with beer and lays off it until the final chords of the last song come signaling the end of the set. He then begins pounding the snare, sending suds everywhere, including onto my guitar. Pete is pissed seeing me there. After he reduces his guitar to rubble, he runs back through rolling floor toms and crashing cymbal stands and grabs the Esquire. I am screaming, "*Nooooooooo*" as he throws it up into the air for what should be the final moments of my guitar's existence. But to my surprise, he catches it and chucks it off the stage. I can't believe I run across the stage right by Pete and leap off. That jump would kill me today. And I can't believe that I get to the guitar and then find myself in a wrestling match with someone way stronger than me, but I'm not fucking letting go of *my* guitar! But it's my buddy Dave Pityer, and we realize who each other is, and the guitar was saved!

Civic Auditorium, San Jose, California. Wednesday, February 21, 1968. *Photo above by Frank Zinn, Richard Martin Frost Archive; photo at left by Dave Pityer, courtesy of Craig Patterson*

John Darsey of Gilroy, California

Fillmore Auditorium, San Francisco, California, on Thirsday, February 22, 1968

I saw the Who twice in 1968; first time was February 22, at the old Fillmore Auditorium, with Cannonball Adderley, the Vagrants (with Leslie West), and the Nice.

This show was during a streak at the Fillmore that included the Who, Hendrix, John Mayall's Bluesbreakers (with Mick Taylor), Cream (two weeks), and Traffic, all in a six-week period! And only $3 for each show! And two sets from each band each night! Those were the days.

This particular night, I was going up with friends. We gathered at someone's house, and somebody had made pot brownies . . . never tried them before, but I was up for anything in those days, so I tried one. It started coming on during the Vagrants' first set.

From the Who's first set, I recall they were playing songs mostly from the *Sell Out* album—it was great hearing songs like "I Can See for Miles." Of course they closed with "My Generation," with Pete smashing his guitar. After the set, I went to the bar for a coke, and one of the road crew (I guess) came in with the busted body. I asked for it, but

he was looking for someone to give him something for it, and I was broke . . . I did get the magnet from one of the pickups, though. I carried it as a good luck charm for a few years, but it's lost to time now!

Second time was August 14 or 15, with James Cotton and Magic Sam. This time the Who had a new mini-opera they'd been working on: "A Quick One While He's Away."

Civic Auditorium, San Jose, California. Wednesday, February 21, 1968. *Photos by Dave Pityer, courtesy of Craig Patterson*

Dressing room of the Fillmore Auditorium, San Francisco, California. Thursday, February 22, 1968. *Both photos by Frank Zinn, Richard Martin Frost archive*

Fillmore Auditorium, San Francisco, California. Thursday, February 22, 1968. © *Jim Marshall Photography LLC*

Fillmore Auditorium, San Francisco, California. Thursday, February 22, 1968. *All photos by Paul Sommer, thanks to Brian Lux*

Fillmore Auditorium, San Francisco, California. Thursday, February 22, 1968. *Photo by Frank Zinn, Richard Martin Frost archive*

John and Keith at their hotel in the Tenderloin district, in San Francisco, before their appearance at Winterland. Friday, February 23, 1968. *All photos courtesy of Dawn Hall of Douglas Kent Hall estate, thanks to Princeton University Library*

John and Keith at their hotel in the Tenderloin district, in San Francisco, before their appearance at Winterland. Friday, February 23, 1968. *All photos courtesy of Dawn Hall of Douglas Kent Hall estate, thanks to Princeton University Library*

Pete and John tuning up in the Winterland dressing room. Friday, February 23, 1968. *Dawn Hall of Douglas Kent Hall estate, thanks to Princeton University Library*

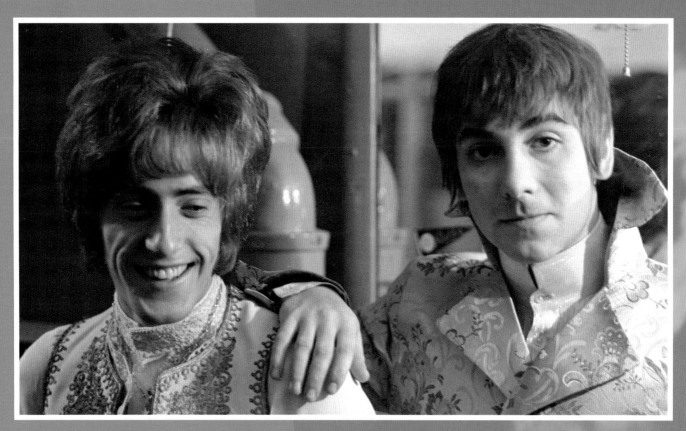

Winterland dressing room before the show. Friday, February 23, 1968. *Dawn Hall of Douglas Kent Hall estate, thanks to Princeton University Library*

Winterland dressing room before the show. Friday, February 23, 1968. *Dawn Hall of Douglas Kent Hall estate, thanks to Princeton University Library*

Winterland, San Francisco, California. Friday, February 23, 1968, before the first set. *Photograph by Frank Zinn, Richard Martin Frost archive*

Winterland, San Francisco, California. First set. Friday, February 23, 1968. *All photos courtesy of Dawn Hall of Douglas Kent Hall estate, thanks to Princeton University Library*

Winterland, San Francisco, California. First set. Friday, February 23, 1968. *All photos courtesy of Dawn Hall of Douglas Kent Hall estate, thanks to Princeton University Library*

Unknown guest. Winterland dressing room, February 23, 1968. *Dawn Hall of Douglas Kent Hall estate, thanks to Princeton University Library*

A kid sitting onstage and enjoying John's playing. Winterland, San Francisco, California. First set. Friday, February 23, 1968. *Dawn Hall of Douglas Kent Hall estate, thanks to Princeton University Library*

Winterland, San Francisco, California. First set. Friday, February 23, 1968. *Dawn Hall of Douglas Kent Hall estate, thanks to Princeton University Library*

Richard Martin Frost

Photographer Frank Zinn titled the string of the following three pictures "Townshend Terror at Winterland"—Pete putting up his dukes to stop a guy at the front of the stage from grabbing Roger's ankles. Frank told me that the guy started playing cat and mouse with Pete, daring him to smash his hand with his guitar. As Frank tells it, the guy got his wish.

Winterland, San Francisco, California. First set. Friday, February 23, 1968. *All photos by Frank Zinn, Richard Martin Frost archive*

Winterland, San Francisco, California. Second set. Friday, 23 February 1968. *Frank Zinn, Richard Martin Frost archive*

Winterland, San Francisco, California. Friday, February 23, 1968, second set. *Photograph by Frank Zinn, Richard Martin Frost archive*

Winterland, San Francisco, California. Friday, February 23, 1968, after sets. *Photograph by Frank Zinn, Richard Martin Frost archive*

Craig Patterson

Winterland, San Francisco, California, on Saturday, February 24, 1968

When the boys and I went to the Winterland show on February 24, it had been only three days since we had seen the Who in San Jose. We were still recovering from *that* concert! Our friend Kevin Jarvis didn't go to this show with us, which was unusual, but we figured that he was still recovering from his successful rescue of his guitar from the clutches of Pete Townshend at the San Jose Civic gig. It was probably too soon for him to face Pete again!

The Who were topping a bill that included the Vagrants, a New York band featuring Leslie West, who was unknown at this time. West was a hell of a guitarist, using a Gibson Les Paul Junior, which was dwarfed by his plus-size frame. The Vagrants were *loud*. Cannonball Adderley and his jazz group rounded out the bill. Bill Graham loved putting bands and solo musicians of very different genres together for his presentations. The man was a *pioneer* (in June 1969, Graham would pair the Who up with Woody Herman and the Herd, a big band first formed in the 1940s. They also turned out to be very loud).

We brought a chipboard guitar case with a beat-up acoustic guitar into Winterland with us. My best friend, Randy Tinch, had dredged it up somewhere. We wanted to give it to Pete, or, failing that, to get his attention so that I could take a couple of shots of him by using my trusty Kodak Instamatic. After all, this plan had sorta worked at the San Jose show, and *this time* we were eager to give him the guitar *and let him keep it*. We were allowed to bring the guitar into Winterland with absolutely no questions, or even a cursory examination from Graham's staff. *This is how things were then.*

Scrambling through the lobby, we wound up sitting on the floor two "rows" back, on Pete's side of the stage. In those days, "festival seating" was still doable. After the Who walked onstage for their first set, our plan was to wait a couple of songs and then offer to hand over the guitar (in its case) to Pete and snap off a couple of pictures. Hey, maybe he'd smash the thing right then and there!

However, we became starstruck when Pete looked down at us and didn't acknowledge the guitar or us.

The band played exceptionally well that night, and *loud* of course. Pete had his Marshall tops and four Sound City cabinets, with their ripped grill cloths. Right before the end of the set, Keith Moon got up from behind his "Pictures of Lily" drum kit with a medium-sized cymbal in one hand. He walked to the front of the stage between Pete and Roger and handed the cymbal to a bearded guy in the front row. Just like that. The crowd went, "*Ooooooh!*" When the set had ended, we still hadn't made a move to give Pete the guitar (however, I *had* fired off a couple of shots anyway). So the guy with the cymbal, whose name was Jim, saw our

Randy Tinch giving Pete the Kay guitar he and Craig Patterson had carried inside Winterland. Leslie West, who was playing in the Vagrants that night, sits behind Pete. Winterland dressing room, between sets. Saturday, February 24, 1968. *Photo by Craig Patterson*

guitar case and said, "Do you want to give that to Pete?" We said, "Oh, yeah," so Randy and I followed Jim to the backstage curtain, where we were allowed inside. I was extremely nervous; this was *unbelievable*! We were pretty certain that we were going to be *discovered*, two teenage kids with a crappy guitar case between us, *and be asked to leave*. But that didn't happen.

The first person we encountered was Roger Daltrey. I offered him a Marlboro, and he took it. I nervously asked him what kind of cigarettes he smoked when he was home in England, and he smiled. "I roll me own," he said. We looked for Pete, but he was chatting with a journalist at the back of the room. I asked Roger where John was, and he said that he was roaming around behind the stage, so we didn't end up meeting him. Keith walked by and was sweating like crazy, chugging Coors beer, one in each hand. He took off his T-shirt and mopped himself with it, as someone piped up, "He should have used Odorono!"

While we waited for Pete to finish with the journalist, Randy struck up a conversation with Leslie West, who was sitting in a folding chair just inside the entrance to the dressing room. "Where are you guys from?" Randy asked.

"New York," West replied. Randy, a real wise guy, asked him, "Oh . . . are all people from New York as fat as you?" Leslie just ignored us after that.

Pete was through talking with the journalist and sat down near us, next to Leslie West. I had my camera at the ready as Randy offered Pete the guitar case. "Pete, this is for you from my friend (indicating me) and I." Pete said, "Oh well . . . thank you . . . What kind of guitar is it?," as he was opening the latches on the case. Randy replied, "It's a Kay," and Pete said, "Well, you know, I've already got a Kay . . ." "Not like this one," said Randy. At this point I took a beautiful picture of Randy, Pete, Leslie West, and the guy that got us backstage, Jim, looking in anticipation as Pete opened the case to reveal the beat-up Kay acoustic guitar. Pete gave us a little smile and said to Randy, "Yeah . . . you're right," and "Thanks, I needed another guitar case." So *that* made us feel good.

We hung out for a few more minutes, and as we edged our way out of the backstage area, I found the nerve to ask Pete, "Can you do 'Summertime Blues' again?" He said, "Oh, I'll have to ask John; he makes up the set list."

When they came back out for their second set, Randy and I were back in our second-row seats. Pete looked down at us and gave us a little nod, walked up to his microphone, and said, "We've had a request to repeat this one . . . it's Eddie Cochran's 'Summertime Blues.'" I swear the band ripped into the song without so much as a count in. Request fulfilled.

The term "I can die now" was made for moments like this.

Winterland dressing room, between sets. Saturday, February 24, 1968. *Photo by Craig Patterson*

Winterland dressing room, between sets. Leslie West warming up (*on the left*). Saturday, February 24, 1968.
Photo by Craig Patterson

Winterland, San Francisco, California. Saturday, February 24, 1968. *Photo above by Craig Patterson; two photos at right by Steve Caraway, courtesy of Craig Patterson*

Winterland, San Francisco, California. Saturday, February 24, 1968. *Photo at left by Craig Patterson; photo above and below by Steve Caraway, courtesy of Craig Patterson*

Winterland, San Francisco, California. Saturday, February 24, 1968. *All photos by Frank M. Stapleton*

Winterland, San Francisco, California.
Saturday, February 24, 1968. *All
photos by Frank M. Stapleton*

Winterland, San Francisco, California. Saturday, February 24, 1968. *All photos by Frank M. Stapleton*

Cannonball and Nat Adderley opening for the Who at Winterland. Saturday, February 24, 1968. *Frank M. Stapleton*

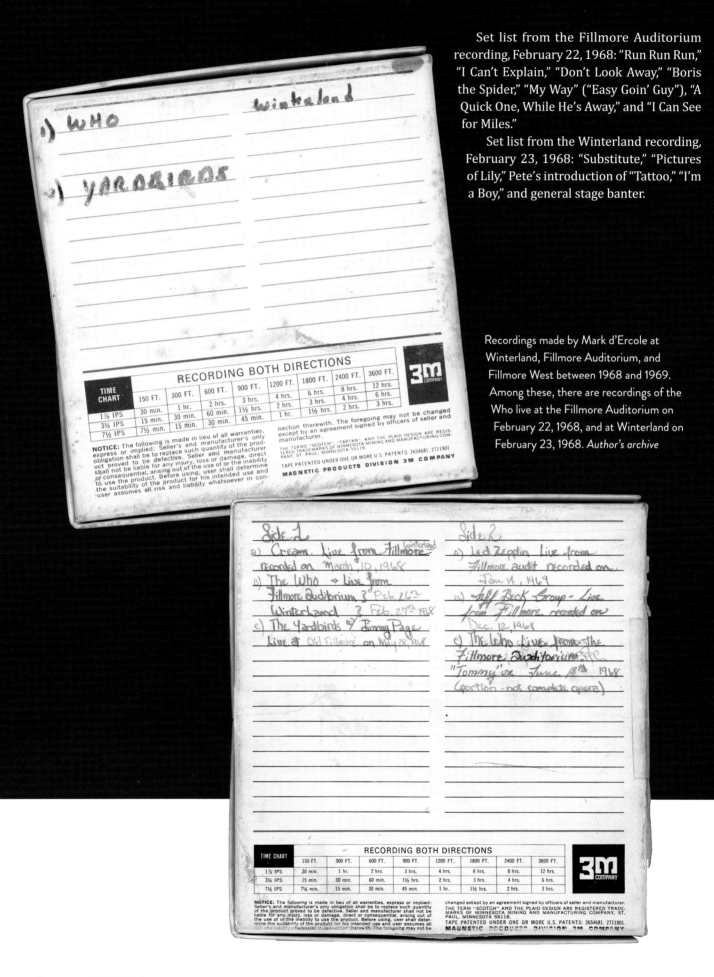

Set list from the Fillmore Auditorium recording, February 22, 1968: "Run Run Run," "I Can't Explain," "Don't Look Away," "Boris the Spider," "My Way" ("Easy Goin' Guy"), "A Quick One, While He's Away," and "I Can See for Miles."

Set list from the Winterland recording, February 23, 1968: "Substitute," "Pictures of Lily," Pete's introduction of "Tattoo," "I'm a Boy," and general stage banter.

Recordings made by Mark d'Ercole at Winterland, Fillmore Auditorium, and Fillmore West between 1968 and 1969. Among these, there are recordings of the Who live at the Fillmore Auditorium on February 22, 1968, and at Winterland on February 23, 1968. *Author's archive*

Ursula Stewart

The photos were taken at the Edmonton Inn, in their hotel rooms, the night before their March 2, 1968, concert at the New Edmonton Gardens in Edmonton, Alberta.

We pretended to be doing an article for the school paper at the school we were going to, Harry Ainley High School.

Keith Moon had a black eye from getting into a fight after their last concert. Pete and John were very grouchy!

Edmonton Inn, Alberta, Canada. Friday, March 1, 1968. *From left to right*: Bob Pridden, Linda Orbeck Beaumont, Keith Moon, Wendy Orbeck Crowley, Mary Redge Willett. *Photo by Ursula Stewart*

Edmonton Inn, Alberta, Canada. Friday, March 1, 1968. *From left to right*: Linda Orbeck Beaumont, Roger Daltrey, Wendy Orbeck Crowley, Ursula Witschl (now Ursula Stewart). *Photo by Ursula Stewart*

Edmonton Inn, Alberta, Canada. Friday, March 1, 1968. *All photos by Ursula Stewart*

David Miller

Grande Ballroom, Detroit, Michigan, on Saturday, March 9, 1968

The first time they played at the Grande Ballroom, they seemed a little awestruck with it, almost intimidated. They were dressed in their extreme Mod outfits: red velvet pants, frilly lacy shirts, Mod haircut. I ran the lights and sound, which were Altec Lansing theater speakers, Altec Lansing amp with five mic inputs. The lights above the front of the stage were five incandescent outdoor flood bulbs maybe 150 watts each: red, blue, green, and yellow and white. The other pendragon oil-and-water light show had a spot and oil and water in glass bowls placed on overhead projectors, which made great effects. The light show was shot from the rear of the ballroom dance floor, and in an elevated wooden platform large enough for Chad and Clyde—the light-show guys—to work the equipment in the light-show platform. The Grande was always alive with the local crazy hippie crowd, long hair, black lights, head shops, soda bar, local drug dealers (weed and psychedelics mostly), and no violence. The MC5 were a regular band there and played a very hard, loud brand of rock and roll. Maybe that is what gave me the impression that the Who seemed a little intimidated with the place. Or maybe it was just their English MO?

The dressing rooms at the Grande were very small rooms on either side of the stage, which was approximately 10 feet by 25 feet and about 20 feet tall. The ballroom's legal capacity was about 1,600 people.

Each of the Who shows was sold out. After we set up the equipment, wall of Marshall amps and double-bass drum set, and after mic check, I offered them a toke on a joint I was smoking, which they declined, and then I introduced them to a waiting joyous crowd. After the first song and the crowd went fucking wild . . . their shyness melted away, and they just proceeded to kick the shit out of a wonderful set of their music, with a crescendo of Pete shredding his amps and then windmilling his guitar to pieces while Roger twirled his mic and Keith destroyed his drum set. The crowd had never seen anything like it, and from then on and after, the Who had broken their Grande cherry; they would be wildly welcomed back to a place they felt was like a home away from home.

They played May 9, 10, and 11, 1969. The first tour to North America started in Detroit at the Grande.

I got to know them a little, and I remember Roger being kind of fascinated with the long buckskin shirt I was wearing, and which I had made, very crude or rustic with about 9-inch fringes across.

Grande Ballroom, Detroit, Michigan. Saturday, March 9, 1968. *Photo by Joseph Crachiola*

Christine Currie

Grande Ballroom, Detroit, Michigan, on Saturday, March 9, 1968

I met the Who when I went to see them at the Grande Ballroom with a friend of mine.

Townshend invited us in the dressing room; we knew sign language, and we stood by the dressing room door and pretended we were mute. Townshend believed that, but at a certain point I accidentally talked, so Townshend immediately pointed his finger at me! Later that night the singer began flirting with me, so I left. I was still a virgin. I remember when I was leaving, one guy had a chair and said, "One of the Who sat on this; it will be valuable in the future!"

Later, my friend Cindy went to the hotel where the Who were staying, and spent the night with Keith Moon. She told me that while she was in the bed with him, he talked to his wife on the phone!

Grande Ballroom, Detroit, Michigan. Saturday, March 9, 1968. *Photo by Ruth Hoffman*

Grande Ballroom, Detroit, Michigan. Saturday, March 9, 1968. *Both photos by John B. Brown*

Tony Palmer

Opera House, Exposition Gardens, Peoria, Illinois, on Sunday, March 10, 1968

My connection to the Who came from Kit Lambert, because he was the godson of the great composer William Walton, whom I knew very well, and son of Constant Lambert, who was one of the founders of the Royal Ballet. Kit Lambert and I got on absolutely immediately. He said, "I want you to do lots of films of my group, called the Who." At that point I worked for the BBC, and we had a weekly arts-and-entertainment show called *How It Is*, and I put the Who on as often as I possibly could, without making it look too obvious! Having been included in this BBC arts magazine, Kit said, "We are shortly going on tour in the States, and I know you are going to make a film (later called *All My Loving*). You must have them in the film!" I said, "Absolutely!" So, we filmed them in Peoria, Illinois, and that was an extraordinary evening. The irony was that where we filmed them was in the local opera house: one year later, Pete and I talked about whether I thought (although the original idea had come from Kit Lambert) that *Tommy* was a rock opera. Pete asked me did I think it was a good title and would it make a good impression in the eyes of the pop world by calling it an opera? I reminded him, "Oh, absolutely. After all, we had already filmed you in an opera house in 1968!"

Dennis Quinn

Fillmore East, New York, on Friday, April 5, 1968

There were supposed to be two shows that night, an 8:30 and a 10:30. We had reserved second-row-center seats for the 10:30 show. I think the seats were like $5. Would you believe that? After waiting outside in the cold for a couple of hours to get inside and sit down, the people coming out of the 8:30 show were saying how bummed they were because the Who didn't perform the early show. When my two buddies and I got inside, we found four other guys in our seats. We told them they needed to get up, but since the Who hadn't come on for their 8:30, they refused to get up. An argument ensued and, all of us being teenagers from New York, of course a fight started. It spilled out into the aisle as the ushers came running down and tried to stop the fight and find out what the cause of the fight was. For a few minutes we tried to explain what was going on, when all of a sudden the lights went down, those guys ran back to their seats, and as a crowd of people rushed the stage, we were pushed right up against the front of the stage, and on Townshend's side. I figured, okay, I'd rather be sitting second-row center, but standing at the edge of the stage in front of Pete would be cool.

Fillmore East, New York. Friday, April 5, 1968. *Photo by Dennis Quinn*

As the show went on, I noticed a beautiful blonde standing next to me, taking photographs, with what was obviously professional gear. I had a cheap Kodak Instamatic myself. Turns out she was the house photographer for the Fillmore, a lady named Linda Eastman. A year later that beautiful blonde married Paul McCartney. So, as the show went on, we were both taking pictures of the band.

At the end of the show, the stage was littered with debris from Keith's drums, and other assorted equipment, and Pete wrapped his strap and guitar cable around his guitar and walked to the edge of the stage, holding the guitar over his head, looking like he was about to toss it out into the audience. I'd seen about a half dozen or more shows before this one, including being front-row center at their very first US appearance at the RKO 58th St. Theater in Manhattan a year earlier. So I'd already seen him throw pieces of guitars he had destroyed into the audience before, but never a whole guitar in one piece.

As I'm looking over to my left, watching him standing there with the guitar over his head, I realize the guy sitting in what should have been my seat is about to have Townshend throw his guitar right at him. My first thought was "If he catches that guitar, he's not getting out of here alive." As I'm thinking this, Pete lowers the guitar and walks over to right in front of where I'm standing. He looks down at me and extends the guitar out, right in my face.

I wasn't sure what was going on, but I reached up, not grabbing the Strat but just putting my hands on it, he grins at me, lets it go in my hands, and walks off the stage.

Now people all around me are grabbing at the guitar, and as one guy snatches the strap off it, my buddy, a 6-foot-5, 250-pound football player, grabs him by the back of his shirt, pulls him back over the seats and clocks him upside the head. And as he hits the floor, people start backing away from me.

I was lucky to have on a heavy wool cape, the kind the British bobbies wore in winter, and as I put the guitar under my cape, my two buddies ran blockers for me, as we pushed our way up the aisle and out the front doors and into a cab.

Now we're headed back to Brooklyn, and my friends are like, "Quinn, you've got Townshend's guitar."

"Townshend gave you his freakin' guitar, man."

I was pretty much dazed and confused all the way home and for days later. Funny thing, for years after that night, at gigs or at parties, I was always introduced as "This is the guy who has Townshend's guitar." Never "This is my friend Quinn," but always "This is the guy who has Townshend's guitar." I can live with that!

Dennis Quinn in the 1970s playing the Stratocaster Pete handed him at the Fillmore East on April 5, 1968.

Fillmore East, New York. Friday, April 5, 1968.
Photo by Charlotte von Segesser

Photographer Charlotte von Segesser brings the Pearly King jacket back to Pete after fifty-two years. She got it after the Fillmore East concert on April 5, 1968. *@mr_mattmyers*

Thom Lukas

My First Introduction to the Who

The first time I came across the Who I remember well, I remember very very well . . . it's just amazing; I feel so privileged to, because I was listening to the radio at night in bed very quietly, because I think I didn't want to disturb anybody. It might have been very late. I was about twelve years old—it was 1965. I was listening to WINS radio station, a program hosted by Murray the K. Every night I listened to Murray the K because he played the best songs of any of the disc jockeys on the New York stations; he was cooler than the other disc jockeys. He wasn't a natural-style disc jockey; he was like a jiver, a hip guy, an older guy who acted young, but for some reason it was appealing to a twelve- or thirteen-year-old kid.

One time he said he was going to England with his friends the Beatles; they were going to do some shows, and the Beatles invited him over. He would call in during his show—somebody else was hosting the show for the week that he was gone, but during each show he called in, so you would get Murray the K talking on the telephone from England. And he would say, "Oh, I'm backstage here with my friends the Beatles, and they just came off the stage, and you won't believe what I just saw! I just saw this group open for the Beatles, and these guys are called the Who! They're amazing!"

That was my first introduction to the Who, opening for the Beatles at some show in England, and Murray the K was there; he was hyping them up. I think he played some of their live set; I think he played "I Can't Explain." Thirty seconds of "I Can't Explain" being played live over the telephone from England. The song had not been released in America, probably wouldn't be for many, many months. That was an incredible thing! And there were very few people I could talk to about it . . . my chest was exploding.

I remember a few weeks or a few months later I saw a story about the Who on the cover of an English magazine called *Rave*. There was a magazine in America called *Sixteen* that was similar, but *Rave* was printed on glossy paper, and *Sixteen* was printed on newsprint, the cheaper paper. And it was also a cross between *Sixteen* magazine, which was for teenagers, young girls really, and maybe a slicker magazine like *Vogue* or something like that. So it was half rock and half fashion, but it wasn't just girls' fashion; it was the fashions of these bands—you saw the bands presented as like models, and their clothes were emphasized. That's where I saw pictures of the Who for the first time.

Murray the K's Music in the Fifth Dimension: RKO 58th Street Theatre, New York, on Saturday–Sunday, March 25–April 2, 1967

We found out they were coming to the RKO 58th St. for one week during Easter 1967, when I was about fourteen. It was on the Upper East Side, where rich people lived, a businessy area. It was near two of the biggest department stores in New York, like Bloomingdales was for the wealthy people and Alexander's for the poor people, right in the same area, not far from Sutton Place, where some of the wealthiest people in the world lived, where Woody Allen got his poster idea for *Manhattan*. Those were the first million-dollar homes around Sutton Place Park. That's just a few blocks from the RKO 58th St. I lived in Ridgewood Queens, so I had to come into Manhattan on the train—two trains to get to Manhattan. Me and my best friend decided we were gonna go, and we knew the RKO 58th St.—we had been there seeing movies, and I don't think there had ever been a rock show there; Murray the K usually had his rock shows not in Manhattan, but in Brooklyn. It was kind of hard for kids like me to go to a show in Brooklyn because that area was segregated, a Black area. It was a cultural experience going there—you walked past record shops and they were playing James Brown really loud. It was very new for me as a kid, because I was into pop music, I knew about that excellent R 'n' B and Black music through these English bands, but it took a while to appreciate that. So we were surprised this Murray the K show was in Manhattan, featuring the Who and "The" Cream, it said in the prints. The Cream—we knew it wasn't "The" Cream; we knew it was Cream—I got their first album.

I had seen *The Who Sings My Generation* album cover a million times in record stores in Greenwich Village—the cool record stores in Greenwich Village would feature those English albums in the windows, and we would just stare at those album covers for twenty minutes, just staring at the English album covers. They were double the price of the American ones, and we could never buy them—they were too expensive—we could barely buy an American album, Beatles or Rolling Stones . . . I remember also seeing the Bluesbreakers, Eric Clapton on the cover; they would feature these cool albums.

I was ready for the Who at the RKO 58th St. After the first show, I stayed for two more shows, then I came back another day for another show. I tried to do a third day, but I couldn't get in because the train had gotten stopped between two stations. So, we were late to get in; if you didn't get in as people were going out, you couldn't get in! We walked in for free by walking backward as people were leaving—and we couldn't pay to get in; it was like $3.50—

it was a fortune for a kid. And plus we just didn't like the idea of paying for shows; we felt we should be able to get in for free. That's a crazy idea, but that's what we thought at the time, because we had luck doing that several times.

Everything started happening in 1967. I saw them again at the Village Theater in July 1967; I tried to get backstage with them. A wonderful experience for a kid . . . I couldn't get backstage, but I could talk to Keith Moon before they opened the stage door for him and for his blonde companion . . . it was a sunny day.

That same year, I got a job working at a candy store that sold magazines. It was on the corner of my high school, a boys-only high school, like a private high school, but it was a public high—it was free—but I had to take a test to get in; it was like an exclusive boys' high school. And it was on 15th St., 1st Avenue, Manhattan. And on the corner of 16th St. and 1st Avenue was the candy shop where I worked; it was directly opposite Beth Israel hospital, the hospital where Andy Warhol died.

The two owners of this shop were Auschwitz survivors, an old Jewish couple; they had tattoos on their wrists. They gave me this job of importance because I was handling money; I was fourteen years old. It gave me an opportunity to have money on my own, and I remember the first thing I bought with the money I saved. It was scuba-diving equipment, in the summer of 1967. My mother thought it was wasting money, that I didn't know the value of money, to be able to buy scuba-diving equipment. The second opportunity I got to buy something from working at this great candy shop was to buy a secondhand professional camera, a 35 mm camera. One of the customers that came in was a photographer for the *Daily News*, one of the biggest newspapers in New York City.

He said his job was just to listen to news stories on his radio from the police—he had a police radio on his car—and he would rush to any police story that sounded like it would be good for photography, and he would take pictures and then rush to the *Daily News* building, develop the photos, and very often they'd use his pictures. He said he was ready to move up, and he just asked me one day—he would come in about once a week and he would buy porn magazines—but one day he said, "You know anybody wants to buy a camera?" And he put the camera on the counter. This was a Miranda F camera; it had three lenses. The most impressive thing was the 135 mm telephoto lens that he had. I had never seen a camera with such a great big lens. And I knew if I had that camera, I could get into any concert in the world. I could say, "I'm a photographer!"—I knew it instinctively! And he said the camera lens had a piece missing in the front; it was like a tiny animal had taken a bite out of the metal. "That doesn't affect the picture quality. I was in the middle of a riot in the East Village a few weeks ago, and somebody threw a beer can at me; they were trying to hit the police. It hit my camera lens, so it saved my eyesight," he said, "so maybe it is a lucky camera for you!" Actually it looked like the camera had survived being in Vietnam! This camera gave me weight; I didn't look like a foolish teenager with pimples. I was shy and insecure, but when I had this camera around my arm, never around my neck, people just looked at it and made a decision right there: this guy is a serious photographer.

Thom Lukas working at the candy store, New York, 1968. *Photo by Michael W. Ewanus*

Fillmore East, New York, on Saturday, April 6, 1968

I was there when the Fillmore East opened. Tim Buckley, Albert King, and Big Brother were on the bill. Big Brother was an amazing band. In some ways they were like a "West Coast Who," because they dressed really cool! They looked like Indians. They were hippies/Indians; they had leather, buckskin like Roger would wear at Woodstock; they had that stuff; they had all kinds of things. Janis had clothes like from the Wild West; you know, velvet, all kinds of interesting things.

Just having the camera, I thought I couldn't get in that night, because everybody in the world in New York City, all the press people, everybody in the world wanted to get in. Completely sold out. Bill Graham had a great reputation from the West Coast; the buzz was that Albert Grossman managed Big Brother. You couldn't get a seat there. It was sold out. And there was no sneaking in that night; security was extra tight. Bill Graham was going to make sure this was the perfect opening.

That theater was my childhood movie theater; I used to go there almost every week to see movies as a kid. It was called the Loew's Commodore. It cost $0.75 to get in. And for some reason, each reincarnation of this theater made you forget about the previous incarnation. I never thought of it as my childhood movie theater; I never thought of it as the Village Theater once it became the Fillmore East, because Bill Graham really transformed it: he painted it; he did detail work in the painting; his security people were very professional, never threatening; they wore uniforms; they were very respectful of the audience. He was so respectful of the audience—he treated us like adults, not kids, and that was nice. And part of the reason was the people he hired—he hired Jerry Pompili and hired Kip Cohen. Kip had studied theater design, lighting design at Carnegie Mellon University in Pittsburgh. And he worked on Broadway, so he knew how to run a Broadway show, and Bill Graham didn't care how much it cost to get Kip Cohen. He wanted the best people working for him. Kip's and Jerry's personalities were night and day. Kip was a real gentleman; Jerry was a little bit thuggish, tough. I never dealt with Jerry. Once he tried to get me to sit down when I was shooting Ten Years After, their encore, and I stood on a first-row seat, one of those beautiful velvet seats; I was inches away from Alvin Lee's face to get some shots, and Jerry went crazy—he was on the side of the stage; he was going, "Down! Down! Down!" But everybody was standing up, everybody was going crazy, because the band was playing "I'm Going Home," and I just ignored him.

A few weeks later, Kip Cohen told me, "You were lucky to survive that, because Jerry wanted to kill you!"

One more guy who came in the candy store regularly was another student of my high school, and he was older and more serious, and he would buy the record industry magazines, which nobody else bought. He bought *Cashbox* and *Billboard* every week or every month, whenever they came out. Somehow we got talking about the Who, and he asked me, "Are you going to see the Who's show coming up?," and he showed me an advertisement of that concert. He's the first guy who explained to me the brilliance of Pete's lyrics. He said, "Look at these lyrics, man: 'Me and my brother were talking to each other about what makes a man a man'; this is amazing!" But he also may have been the one who advised me to be careful, because I said, "I'm going to photograph the Who," and he replied, "Be careful; sometimes Pete gets a little wild." I took that into consideration, even though I probably ignored that at first and I did get a couple of shots, but when I saw that Pete was getting a little bit wild, I moved over to Roger's side of the stage, and that's where I really felt comfortable, because his clothing was just outstanding compared to Pete's in my mind.

Fillmore East, New York. Saturday, April 6, 1968. *Photo by Thom Lukas*

I had been reading *Rave* magazine, and Roger was like a fashion icon. I could never have clothes like that in a million years, I couldn't wear them, and then the fact that they had a sort of a soft look, a little bit effeminate—pink velvet, white silk, and a shiny vest—but it was just great in my camera lens. And his hair looked so cool. I took as many good shots as I could of Roger, and luckily the security didn't seem to be bothering with that left side of the stage. I think most of the security people were focused on Pete's area because they were anticipating that something might happen on that side of the stage, and also it seemed to be where many of the photographers wanted to stand. That was the more popular side of the stage for taking photos, the right side. I could see there were at least three photographers there already, so I thought it would be more difficult, because photographers seem to be competitive in a sense.

At the time I saw the Who at the Fillmore East, the theater had been opened only for less than a month. Martin Luther King had been murdered on April 4, but I think the Who's audience had no interest in that. Maybe Jimi Hendrix's audience would have an interest in that, but I don't think we were too racially aware of this thing. At least I wasn't, as a fifteen year old. Nobody was wearing arm bands or was angry that the Who were playing. It was a Who audience.

I believe I paid for tickets. I would go regularly to the box office, since my candy shop was walking distance from the Fillmore East, and I would look to see which groups were coming up, and sometimes I would stand near the box office window, which was in the lobby of the theater; you could go there and buy tickets for upcoming shows, and I would just listen to what people were saying, because I didn't really have money to buy tickets. I heard some guys saying it would be sold out—"We only have tickets in the back now; it's gonna sell out soon!" If the show sold out, it would be very hard to get in. So I knew I had to buy a ticket, and I usually bought the cheapest ticket, which was probably $3, and then I would try to get a better seat. That was my strategy, always. To get a cheap ticket but never sit there. And I would just drift from seat to seat, because a lot of times, record companies' people got free tickets and didn't use them. That happened a lot. And I knew which seats they were; they were usually on the aisles, so the guy could go to the toilet or he could leave without bothering people. When the occasional person was going to the toilet for ten minutes, I would just sit there for ten minutes. Hopefully nobody would notice me, and I could get a couple of shots out. For the Who show that I saw that night, I got the cheapest ticket, and I would just stand in the back lobby until I got an opportunity to go down front, but I don't think I had a seat that night; the front was pretty crowded, and I tried to stand on the left side of the stage as much as I could. Some of the ushers were kinder than the other ushers. Basically what I would do is I would stand near the street door. Right to the side of the aisle was a door that exited to the street that they kept closed, and I would try to sink into the shadow, if the guy told me to move. So I tried to go to the stage area, then the guy there would say, "You can't stay here; where's your ticket? Where's your seat?" And they tried to take me back. And I pretended that I was going back and just slide into the side and wait until the guy disappeared to take somebody else.

For this show, my strategy was to not go early to see the first two bands, never. Get there right between the changeover, between the second band and the headliner, just as the second band was ending, so that I got the full charged atmosphere of the audience. After the band, everybody came to the lobby, and you could see how people were dressed, the cute girls and everything, and you could overhear them talking about the Who: "Oh, I saw them last time; they're great, man." You could hear all that, the anticipation, the excitement.

I usually had to work Saturday nights; that was the busiest night because I had to put the newspapers together for Sunday morning. My boss was very kind to me a few times regarding the Fillmore East; once was lending me money to buy a first-row seat for Jimi Hendrix, and this time when he said I could go on Saturday night, and the other time was discussing the Rod Stewart and Jeff Beck show that I had seen the night before. He told me, "What did you do last night?," and I said, "Well, I went to the Fillmore East," and he said, "Did you see the Jeff Beck Group?," and I said, "How did you know?!" He laughed and said, "It's right here in the *New York Times*," and I had never even related to the *New York Times* in my life; that was for rich people and doctors to read. That's when I first became aware that the *New York Times* could be a hip paper! I read that article, and it helped Rod Stewart and Jeff Beck Group to take off in America.

Singer Bowl, New York, on Friday, August 2, 1968

I brought my Fillmore East prints over to the Singer Bowl, with the hope of showing them to the band. My date, Nancy, and I arrived a few hours early, and I spotted Roger standing in front of the stage door. I got his attention by saying that I was a photographer and had some photos to show him. He took them out of the large envelope and studied each picture. He even asked me how I had gotten the special effect on one of the photos. It was a badly printed photo which showed Roger bowing with his necklace hanging that had a picture of his wife, Heather, in it. I made a mistake when I was printing: I underexposed the print as I was printing it, I put it in the developer, and I could see that it was too light, so I did something you're not supposed to do—I took the paper out of the developer and put it back on the easel and tried to print it again and expose it again from the enlarger. I misaligned it by mistake—I got two images slightly misaligned on the same print—but I brought it with me anyway. It was a mistake; you wouldn't usually show a mistake to somebody.

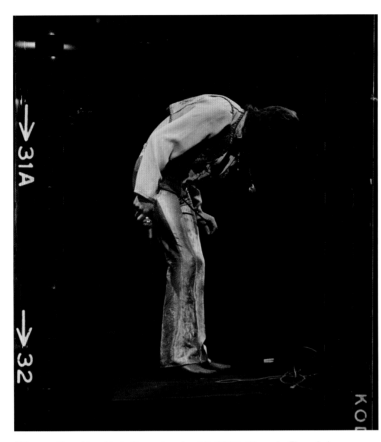

Fillmore East, New York. Saturday, April 6, 1968. *Photo by Thom Lukas*

So, either I didn't have a lot of prints to bring or I never intended to show them to him. But that particular photo of Roger got me lucky: he invited me backstage. "Would you like to come backstage and take some pictures?" he said, and I went, "Oh, it would be great, but I'm here with my girlfriend. Is it OK if I bring her?" He said, "Sure," and waited while I found her. She couldn't believe her luck. That was our first date together. I had met her the Sunday before in Central Park, and this was a Friday night.

As soon as we got backstage, Roger put us in his protected area. Everybody had their own little space, and Roger had his space where all his clothes were arranged, all his belongings, and anybody who was a friend of Roger. I remember just one other person, Eileen. My girlfriend, Nancy, talked to her, and Roger paid attention to me occasionally—"Go around!"—so I took a couple of snaps of everybody, and I got a very standoffish vibe from Peter. Actually not 100 percent negative, because he did look at me when I was taking pictures; he kind of cooperated in a sense, but there wasn't any invitation in his eyes, like "Come and talk to me!"—nothing like that.

My girlfriend Nancy's best friend, Peggy, told me that a friend of hers got hit at the Who's show at the Village Theater. It would be nice if you could interview that girl that got hit, because Pete gave her the remains of his guitar, as an apology. That would kind of connect,

in a sense, Jim Morrison being nice to the girl who got the split head at the Singer Bowl show. So, when Pete is watching Jim Morrison at the Singer Bowl be kind to this girl who has a bleeding head, he might have been thinking back to the show where he hurt a girl in the audience, and then he went out of this way to be kind to her, just to convince her that he wasn't a bad man; it was just this stage character who did it, and I guess Morrison was trying to be the nicest person in the world. In the documentary, when you see Jim Morrison talking, he's just being so sweet to this girl. That was not the Jim Morrison personality that I saw when I had seen him backstage before at the Village Theater. I guess some people could bring out Pete Townshend's sweet personality. One of them was the writer Paul Nelson, I think.

One of the interesting things about being backstage with the Who at the Singer Bowl was Roger, who didn't interact that much with the other members of the band. And I remember him interacting the least with Pete Townshend, who was drinking Seagram's 7 whiskey. Keith looked like the shiest member of the group. He posed for me one or two shots and he looked cool; he had sunglasses on. And John was as kind as Roger was; he said, "We should go somewhere more private to take some shots if you want."

I couldn't believe my luck.

Singer Bowl dressing room, New York. Friday, August 2, 1968.
Photo by Thom Lukas

That night at Singer Bowl, before we said goodbye, Roger put me and Nancy on the guest list for their next concert in New York, at the Wollman Skating Rink in Central Park, on August 7, 1968. The Central Park Schaefer Music Festival show wasn't as much fun for me as it had been just a few nights before, at the Singer Bowl. Singer had been my first date with Nancy; we got backstage, it was private, and we had gotten special attention. The backstage area at Central Park was smaller, and although I had access to the stage, shooting there wasn't so comfortable.

The two shots of Roger and Keith are some of the few I managed to take while on the side of the Central Park stage. It was very high and distant from the audience. In addition, the band looked under pressure. I guess that was because they had to do two shows in one night.

Singer Bowl dressing room, New York. Friday, August 2, 1968. *All photos by Thom Lukas*

I didn't feel at ease, it wasn't intimate, it was too crowded, and there were a lot of stagehands. Central Park was in a sense more like Woodstock would be. You could almost feel how rock was becoming big business. It became corporate very quickly. You can also see that from the pictures I took at the Fillmore East in October 1969, when the Who came back to perform *Tommy*. My photos look distant because access was harder by then.

It was harder to get close because the Who had become too famous, and that's when I lost interest in seeing them live. I liked *Tommy* the record, but I didn't like what they were becoming. I guess it's in contradiction to everybody else, but I thought that was the decline of the Who. Something important was happening for them, but yet, it was not good for me! They started to make money, they finally broke through, they got commercial acceptance, but that's when I lost interest. I didn't think they were dressed so beautifully and uniquely like they had been, either. Their fashion style had changed. Roger looked like he had adopted an American style; he almost looked like David Crosby from the Byrds. Pete seemed to be going more antifashion. I thought, "This is not my band." They became everybody's band.

The Schaefer Music Festival, Wollman Skating Rink, Central Park, New York. Wednesday, August 7, 1968.
All photos by Thom Lukas

Dermot Bassett

Marquee Club, London, on Tuesday, April 23, 1968

Pete accidentally broke his Gibson ES 335 after three numbers. During "Summertime Blues," he spun it up into the air but didn't catch it properly, and the head hit the floor. At the end of the number, Pete said, "I've broke me guitar already"; hit the head and the neck broke off. Then he said, "They gave me this in America," as he pulled the cardboard wrapping off another guitar! At the end of the show, he absolutely destroyed the two guitars together.

Marquee Club, London. Tuesday, April 23, 1968. *All photos by Max Browne*

Marquee Club, London. Tuesday, April 23, 1968.
All photos by Max Browne

Memorial Auditorium, Sacramento, California. Monday, July 8, 1968. *Photo by Dennis McCoy, copyright of Brad Rodgers, www.whocollection.com*

The same moment captured by three different photographers. Memorial Auditorium, Sacramento, California. Monday, July 8, 1968. *First photo by Steve Caraway (courtesy of Craig Patterson); second photo by Dennis McCoy, copyright of Brad Rodgers (www.whocollection.com); third photo by Randy Tinch (courtesy of Craig Patterson)*

Memorial Auditorium, Sacramento, California. Monday, July 8, 1968. *Photo by Steve Caraway, courtesy of Craig Patterson*

Grande Ballroom, Detroit, Michigan. Saturday, July 13, 1968. Second set. *All photos by Ruth Hoffman*

Glenn Coleman

MusiCarnival, Warrensville Heights, Cleveland, Ohio, on Sunday, July 14, 1968.

When the Who came to the US on their second tour, they played Cleveland, Ohio, in a circus tent in the round. I did not go to this show, but close friends did. They found their way backstage and, in poor judgment, stole a few items of clothing. A watch that was on the *Magic Bus* album cover, a pair of purple velvet pants, and a leather jacket. The jacket had the keys to a Holiday Inn room, and they went there after the show. When they were in the room, they stole Pete's passport. Now, like I said, I was not there, but I did see the passport about a week later. The person who stole it has passed away years ago, and the passport was thrown away for fear of getting into BIG trouble. I always thought the song "Sheraton Gibson" was about this experience. When I worked at MCI Recording, Pete came in to check out a recording console. I was afraid to tell him my story about his passport for fear of getting into trouble.

Charlie Andrew

MusiCarnival, Warrensville Heights, Cleveland, Ohio, on Sunday, July 14, 1968

I skipped out of football practice that day, missed the team picture, just to see what the Who was up to. We had seen them the previous year when they opened for Herman's Hermits, and actually met Pete at the Statler Hilton. I still have a piece of a Fender bass that Pete pulled out of a box of spare guitar parts. He was passing out souvenirs from a large suitcase. My buddy's sister Daphne took souvenir orange and banana peels as her mementos.

A year later, on July 14, 1968, we got a ride out to Warrensville Road, site of MusiCarnival. I don't remember where our seats were, but when everyone else moved toward the stage, we went too. I wish I'd ended up on Pete's side of the stage, to catch his windmilling. It was incredibly loud—my ears rang for a week. The crowd didn't understand that if Pete *did* wreck his guitar, it would be at the end of the show. There was a big rush on the stage, and the roadies moved equipment away. After some pleas for order, the stage was reset and the show continued.

MusiCarnival, Warrensville Heights, Cleveland, Ohio. Sunday, July 14, 1968. *All photos by Charlie Andrew*

MusiCarnival, Warrensville Heights, Cleveland, Ohio. Sunday, July 14, 1968. *All photos by Charlie Andrew*

MusiCarnival, Warrensville Heights, Cleveland, Ohio. Sunday, July 14, 1968. *Photo by Robert Kavc*

Gary Piazza

The New Place, Algonquin, Illinois, on Wednesday, July 31, 1968

What a night to remember! It was a warm summer evening in July of 1968 in the Midwest.

My best friend and fellow guitarist and I were heading up Highway 31 to the New Place in Algonquin, Illinois (near Chicago), to hear the band from across the ocean. It was the Who; they were really shaking things up in the rock music world, and we couldn't wait to hear them wail and sing our newfound anthem, "My Generation"! This iconoclastic song was a visceral and explosive "call to action" for young people to rebel against the old guard, social injustices, the Vietnam War, racism, and all of the other societal-programming nonsense that we are still attempting to resolve.

The parking lot overflowed into the grass and off to the side of Highway 31! We had never seen it so crowded; they came from near and far, including Chicago. Once we paid our cover, we eagerly found a spot as close to the stage as possible; we were packed in like sardines, as you see in my photos. Then . . . we eagerly waited in a standing-room-only crowd for the late arrival of the bad boys who rebel against authority and smash equipment onstage! Once they arrived, their equipment manager, Bob Pridden, very efficiently set up. Then, Moon came out and tweaked his kit, followed by Townshend and Entwistle making their final checks and tuning. The energy in the air was electric; you could feel it and taste it! There had never been a group quite like the Who in these parts, and we were more than ready to hear and feel

what they had to say! Roger was in the pocket from the get-go, very comfortable in his skin and fronting the band like a pro that he was. He was quick to fire his mic high up in the air, out in the crowd like a ninja singer, and then, like a musical cowboy, he lassoed it! It was amazing that he didn't clobber someone with all of us packed in so close to the band! To pull off the mic stage antics, they had cleverly placed gaffer tape on the low-impedance mic line up the side of the mic, so that the mic line didn't pull apart from the connecting jack. If they hadn't built in the gaffer tape safety feature, the mic would short out or, worse yet, fly off like a missile when he would lasso it. The warm summer night's air and the hot ride in the van and the previous gig before might have been too much for the glue on the gaffer tape. So when he would shotgun it out to the crowd, sometimes it shorted out and made a horrible noise from the wire breaking the solder joint. This was all very frustrating to Daltrey, who would then look over to Pete; Townshend would shrug and play on while taking no prisoners! He was possibly nonverbally communicating with Daltrey that it was Daltrey's problem or the soundman's problem to fix, not his. It was also the nonverbal onstage language to acknowledge that they had a mic to repair before the next gig. Townshend had his cool 360-degree arm swings down to a science and never missed a searing power chord! Keith Moon was an animal on the drums, yet maintaining a solid beat in his timekeeping with forward motion, while interweaving intricate and very cool syncopations. Then, there was the virtuosic playing of unassuming John Entwistle; low-profile, cool Entwistle was literally playing and rewriting a new bass syntax for melodic and chordal bass playing. Remember gang, this predated bass virtuosos such as Jaco, Stanley Clarke, and Victor Wooten. Jaco Pastorius was still developing his technique and didn't break into the big music scene until 1970, when he joined Wayne Cochran and Clarke in the jazz world the same year.

So let me describe the sound from a musician's ears. It was very basic and raw, especially with tube-driven amp heads, timbre was brightly EQ'd to the upper-end spectrum, and it cut through the humid evening's air and crowd buzz. Entwistle beautifully filled out the bottom end while playing very cool virtuosic riffs, yet he still maintained the bass bottom integrity while Moon smashed and drove the band forward. Townshend sonically filled in the midrange with his own style of Townshend power chords and electrifying lead solos—holy shit, Dorothy, we were not in Kansas anymore!

The band delivered a smashing and riveting fifty-to-sixty-minute set. Yes indeed, they delivered their promise as they really trashed their equipment in a starkly violent and expensive way at the conclusion of "My Generation"! Daltrey drove his mic stand through a speaker in Townshend's stack, and we had instant fuzz tone guitar! Check out my close-up photo demonstrating the violently torn grill cloth.

The New Place, Algonquin, Illinois. Wednesday, July 31, 1968.
All photos by Dr. Gary L. Piazza

The New Place, Algonquin, Illinois. Wednesday, July 31, 1968.
Photo by Dr. Gary L. Piazza

Townshend ran the guitar into his stack, then beat the stage until the defenseless Strat gave up its body for the cause! The very sweet blue vintage 1960s Fender Strat's neck violently ripped away from the tightly secured body. Guys, that neck is bolted on with four long, tempered, heavy-gauge Phillips-head screws; it takes a lot of smashing and torque to pull the neck off this guitar. Keith Moon symbolically turned his kit over and knocked over cymbal stands so as not to hurt his kit.

As a Townshend postsmashing event we also experienced a "guitar neck ballet" too . . . my buddy Bob Hollis played tug-of-war with their soundman, Bob Pridden, for the neck of Townshend's guitar. ¡Olé! Pitbull Pridden was small yet tough as nails, and he did an explosively violent front kick that freed my friend's hands from the expensive Strat neck and sent my friend hurling . . . it was violent and funny all at the same time. I watched all of this in a state of neutrality, then walked over to the van where Pridden was loading, and I struck up a very cordial conversation with him. He was somewhat apologetic since he knew the "Strat neck perpetrator" was my friend.

Being a guitarist and the son of an electrician, I was taught how to built amp bottoms and how to repair my gear on the road and during gigs. So, I had a unique set of questions for Pridden that he hadn't anticipated from a baby-faced, long-haired teenager. He commented that he couldn't let my

friend run off with the neck because he was running low on Strat necks and parts in general. Then, he opened up the van and showed me the bodies and necks hanging in the van for repair or for spare parts. I couldn't believe what I was seeing; it looked like one of those jet plane boneyards! The more I talked with Pridden, the more I could see that the Who and Pridden had this all planned out and down to a "T." I commented on how difficult it must be to maintain the Who's equipment and Townshend's guitars. He just shrugged it off by commenting it wasn't that bad with the bolt on Strats necks and the electronics screwed to the pick guard. Okay, for you nonguitarists, it's kind of a plug and play with a soldering gun, solder, Phillips screwdrivers, and Fender Allen wrench for neck adjustment, Leo Fender was brilliant! Most of you know that Pete also played a Gibson SG, and those necks are through-construction without external bolts; if you snap that neck, it's over while on tour, or it goes to a guitar luthier for months once you get home.

So, after our conversation, and while all the fans were heading out, I lay back and scoured the cement floor for some Townshend memorabilia. And, low and behold . . . gems of the rock god were left behind for mere mortals! I quickly snatched up Townshend's pick, a chard of the blue Strat body, and a broken piece of his guitar's B string.

The following day, I placed all of my Who treasures in a clear-glass medicine bottle as a memento of such an auspicious musical event and placed it on my dresser in my bedroom for braggin' rights later. Yes, indeed, it was my Pete Townshend shrine. I have to tell you, I'm laughing while I'm putting this down and recalling the events that transpired afterward, as I have not thought of this since the late 1960s. We guitarists love this kind of stuff, even grown men!

When it came time for college, I left my rock god gift from Olympus behind. Get this—while I was away at the university studying music, my grandmother came over to our house and took it upon herself to clean my bedroom, and she threw it all out! When I came home for a holiday, I noticed it was gone, and my mom said Grandma Rosa Piazza did a number on your room while you were away at school, and she was really sorry. When I asked Rosa why she threw out my rock god gift, she said in broken Italian English, "Itsa no gooda; it's abrokena junk, Gary!"

All right, a final anecdote: my friend Bob Hollis, who went a hurling from the Pridden kick, always gave me a rough time for taking pictures at concerts, as it embarrassed him and he didn't think it was cool; you know the deal . . . teenage insecurities. I didn't give a shit; still don't! If I would have listened to him, I would not be here today sharing these photos, or the anecdotes. Hollis and I are still best of friends today, and we have a good laugh over all of this. However, looking back twenty years ago, he was the one person of all the people that begged me—I mean begged me and pestered me—for copies of my Who, Led Zeppelin, and Dead pictures, even after all the grief he had given me back in the day. So what did I do . . . I made him beg a little more and wait a few decades. Karma baby!

Addendum: Note of reference for the younger generation: back in those days, you could go to Chicago-area teen clubs and see acts up close and personal for $5, like the Kinetic Playground on North Clark Street in Chicago. I actually preferred this venue over the Fillmore West! You guys will love this digression, if you will; it's a classic example of a 1960s perspective and how things were just forming in a basic way back then. We saw the Yardbirds' last tour at the Crimson Cougar in St. Charles, Illinois. Within the Yardbird construct, Page was foreshadowing Led Zeppelin by forming and working out his signature riffs, his look, the bow/guitar trick, and even guitar works. Keith Ralph, the singer, had an abscessed tooth, gave it a go, but couldn't cut it, so Jimmy Page took over the helm, and what a historical night of music that proved to be. Page even premiered "Black Mountain Side"! We were beside ourselves; we had never seen or heard such things. It was virgin territory, and that musical journey was pure magic!

Much love and peace to all of you; may you find the same joy and magic on your musical journey that I have been blessed with.

Photos and article by Gary L. Piazza, PhD in music; guitarist, vocalist, delta blues guitarist, lutenist, singer/songwriter, composer, arranger, and conductor.

Jim Stark
"Hanging Around with the Who"

It was the summer of 1968, and the British band the Who were scheduled to play at the Illinois State Fair in Springfield, opening for the Association, whose big hit "Windy" had been playing on the radio that year. The Who were gaining popularity in the US and had some hits themselves, obviously, including notably "Magic Bus," which they were playing on that early tour.

My friends and I had formed a rock band called the Fungis (pronounced "Funguys"). We followed closely and played the music of the Who, the Beatles, the Kinks, etc., a.k.a. the "British Invasion."

After learning the Who would be staying at the Holiday Inn East during their state fair performance, my bandmate Trabue (pronounced Tray-Byu) Gentry and I put a plan together that we hoped would allow us to get their hotel room number so we could meet and talk with our musical heroes.

We would pass ourselves off as cub reporters. We had in our arsenal temporary Illinois State Fair press passes, and we dressed in shirt and tie. I played the role of photographer, and Trabue, the reporter. We walked right up to the battery of front desk clerks with our story, asked for the room, and, of course, were summarily shut down!

This was a setback, and we had to rethink our plan. I had noticed that just off the lobby was a gift shop, with a young woman around our age at the register. The shop was empty of customers. Maybe we could ask her? She might be a Who fan too! We considered this and then had a flash: let's use our remaining asset. Built from imitation of our musical heroes were our oft-practiced faux British accents, which we thought we had perfected. So, in we went.

After some storytelling, laughing, and cajoling as "Brit" reporters following the band on the US tour, the gift shop girl pried the room number out of the front desk clerk who had previously rejected our requests. We could barely believe this unexpected "gift" from the shop! Excitedly, we made our way upstairs to room 205 and knocked, and Pete Townshend himself opened the door and let us "cub reporters" in!

We began by being the reporting team, asking various questions about the tour, the music, and their impressions of the States. We took notes and even talked about our band a little bit. These notes have been lost to history. Overall we were being totally amazed. It was a series of incredible moments.

Pictures of this encounter were taken by me (as "the photographer") on a well-used 35 mm viewfinder camera. I appear only once in the background mirror as I took the picture of Roger Daltrey. When he took out his soldering iron and plugged it in, I was puzzled and asked. He explained how he was "triple" soldering his microphone leads for his signature moves onstage later that night. Who knew rock stars did their own soldering! By the time the leads were secure, we were all just joking, taking it all in, smoking cigarettes and hanging around with the Who. Pete and Roger were laid back and friendly. A fellow called Bope, the assistant road manager, was also present.

A couple other moments stand out. We asked to see Keith Moon, but they expressly forbade it, saying, "No, no, no—it wouldn't go well!" They did give us John Entwistle's room number, and we got a pic with him and his famous French horn.

We returned to the previous room with Pete and Roger, where they asked if we had a vehicle. A bass amp speaker cabinet had been left at the airport by mistake, and they needed to retrieve it, and could we help? We called Trabue's dad, and he made the trip and brought it back to the Holiday Inn. He pulled in with top down on his dark, metallic-blue 1967 Mustang convertible with the cabinet hanging out of the tiny trunk, all roped down! We all shared a laugh at this sight.

Time was now up for our "interview," and we accompanied Pete down to the lobby, where he wanted to, as he said, "post some letters back home." In his biography, he mentioned how important it was to him to always write home, to stay connected while on the road. That farewell pic captured the image not just of those letters in his hand, but the sense of their adventure, in those early days, starting to fulfill their destiny.

That night, we were on-site adjacent to the backstage area when the band arrived, and we were greeted with waves and smiles from Pete and Roger as they got out of the limo. It was a magical day made only more complete as "Magic Bus" rocked out over the infield to the cheers of thousands of young fans, including us. Bope was there too, playing the claves right on the microphone for the song's intro. All was well on that "rockin'" August summer night!

This brief time hanging around with the Who was one of the best moments of our teenage lives. We must ask for forgiveness for our innocent duplicity and are forever thankful to the Who and, of course, the gift shop girl! ©Jim Stark 2020.

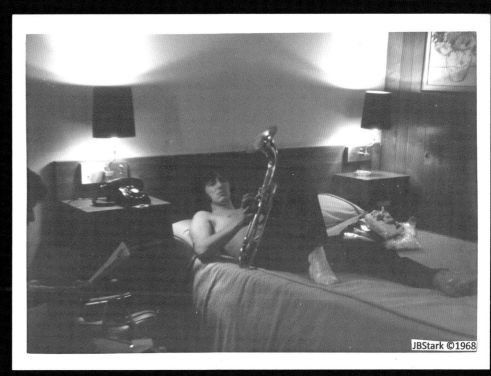

"Entwistle's famous French horn. We Midwestern kids were shocked at boots on the bedspread! What would mom say?" Image included in the exhibition *ROCKED and ROLLED* at the Illinois State Museum, Lockport, Springfield, Illinois (2019–2020). *JB Stark*

"Pete and Bob Pridden, 'Bope,' were using this portable reel-to-reel to keep track of new musical threads on the tour." *JB Stark*

JBStark ©1968

"Roger solders while we loosen our ties, smoke Marlboros, and hang around with The Who. Notice the teapots on the sink in the back. They are British after all!" Image included in the exhibition *ROCKED and ROLLED* at the Illinois State Museum, Lockport, Springfield, Illinois (2019–2020). *JB Stark*

JBStark ©1968

"We walk to the lobby with Pete. He posts letters to his people back home. We say thanks and trade farewells." Image included in the exhibition *ROCKED and ROLLED* at the Illinois State Museum, Lockport, Springfield, Illinois (2019–2020). *JB Stark*

John "Spider" LeQuesne

Jaguar Club, Saint Charles, Illinois, on Saturday, August 10, 1968

On Saturday, August 10, 1968, I went to see the Who for the third time in three weeks with my good friend and bass player, Greg, this time at a club called the Jaguar, in St. Charles, Illinois. I had met them just a couple of weeks earlier after their show at the New Place and had seen them just a few nights before this, at the Majestic in Lake Geneva. For all three shows, I would stand at the very edge of the stage, right in front of Pete for every minute of the concert. Just a couple of songs into the show, Pete looked right at me and my buddy and said, "It's nice to see some people we've seen before!" This night was to be magic. At one point in between songs, when Pete was tweaking the volume of his amps, I yelled out, "Summertime Blues!" . . . and they played it. They went right into it. To this day, it amazes me that the Who took a request from this young kid from Chicago. I was fortunate to see them eighteen times and would get to meet them a couple of more times, but that night at the Jaguar was simply amazing.

"Pete swinging upside down from a pipe that ran above the stage, above Keith's drum kit. What's cool is, he had just smashed (and I mean disintegrated) his Gibson SG on that pipe, just before he was swinging on it." Jaguar Club, Saint Charles, Illinois. Saturday, August 10, 1968. *John "Spider" LeQuesne*

"Moon trashing his drum kit, while Pete & Roger look back. Entwistle is still playing till Moon is done kicking over his drums." Jaguar Club, Saint Charles, Illinois. Saturday, August 10, 1968. *John "Spider" LeQuesne*

John Entwistle and Keith Moon are hosts at KYA radio station in San Francisco, before their Fillmore West appearances of August 13–15, 1968. On the final of these three nights, Pete told the Fillmore West audience: "On the radio today we made them play 'Cobwebs & Strange' and . . . it broke the radio!" *Photo by Frank Zinn, Richard Martin Frost archive*

John at KYA radio station in San Francisco, August 1968. *Photo by Frank Zinn, Richard Martin Frost archive*

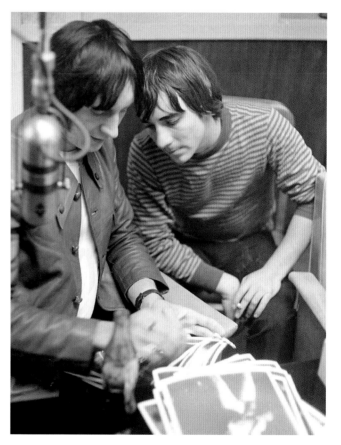

John and Keith at KYA radio station in San Francisco, August 1968. They are going through Frank Zinn's shots taken at the Who's last West Coast appearance at Winterland in February 1968. *Photo by Frank Zinn, Richard Martin Frost archive*

Mark d'Ercole

Fillmore West, San Francisco, on Tuesday–Thursday, August 13–15, 1968

You know all the best things in life come by surprise
Just like you met the one you love
When you see a singer who tears you apart
he rarely comes down from above

I don't know what I expected to see that night
I don't remember much at all
All I know the music was the best I'd heard
with clouds of smoke and fireballs.

Music shot out loud like cannon fire
with wooden pieces mad in flight
The last thing ever in my mind I see
was the man jumpin' down out of the lights
oh the man jumpin' down out of the lights

He made more noise with silence
than others make with bombs
He cast his fate and his soul and self
upon his worshipper's arms
he danced upon their outstretched hands
like a half moon that is cast on clouds
he always knows just where he lands
on the top of the notes he plays so loud

It was the most wonderful thing that ever happened to me
It was the most wonderful thing that ever happened to me
It was the most wonderful thing that ever happened to me

This man, this sight, this light, this rumble flowin' by
like tension just before a fight
I know I'll never see the likes of him
Oh the man jumpin' down out of the lights
the man jumpin' down out of the lights

I wrote this song called "The Man Jumping Down out of the Lights" coming home from the Who's concert at the Fillmore West on Thursday, August 15, 1968. The verse "It was the most wonderful thing that ever happened to me" came from a guy I heard repeating this thing while coming out of the Fillmore that night. He was crying.

Fillmore West, San Francisco, California. Tuesday, August 13, 1968.
Mark d'Ercole

Fillmore West, San Francisco, California. Tuesday, August 13, 1968.
Mark d'Ercole

Recording of the second night of the Who at Fillmore West in August 1968. *Courtesy of Mark d'Ercole; Author's archive*

Recording of the third night of the Who at Fillmore West in August 1968. *Courtesy of Mark d'Ercole; Author's archive*

There is another verse of that song I wrote that goes, "With wooden pieces mad in flight"—those were the pieces of Pete's guitar that were coming down on me when Pete threw his broken guitar in the air. I was sitting onstage that night.

I was watching James Cotton off to the side on the right, when someone tapped on my shoulder: it was Roger Daltrey, who asked me for a light for his cigarette.

I went, "Oh! You're Roger!"

I asked him what he was doing being out from the backstage, and he told me he wanted to see these blues guys, James Cotton and Magic Sam, who were opening for them. We started talking, and the other members of the band came out one by one. The next to come out was John Entwistle.

We talked about where they were staying in the city and what they wanted to know about places and restaurants to see in San Francisco. The next to come out was Keith Moon. I asked him if he liked the city, and he replied, "We come to San Francisco to get laid." He was acting very skittish and like he was high on something. Very ADDish.

Last, Townshend showed up to tell them the manager wanted them to come back to the dressing room.

As they were going, I tapped Roger on the shoulder and said, "Hey, would you play one song?"

He said, "Sure, which one?"

"Play 'I Can't Explain.'"

"Oh, we play that every time, no problem . . . You just stand over there by the stairs and wait for us."

So I walked over and found the little staircase that went up to the stage. It was obscured from view by the large PA column. I waited right where the steps that lead up to the stage connect with the stage floor itself. Back in the day you could almost walk up and sit on the stage. There was no security, no bouncers, only a black guy called Elvis who was at the entrance collecting tickets as you went in. You were one with the musicians.

As the place got ready, Bill Graham walked up the stairs to begin introducing the Who while they were still standing on the stairs in line. Pete was a foot in front of me (turned to my left), and the beautiful, gorgeous SG was less than that. The neck was right there. I'm not sure Pete was even looking at me, since he was probably waiting for the go signal from Bill. The neck of his guitar was right there, so I tried to place my hand on the fingerboard to see how high the action was. I remember saying, "Thick strings!," and Pete nodding.

Just then a person in a big pioneer dress, a woman, I think, but I'm not sure, came running from all the way across the stage. I turned and this person stuck a flash camera right in Pete's face and pulled the trigger, and the flash went off! Pete covered his eyes and yelled, "Oh Christ, I'm blind!" I distinctly recall saying to myself, "How could he ever forget that?"

Right then Bill said, "Welcome now, the Who."

As they ran up onto the stage, Daltrey yanked my arm and I scooted to a place behind the PA column and watched the show from about 7 feet to Townshend's left.

When he decided to destroy the guitar, he climbed on top of his amps, shredding the last chords of "My Generation" before then dropping his SG onto the floor to jump on it. I'm not sure if he succeeded in breaking his axe on the first strike; I recall he partially snapped the body, but it was the second or third strike that completely separated the pieces. He then threw the mass up into the air, and that's when I suddenly realized it was coming right down on me. I can still see it coming. I ducked and put my hands up to protect me. I felt sharp things like needles, which were probably the strings or the edge of the broken wood. I put up my hands to block the falling broken pieces connected only by the strings. Suddenly I was trapped under a mob, with the guitar on top of part of me, when I was absolutely swarmed by a wave of people jumping onto the stage, grabbing

Courtesy of Alex Kipfer, Swiss Who Archive, www.thewho.ch

different parts of the instrument. Pieces of the SG were scattered all over the stage area. That's how I ended up getting a piece of it too.

On the last day of college, someone stole it off the wall where I had it hung during moving day, when everyone was bringing their boxes of stuff down to their cars.

Pictures unfortunately can't truly give you the overall feelings of what it was like to be in the room itself with the band playing. I remember many times as the songs rolled out and the histrionics were happening on the stage in front of me, not just when I sat on the stage with the Who. It was the vibrations in the air that would roll over you like a wave. A physical, not just aural, sensation.

I remember pleading with the universe to please let me not forget this. Closing my eyes to hope that the visual memories would become indelible. And they have.

The combination of the three—the visual, the aural (the great songs), and the physical—really isn't duplicated by the modern massive sound systems in stadiums and arenas today. The reason was because the sound was shaking that whole building, not just the atmosphere. I often felt like I was in some big carnival ride that was shaking me all over (no pun intended). I never took LSD or any hallucinogen, but I can't even begin to imagine what that must have been like for the many who were.

Fillmore West, San Francisco, California. Wednesday, August 14, 1968. *Photo by Jeff Wong, courtesy of Craig Patterson*

Fillmore West, San Francisco, California. Wednesday, August 14, 1968. *Photo by Jeff Wong, courtesy of Craig Patterson.* The same moment was also captured by photographer Baron Wolman and published in *Rolling Stone* 17 (September 14, 1968), pp. 12–13.

Fillmore West, San Francisco, California. Wednesday, August 14, 1968. *Photos by Jeff Wong, courtesy of Craig Patterson*

JUN • 70

JUN • 70

Fillmore West, San Francisco, California.
Wednesday, August 14, 1968. *Photos by
Jeff Wong, courtesy of Craig Patterson*

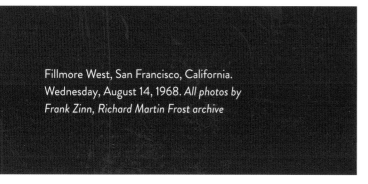

Fillmore West, San Francisco, California.
Wednesday, August 14, 1968. *All photos by
Frank Zinn, Richard Martin Frost archive*

Fillmore West, San Francisco, California. Tuesday, August 13, 1968. *Photo by Frank Zinn, Richard Martin Frost archive*

Fillmore West, San Francisco, California. Tuesday, August 13, 1968. *Photo by Frank Zinn. Richard Martin Frost archive*

Fillmore West, San Francisco, California. Thursday, August 15, 1968. *All photos by Frank Zinn, Richard Martin Frost archive*

Fillmore West, San Francisco, California. Thursday, August 15, 1968. *Photo by Frank Zinn, Richard Martin Frost archive*

"Before the last number, Pete changed to a 'throwaway' red solid body. When the guitar broke in half, he threw the shattered mess into the crowd. Ten minutes later, as we walked back to our car, an old model black Chevy with four young occupants roared by with one of them dangling the fractured guitar out a side window as a trophy."—Don Baraka

Fillmore West, San Francisco, California. Thursday, August 15, 1968. *Photo by Henry Pile*

Fillmore West, San Francisco, California. Thursday, August 15, 1968. *All photos by Dennis McCoy, copyright of Brad Rodgers, www.whocollection.com*

1969

Got a Feeling '69 Is Gonna Be a Good Year

On May 19, 1969, the Who played the Rockpile in Toronto, the tenth gig of their North American tour. This was their seventh time in North America, and the decibels of the four guys from Shepherd's Bush smashed through the walls of the most-prestigious venues in the northeastern United States. From the Grande Ballroom in Detroit, Michigan, through the Boston Tea Party in Massachusetts and the Fillmore East in New York, to that thunderous night in Canada, the Who put on a show that would immediately become the benchmark for live performances in general while becoming representative of the band itself both for its musical and visual incisiveness. In less than two years from their first anarchic shows in America, the Who soared to an artistic peak and level of maturation only rarely seen in concerts previously. Somehow the four members of the band created and sustained a wall of sound, harmonics, crescendos, and counterpoints usually associated with a 106-member orchestra playing the final movement in a massively popular symphony. It was the year that the band reached superstardom and all that came along with it.

That night, on May 19, 1969, the Who played what Townshend casually introduced to the audience as "the first bit of our latest album, which is a departure for us."[1] He was referring to *Tommy*, a double album released only two days prior in America, with another four days yet to pass before its release in the band's home country, England. Townshend, always eloquent and often ironic, purposely used the term "departure" to introduce the album. *Tommy* would indeed eventually become known as the fulcrum between the past and future Who. Artistically speaking, *Tommy* was by far the Who's biggest step in artistic originality since they burst onto the music scene in 1965: "I think that, in retrospect, [*Tommy*] is as important now to The Who as a definitive work as was *My Generation* previously to it," said Pete.[2]

At the same time, it was no small matter that the album put an end to the financial troubles that had plagued the Who since the beginning of their career, a constant yet changing form of stress that had threatened to utterly disrupt their internal balance and creative output.

Tommy provided the band and its individual members stability while, along with several other musical works by equally innovative artists, radically changing the direction of popular music from the three-minute single to "album rock." It helped add a level of depth to a genre that had not until then been taken as seriously as others. In 1974, during a *Rolling Stone* interview, John stated that before they started to make money with *Tommy*, the band had come close to splitting up at least five times.

With huge success comes ever-larger expectations, and for the Who that meant new tensions from which other successes and near tragedies would arise. In a nutshell, *Tommy* was what the band had been aiming toward, and from which it would try to escape for years to come. It was a huge success, such that for many new to their music, the band's name was assumed to be "Tommy," and the album, "*The Who.*"

Composing the Opera

It is necessary to point out, first of all, how the term "rock opera" was applied to *Tommy*.

Pete reveals:

We never really used the title "Rock Opera"; that was something which came as a natural development in conversation. Because it's not essentially a musical; it's not something which is gonna be staged as such. It's not as simple as a musical. The ingredients to the songs aren't there to put across a mood or a feeling of an age, or a feeling of a society. They're meant to tell a story in a literary manner. Of course, a very few operas have done this; most operas have got very shadowy sort of plots. The good thing about opera is that the performance is by the singers and the music itself. It's something I'm very fond of, the opera, and our manager too. My favorites are Wagner and Mahler, people like that. And I don't really like Italian opera, which I think is what most people think of when they think of opera.[5]

Writing an opera had long been the dream both of Pete Townshend and the Who's producer Kit Lambert. It was a project the two had been moving toward since 1966. Kit would complain about all the hang-ups of the genre, especially when performed to those unfamiliar with it: in particular, its audience—being mainly middle class—lining up for tickets because it was the thing to do, and then standing up, clapping and cheering before the end because it didn't know the piece well enough.

Somehow though, through *Tommy*, Kit hoped for a personal "vendetta" over the establishment:

> He wanted to take a rock group into Covent Garden, shit all over the stage and storm out again. He wanted to do this because he loved the opera and wanted to bring it back to its proper musical level.[6]

Pete's ambition of composing an opera dates back to 1966, influenced by Kit Lambert (whose father was a respected composer), who exposed Townshend to the genre, and from that time there were three attempts to develop a theme-based form of rock music before realizing it in *Tommy*. Roger tells us about it:

> Actually, Pete has been writing these operas for some time, and a lot of our hits come from them. "I'm A Boy" was from an opera he wrote about living in the year 2000 when there is a machine that helps you select the sex of your baby. That song was about a woman who couldn't believe that the machine had made a mistake and she's gotten a boy instead of a girl.[7]

"A Quick One, While He's Away," from the same year, marked a step forward for being a story of adultery in six movements within an eight-minute song. Then, in 1967, Pete wrote "Rael," a second mini-opera in twenty-five acts played over eleven minutes, eventually reduced to five:

> It takes place in the year 1999 when China is breaking out and is about to take over the world. The hero, or at least, central character, loses his wife and decides to go and live in this tiny country, which is about to be over-run by the Chinese. The hero goes through hundreds of different situations and there is music for each. He goes out in a boat and gets shipwrecked, he has a bad nightmare, and so on. I have used sound effects for a lot of the situations with music over them. I have written music to set the scene in some parts, but I haven't tried to bring impressionist music in. This sort of stuff has been done so superbly by people like Ravel and Debussy that it's not worth touching. I used the sound tracks of storms and things because I thought, why mess about trying to get sounds when you can have them right there on tape?[8]

In the end, we have "Glow Girl," a song written in early 1968, which did not belong to any operatic project but is equally important in tracing the origins of *Tommy*. The song is about the reincarnation of a young man into a new life as a girl following a plane crash. Its spiritual vibes and,

most of all, the final refrain, "It's a girl, Mrs. Walker, it's a girl," make this song the final link to *Tommy*.[9]

In time, through the press's constant association of the name *Tommy* to the term "rock opera," it was inevitable that Pete Townshend became known as the father of this new genre of musical expression. He points out that

> the mini-opera "A Quick One, While He's Away" was so popular on stage that I decided to do a complete opera. Previously only the Pretty Things and Keith West had attempted any sort of pop opera, and Keith West's was never finished. *Tommy* is an attempt to link all four sides of the double album musically. It's a progressive step, but . . . also a revolution. There are some fairly short tracks and long tracks which allowed us instrumental freedom and which give the underground people something to get their heads into. Judging by double albums I'd heard previously—such as The Beatles'—all the tracks seemed to be about the same length, and one tends to lose interest.[10]

In his first operatic attempts of "A Quick One" and "Rael," and even with *Tommy*, Townshend did not aim to follow traditional criteria of the opera format too closely but, rather, developed an original revisitation of it. As he explained at the Rockpile concert in Toronto:

> It's a story which is told using some techniques which have been used before by very, very, very old men that are probably rotting away now, still sticking to some rock formula and trying to keep the adrenaline of rock and roll.

Similarly, at the Guthrie Theater, Minneapolis, on June 8, 1969, Pete pointed out this:

> We're trying to make a step forward and still be rock and roll. This is a kind of paradox, because rock and roll hardly ever goes up and down. One day you're up, next day you're down.

"A Quick One," "Rael," and *Tommy* are, in fact, *pieces d'opéra* in which rock-and-roll criteria meet the operatic criteria, essentially claiming the same level of authenticity and dignity. Pete continued:

> It is something we wanted to do ever since we finished *The Who Sell Out* and ever since we did the mini-opera on the *Happy Jack* album. The very nature of those two events indicated to us that the thing we wanted to do was to get an album, to have a storyline, and to have the whole thing tight musically, and still retain the rock-and-roll nature of the thing. We started to think about this probably about two years ago.[11]

Kit Lambert, however, interpreted Pete's decision as one of the symptoms of a spontaneous phenomenon that was taking place in the pop world in general, in which the genre was being reassessed as the new classical music:

Fortunately, the musical frontiers are now beginning to disappear; classical influences are being absorbed by pop and pop by classical. . . . Opera as we know it now is absolutely defunct. One needs a completely fresh approach. And I think pop is going to provide it.[12]

Pete rejected Kit Lambert's suggestion to feature strings and other instruments that would, he feared, refer to classical opera too directly. His choice to blend innovation and tradition turned out to be successful, and by the end of the year *Tommy* would rouse enthusiastic feedback from the press. Journalist Stu Ginsburg, for example, wrote this:

The Who have come up with . . . something that is done extremely well in all aspects. We can hope for a full dramatic production of it. Perhaps Tommy will lead to a new area of musical expression. It certainly has combined the classical form of the opera with the musical form of contemporary rock. That's the first stop.[13]

Composition Stages

Tommy probably lived in Townshend's subconscious from the earliest days of the Who and went through several changes before taking its definitive form. What contributed to that was an event in 1967, when Pete came across the book *The God Man*, written by C. B. Purdom and dedicated to Meher Baba, an Indian guru born in 1894 who died in early 1969. In 1967, Pete was introduced to this work by his friend Mike McInnerney, the artist who would later, with an airbrush and paint, create the artwork for the *Tommy* album and booklet. In time, Pete would find in Meher Baba's teachings many of the answers to questions he had long been obsessed with:

Every time I came up with a world-wise theory that had taken me years of thought to get clear he [Mike] would say, "That's such a coincidence man, this guy Meher Baba said something similar to that in this book, *The God Man*."[14]

This quote by Pete appeared in the November 26, 1970, issue of *Rolling Stone*, in an article whose title could be anything but ambiguous: "In Love with Meher Baba." Pete referred to him as an "Avatar," God's incarnation on earth, a new messiah, and attributes the spark that led his inspiration toward *Tommy* exclusively to him:

The idea for Tommy came completely, directly from me discovering . . . that an avatar, a messiah, was on earth for seventy years and we were born into his avataric life.[15]

During a historical time of transition such as 1968, where the Western and Eastern worlds were influencing one another, and charismatic spiritual teachers from India were entering the music world through avenues such as the Beatles establishing themselves as spiritual advisors, Pete Townshend clarified that Meher Baba seemed different to him:

He is not a maharishi or any of those things: he is today's avatar. Nothing higher, nothing lower, nothing bigger, nothing smaller: the avatar. And that's the end of it. That's basically where most of the philosophical things came from.[16]

Pete focused on the fact that Baba did not come to form a religion or to organize a cult under his name, but "to bring together all religions and cults, revitalizing them for individual and collective needs."[17] Since the "Word" had already been spoken long before his arrival, Baba's purpose was "not to teach, but to awaken,"[18] because all that needed to be said had already been said. Pete added:

For all intents and purposes, he said exactly the same thing that Christ said, that Mohammed said, that Zarathustra said, that Krishna said. As far back as the eye can see, they all said the same thing, all the major world religions are based on exactly the same thing . . .
There is no point meddling with an already perfect divine scheme. There is no point meddling with it because it is already there and no matter what you do, you are never going to change it.[19]

For this reason, on July 10, 1925, Baba took a vow of silence: "You have had enough of my words, now is the time to live by them."[20] Meher Baba also took a critical stance toward drugs, considering them "harmful mentally, spiritually, and physically."[21] Townshend initially fully embraced Baba's teaching, especially after his terrible experience with acid coming back from the Monterey Pop Festival on June 1967:

What I am trying to put across is that I still love the idea of getting stoned, I remember the days of colorful highs with acute nostalgia; I would be a fool to myself if I didn't allow myself the luxury of a past. The crux of it is, that I am now stoned all the time. It's hard to take, I know, but it's true. It's not a dizzy, smashed high, it's a fairly alert and natural one; just about as natural as you can get.[22]

Meher Baba's influence on Pete became apparent at the start of the Who's six-week American tour that began in February 1968.[23] It was in California that Pete jotted down the first ideas and concepts for what would become *Tommy*. In those days, Pete became very much aware of the growing correspondence and synchrony between his expressed musical ambitions and what the audience wanted to hear, something that was a far cry from the simple hit-single structure of pop music reflecting the deeper and expanding "seeker"-type consciousness of that time.

Pete's growing self-awareness gained through Meher Baba's influence on his development as a person would become the main source of inspiration for the Who's music, as well as the tool that would afford reassessment of the band's past, which, from that time on, would look increasingly like a sequence of steps necessarily and unconsciously aimed toward the realization of *Tommy*.

The first public announcement of the new Who project was made by *Rolling Stone* magazine, when director Jann Wenner published the whole Pete Townshend interview over two issues in September 1968. There, Pete spoke openly about *Tommy*, still in its early stages, which he then referred to as *Deaf Dumb and Blind Boy*:

It's derived as a result of quite a few things. We've been talking about doing an opera; we've been talking about doing like albums, we've been talking about a whole lot of things, and what has basically happened is that we've condensed all of these ideas, all this energy and all these gimmicks, and whatever we've decided on for future albums, into one juicy package. The package I hope is going to be called "Deaf, Dumb, and Blind Boy." It's a story about a kid that's born deaf, dumb and blind and what happens to him throughout his life. The deaf, dumb and blind boy is played by The Who, the musical entity. He's represented musically, represented by a theme which we play, which starts off the opera itself and then there's a song describing the deaf, dumb and blind boy. But what it's really all about is the fact that because the boy is deaf, dumb, and blind, he's seeing things basically as vibrations which we translate as music. . . . The boy sees things musically and in dreams and nothing has got any weight at all. He is touched from the outside and he feels his mother's touch, he feels his father's touch, but he just interprets them as music. His father gets pretty upset that his kid is deaf, dumb and blind. He wants a kid that will play football and God knows what. One night he comes in and he's drunk and he sits over the kid's bed and he looks at him and he starts to talk to him, and the kid just smiles up, and his father is trying to get through to him, telling him about how the other dads have a kid that they can take to football and they can teach them to play football and all this kind of crap and he starts to

say, "Can you hear me?" The kid, of course, can't hear him. He's groovin' in this musical thing, this incredible musical thing, he'll be out of his mind. Then there's his father outside, outside of his body, and this song is going to be written by John. I hope John will write this song about the father who is really uptight now. The kid won't respond, he just smiles. The father starts to hit him and at this moment the whole thing becomes incredibly realistic. On one side you have the dreamy music of the boy wasting through his nothing life. And on the other you have the reality of the father outside, uptight, but now you've got blows, you've got communication. The father is hitting the kid . . . and the kid doesn't catch the violence. He just knows that some sensation is happening. He doesn't feel the pain, he doesn't associate it with anything. He just accepts it. A similar situation happens later on in the opera, where the father starts to get the mother to take the kid away from home to an uncle. The uncle is a bit of a perv, you know. He plays with the kid's body while the kid is out. And at this particular time the child has heard his own name, his mother called him. And he managed to hear these words: "Tommy." He's really got this big thing about his name, whatever his name is going to be, you know "Tommy." And he gets really hung-up on his own name. He decides that this is the king and this is the goal. Tommy is the thing, man. He's going through this and the uncle comes in and starts to go through a scene with the kid's body, you know, and the boy experiences sexual vibrations, you know, sexual experience, and again it's just basic music, it's interpreted as music and it is nothing more than music. It's got no association with sleaziness or with undercover or with any of the things normally associated with sex. None of the romance, none of the visual stimulus, none of the sound stimulus. Just basic touch. It's meaningless. . . . Slowly but surely the kid starts to get it together, out of this simplicity, this incredible simplicity in his mind. He starts to realize that he can see and he can hear, and he can speak; they are there and they are happening all the time. And that all the time he has been able to hear and see. All the time it's been there in front of him, for him to see. . . . The music has got to explain what happens, that the boy elevates, and finds something which is incredible. To us, it's nothing to be able to see and hear and speak, but to him, it's absolutely incredible and overwhelming; this is what we want to do musically. . . . The main characters are going to be the boy, and his musical things, he's got a mother and a father and an uncle. There is a doctor involved who tries to do some psychiatric treatment on the kid which is only partly successful. The first two big events are when he hears his mother calling him and hears the word, "Tommy" and he devotes a whole part of his life to this one word. The second important event is when he sees himself in a mirror, suddenly seeing himself for the first time: he takes an immediate back step, bases his whole life around his own image. The whole thing then becomes incredibly introverted. The music and the lyrics become introverted and he starts to talk about himself, starts to talk about his beauty. Not knowing, of course, that what he saw was him.[24]

It is clear that in Pete's first conception of the work, parricide is not mentioned and does not seem to be the cause of Tommy's trauma. It would take eight months before *Tommy* would get a definitive structure—eight months spent on and off the road, before and after gigs encompassing two American tours. Photographer and friend Tom Wright recalls:

Pete was always writing in his notebook or reading any of the half-dozen paperbacks he kept strewn in his bus booth, the area that was supposed to be the "kitchen" but wound up as Pete's writing suite.[25]

On August 30, precisely twenty days after the last tour gig in Arizona, the Who locked themselves up in IBC's Studio A to give shape to the new album.

John Entwistle gave a detailed account of that period:

We're working quite hard at the moment—we spend every day recording numbers for our new album *Deaf Dumb and Blind Boy. . . .* It's like going to the office every day—we've set aside the hours between two in the afternoon and midnight for recording, and we try to stick to it. Obviously, it can't be rigid—if we're working on something then we continue outside the "office hours." Or if we've finished what we're doing then we go home. The thing is that by setting aside the time like that it makes it easier for us to get together—as you can imagine, it's not easy to get all the Who together in the same place at the same time.

We're spending all our working hours recording the album at the moment. It's been a long while since we had enough time to completely work things out for recording. The last album was a bit rushed—doing a track here and a track there between gigs. It just doesn't seem to work that way. We want to finish the album before we start to do too many appearances, or before we return to the States. In fact, I don't think we'll be going back to America until early next year.[26]

John gave some more to *Record Mirror*:

Pete made up the whole plot of the story and we're all leaping about the place doing different things to fit into it. We intend to do it live. The opera will probably take up most of our act—it won't be an elaborate thing with scenery or anything like that. We've always done a mini-opera in our stage act, and this will be like that but much longer. We won't really know how it'll develop until it's much nearer completion—we've only been recording for two days now.[27]

The band stuck to a tight schedule, recording during the week and often playing live on weekends both to pay for the studio—it would amount to £36,000—and to study audiences' reactions to the new material.

I'm Free

The first sign of the new work was the single "Pinball Wizard," released in England on March 7 and in the US on March 22, 1969. Decca advertisements featured the curious line "From the opera *Tommy 1914–1984*," one of the many temporary titles given to the album before its release, this one in particular suggested by Kit Lambert via a script he gave to the band. "Pinball Wizard" skyrocketed to no. 4 in the UK charts and no. 19 in America, marking the long-awaited redemption of the Who as a commercial artist, at least since the disappointing reception of "I Can See for Miles" a couple of years earlier. "Pinball Wizard" provided a concrete, commercial focus to *Tommy*, providing, in a sense, an existential redemption for the work, just as *Tommy* had for the Who. How the song came about, and how it was initially received, is even more interesting. Once Nik Cohn read the subject of the opera, he admitted that Pete was on to something extraordinary, yet it lacked that certain "je ne sais quoi" that would make the work catchier, less tortuous, and, of course, more commercially successful. Cohn suggested to Pete the expediency of a pinball champion, one that he himself had used for his tale *Arfur: Teenage Pinball Queen*, and although it was suggested by a respected music journalist, it would prove ironic that a large part of the press world would come to label the new Who single and album a sick manifestation of Townshend's mind, the taunting of a deaf, dumb, and blind boy.

The BBC, as it happens, have already slightly baulked at "Pinball Wizard"—Tony Blackburn has said he finds the words distasteful—so what their reaction will be to Tommy is anyone's guess.[28]

The ultimate test would take place at Ronnie Scott's Jazz Club, on May 1, 1969, the historical Soho venue the Who chose to introduce their new work to the press. That night, Townshend said rather sarcastically that it was all about what he thought of the harsh criticism certain journalists had given the single "Pinball Wizard," most of whom were sitting at Ronnie Scott's tables in the audience that evening:

No matter what Auntie [BBC Radio 1] thinks, it's not sick. In fact, the sickest thing in this country is Auntie herself![29]

Journalist Lon Goddard gave a detailed account of that day to *Record Mirror*:

From twelve o'clock onwards, an influx of journalists, publicists and assorted ravers were to be seen conglomerated in deepest Soho, preparing themselves with liquid medication for an occasion most rare and beautiful (and likely to go berserk). This was Thursday the first of May and The Who were going to lay it on big at Ronnie's. The evening reception was to be in honour of their forthcoming album, entitled simply, *Tommy*. At six sharp, the pubs in the city of bright lights and lit people, began to drain. By six-thirty, there existed a severe retail booze depression outside and the scattered tables within Ronnie Scott's club were seething with the pop industry. Crawling over hors d'oeuvres and threatening to over-run the bar in great teeming hordes, they distributed "Hellos" and "what-are-you-havings?," then meticulously selected tables and sat waiting, gorged and heavy. There were affectionate cries of "Blank off" as Pete Drummond [*sic*], Roger Daltrey, Keith "Mooney" Moon and John Entwistle assumed their positions. Pete began to explain the nature of the LP.

"There is a story to the music; it's the story of Tommy. Tommy is born and with the advent of the war, his father goes off to fight. Tommy's mother, meanwhile, gets randy and takes a lover. One day, Tommy sees something he shouldn't and is told to keep quiet about it. The shock causes him to go deaf, dumb and blind."

Exclamations of "Sick!," "Sick!"

"No, it's not sick, ha ha," replies Pete as Keith confirms this from the drums in back.

The next scene introduces Tommy to Gypsy the Acid Queen, who declares that she will take him into a room for a while and make a man out of a boy. Following this episode, Tommy becomes renowned as a pinball wizard. The LP ends with what appears to be a musical philosophical question: What happens to Tommy after his disturbed childhood? Where went the pinball wizard? The Who gave us a good solid hour's worth of quality listening and excellent showmanship, leaving amid chortles of "More!," "Get

off!" and "To the bar!" All in all, it was a great pop-religious happening and ends of the scale from Dave Dee to John Peel turned up to urge the play on. Then the pubs became enormously popular once again.[30]

Even after this episode, Pete kept defending his opera from the press's cutting words:

I don't consider the album to be sick at all. In fact, what I was out to show is that someone who has suffered terribly at the hands of society has the ability to turn all these experiences into a tremendous musical awareness. Sickness is in the mind of the listener and I don't give a damn what people think.[31]

Townshend's bitterness and preoccupation would cool off as soon as the Who ventured on their first 1969 North American tour. Perhaps having been too used to the cold response of the English audience, the Who could not have imagined the unexpected musical and cultural impact that *Tommy* would have in America, and how the success of the album would take the band through three American tours up until late 1970.

Tommy was released as a double LP by Decca Records in America on May 17, 1969, and on May 23 by Track Records in the UK because of its complex packaging production. The English print of *Tommy* is richer than the American: both feature a booklet with lyrics and illustrations to guide the listener through the story, but only English booklets feature a five-number matrix. In addition, the English printing was to have included an introduction by Kit Lambert, but the idea had been dropped.

In its definitive form, *Tommy* has a much more complex plot than what emerged from Pete's initial references to the album.

How Do You Think He Does It?

As a former Ealing Art College student, Pete knew well that according to classical tradition, art generates itself from the impulse to express the most-profound elements of our psyches, in search of catharsis. In this respect, it can be said that the creative process, along with other functions, works as a metabolic and psychological mechanism for the experience and release of—or perhaps in some ways, the sublimation of—negative experience.

Townshend seemed to embrace this point of view by explaining the genesis of *Tommy* with these words:

I wanted to express childhood feelings because they are the most intense feelings you get. I've also tried to get a social meaning to the '60s, a political meaning and a spiritual meaning. [32]

That is to say, *Tommy* served as both a personal and generational redemption. Although Pete excluded any reference to his own past life through *Tommy* ("Nothing to do with my life or any of that!"),[33] the album seems to conceal the underlying necessity for Pete to trace back and process a trauma he experienced as a six-year-old child, when he was left in the custody of his wicked, insane, and authoritarian grandmother Denny. Back then, the guitarist's mother, Betty, had had too many challenges with her marriage to look after Pete properly, and one day she received the news of the aggravation of Denny's emotional troubles and mental health problems. In a not-so-smart move, she sent Pete off to keep Denny company, especially now that Denny's lover Mr. Buss has walked out on her. The time Pete spent with his grandmother would turn out to be a real *discensus ad inferos*, a period that Pete, in his autobiography *Who I Am*, describes as the darkest of his life.

From Pete's words, we can gather that these episodes and some of the people whom he met while living with his grandmother are not so different from those that Tommy experienced. Emotionally ignored and neglected at an age when we need more attention and care than ever, Pete is the real deaf, dumb, and blind boy saved by the thaumaturgic property of music.

On the other hand, Pete's intention in composing *Tommy* was not merely one with which to handle his personal demons. Townshend's private trauma became a means by which he could voice the story of a whole generation of young people, a postwar-babies' generation for which he became a public spokesperson: those children born in the mid-1940s who, like Pete, suffered the gratuitous iniquities of World War II.

England was eventually, with its Allies, victorious in the war against Nazi Germany, but at an unprecedented cost of lives and money so high that it harmed the pride and prestige of the country. While adults were encouraged by Churchill to keep leading a lifestyle that celebrated a national identity—though now well faded—the new generation was left to its own devices. Townshend was among those children. They, more than enduring postwar financial troubles, were fated to witness the indifference of their parents, who were themselves trying to come to grips with the moral and material reconstruction of the country.

In such a context, sensitive children such as Pete Townshend are the ones most often exposed to social marginalization and bullying. And from this perspective, the music of the Who in 1969 became an unconscious attempt to reprocess traumatic experiences, with *Tommy* as both the key to and manifestation of that phenomenon. And from a social and collective point of view, the music of the Who, *Tommy* in particular, and later *Quadrophenia*, serves as a mirror, one that reflects a person's own identity in a sea of common experience.

Pete recalled:

For a while I used the term "mirroring" to describe the transaction between The Who and their fans. The Who, I mused, merely mirrored their audience, they reflected them. [34]

The metaphor of the Who's music as a mirror and their live concerts as a vessel is also very close to the definition that *Rolling Stone*'s director Jann Wenner gave to rock and roll: "Rock and roll works as common experience and private obsession. The two cannot really be separated. Indeed, one fuels the other."[35]

The realization of this metaphor at its zenith and its most powerful came about in 1969 on stages such as Woodstock, when the refrain of "See Me, Feel Me" and "Listening to You," sung at the first rays of dawn, sounded like the definitive existential and spiritual litany of a whole generation.

Tommy came along at a time in our lives when everyone was searching for answers in their life. The ambiguity of Tommy allowed it to answer many things for many different people. But in fact, it didn't really answer anything.

That was the beauty of it. [36]

CHAPTER 8

1969

Anyway Anyhow Anywhere

Bill Graham

Fillmore East, New York, on Friday, May 16, 1969

What follows is the transcription of part of an audience recording owned by the author from the Fillmore East, on Friday, May 16, 1969, when Bill Graham had to stop the Who's set to order the evacuation of the building due to a fire next door. According to the recording, the Who were halfway through "See Me, Feel Me / Listening to You" when the plainclothes cop came onstage and was kicked and punched by Pete and Roger. Unaware of what was really happening, the Who continued their set onto "Summertime Blues." They did not go further, since Bill Graham asked the band to stop playing to make an announcement:

Do you want to hold it just for a moment, please? Do you want to hold it just for a moment, please?[Audience member: "Let the place burn down!"] Do us a favor, please. Very slowly and very calmly, please . . . The building across the street . . . there is a fire . . . [unintelligible] . . . As a precautionary measure, the fire department has asked us to vacate this building . . . there is nothing . . . there is nothing we can do. We're terribly sorry. Get off the chandelier [?] . . . Thank you. Would you kindly, slowly . . . very slowly, please . . . [unintelligible] on this side, or that side.

The Fillmore East is evacuated after a fire in the grocery store next door. Friday, May 16, 1969. *Photo by Charlotte von Segesser*

Steve Richards

Fillmore East, New York, on Friday, May 16, 1969

On May 16, 1969, I took the train from Stamford, Connecticut, to Grand Central Station in New York City, and then the subway down to Greenwich Village to witness a historic performance. It was the first time I got to see the Who. Held at the now-long-gone Fillmore East concert hall, I had ninth-row-center seats. Since the actual album *Tommy* wasn't released until seven days later, on May 23, 1969, this was most certainly one of, if not the first ever, official

performance of their first rock opera. From what I can tell from their listed concert schedule in 1969, it was the first time in the US, and I was damned well in attendance. Several things of note took place that night.

One of my photos, while on the dark side, shows Pete Townshend leaving the stage, shortly after rescuing Roger Daltrey (with some well-aimed Pete Townshend's footwork) from what appeared to be an onstage assault. I suspect the

Who did not know their portion of the show was finished, since they weren't moving. Nobody seated anywhere near the stage like I was could smell any smoke at the time, and that plain clothes officer damned well *did not* show any form of identification as he claimed. The Who *did not* finish their performance. Trust me. No "My Generation" meant no finish. After an abridged version of *Tommy*, they did maybe four more tunes. As I recall, they stopped after "Summertime Blues," and this is where Pete Townshend is seen exiting the stage.

When they finally did get around to evacuating the front rows, the smell of smoke became very strong. In fact, as we were attempting to very slowly exit the theater following many other *very slow* concert attendees, oxygen was at a premium. Becoming very difficult to breathe, you really start to wonder if you are going to get out. Fortunately, everyone got out, and the rest is apparently historically significant only if you were there or are some kind of rock and roll historian.

Fillmore East, New York. Friday, May 16, 1969. *All photos by Steve Richards*

Jerry Pompili

Fillmore East, New York, on Friday, May 16, 1969

There has been a lot of documentation on the "Fillmore fire" episode, with the cop jumping up onstage, but there's a whole lot of things that happened that night, part of the fire. The fire was in this building on the corner of 2nd Avenue and 6th Street, and the Fillmore East was around this building. And in one point, the flames from this fire were blowing totally across 2nd Avenue. I mean, it was *that* bad. When we became aware of it, got together with Bill and devised the plan, which was we would let the Who finish their song, then Bill would get up onstage and calmly talk the audience out. Now, normally, doing two shows at night, under normal condition, we could empty the theater in seven minutes, so we knew we could do this in a lot less time in this kind of situation. So everyone was geared up to do this, and Bill was going to have everyone exit everywhere except the front door, because that was where the fire was located. Meanwhile, I got up to the front with other three or four ushers, and as Bill was up onstage the fire department came rushing into the building, and the less we wanted them to do was running and start screaming, "Fire!" So we literally stopped them in the lobby, and luckily they listened to us and didn't go running into the theater, and we probably emptied the theater in less than three minutes. There was only one minor injury—one of our guys was overcome by smoke up in the balcony, but we found him and got him out—but other than that, no one was injured by the fire.

Mike Jahn, *New York Times* Special Feature

Fillmore East, New York, on Friday, May 16, 1969

Those were the years during which I covered rock and roll and related riots for the *New York Times*, which got me into a lot of yurts. . . . Everyone knew everyone else because they were "around." . . . Steve was another guy who was around. He was a good friend of mine who had a quartet that opened for the Who during one of their 1970s arena tours. How did a folk/rock/jazz fusion quartet get to open for the Who (and get booed for their effort)? Steve was good friends with Pete Townshend, whom I also knew from around . . . ran into him at a guitar store on 47th Street twice and on the street in San Francisco once, following which we went to his hotel room and split a six. I don't recall what we talked about. Probably all the people we knew from around.

One weekend night circa 1969, I got a worried call from Steve, who said something like, "Pete's here. The cops are looking for him." The exact words don't matter when you're in a situation involving guns and jails. It seems that Pete threw a fire marshal off the stage at the Fillmore East—there was a fire next door, and the man interrupted a Who set to ask that the theater be evacuated. Pete gave him the old heave-ho and, later, when told that the NYPD frowns on such things, ran off to Steve's apartment to hide. I told him that Pete should lay low until Monday, when the lawyers were around.

(Extract from Mike Jahn's blog: https://mikejahn.moxietype.com/)

Mark Suall

Fillmore East, New York, on Saturday, May 17, 1969, Early Show

It was the early show. Townshend had just been released from the holding cell at the 9th (?) Precinct after spending the night in jail. I had to listen to WNEW all day to find out if he was going to be released in time for the show. The tension in the Fillmore before the Who walked out onstage was unreal. It was the 1960s. Concerts were infused with a sense of revolution. And Townshend was regarded as one of the leaders of that revolution. So there was something very triumphant about that moment, and you could feel it in the theater. The energy in the Fillmore that night was like something I'd never experienced before or since. The Who were so powerful and intense it was intimidating. I remember looking at people in the audience, standing with their fists clenched, gritting their teeth like they were on a thrill ride. It was like being in a room with King Kong straining to bust loose from his chains. I saw Jimi, the Doors, etc. All fantastic. But that Who concert at the Fillmore was the most intense rock and roll experience I ever had. They looked 10 feet tall.

Fillmore East, New York. Saturday, May 17, 1969. *All photos by Mark Suall*

Fillmore East, New York. Saturday, May 17, 1969. *All photos by Mark Suall*

Fillmore East, New York. Saturday, May 17, 1969. *All photos by Mark Suall*

Fillmore East, New York. Saturday, May 17, 1969. *All photos by Charlotte von Segesser*

Aaron M. Hodgett

Kinetic Playground, Chicago, on Thursday–Saturday, May 29–31, 1969

These two pictures were taken by my father, Gary. He was a great Who fan. That's why and how the Who became my life band as well. I saw the passion that my dad had for the Who since I was a baby, and the influence was passed on straight to my gut. The one thing I picked up and really took to heart was when he would tell me how whenever you would see Pete in the white jumpsuit, Doc Marten boots, and maroon Gibson SG, it was when the Who were in their absolute prime. He was right. When my dad first saw the *30 Years of Maximum R&B* VHS when it came out, and it had "Heaven & Hell" from the 1970 Tanglewood set, he flipped out because that was the first time he saw them play "Heaven & Hell" since he saw them do it live in front of him at the Kinetic Playground in 1969. Surreal. I was lucky enough to see the Who, live, with my dad; mom, Deb; brother, Joe; and sister, Gracie twice in 1996 for the *Quadrophenia* tour in Tinley Park, Illinois, which is a suburb of Chicago, and again in 2002 at Tinley Park, which is my favorite concert that I've ever attended out of the hundreds of shows that I've been to in my life, before my father's tragic passing of a heart attack on July 22, 2005, at fifty-five. My family then saw the Who together one more time at the famed United Center in 2006, because we all knew that Dad would want us all to go for him.

Kinetic Playground, Chicago, Illinois. May 29–31, 1969. *Photos by Gary W. Hodgett, courtesy of Aaron M. Hodgett*

Kiel Auditorium, St. Louis, Missouri. Sunday, June 1, 1969. *All photos by Craig Petty*

Guthrie Theater, Minneapolis, Minnesota. Sunday, June 8, 1969. *All photos by Mike Barich, the Barich Archive*

Guthrie Theater, Minneapolis, Minnesota. Sunday, June 8, 1969. *Photo by Mike Barich, the Barich Archive*

Guthrie Theater, Minneapolis, Minnesota. Sunday, June 8, 1969. *All photos by Mike Barich, the Barich Archive*

Guthrie Theater,
Minneapolis,
Minnesota. Sunday,
June 8, 1969. *All
photos by Mike Barich,
the Barich Archive*

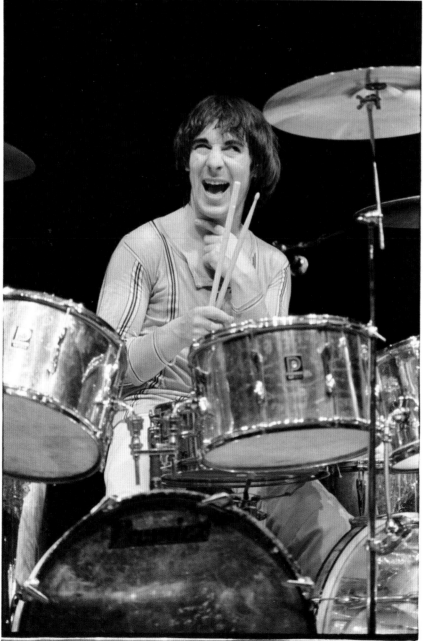

Guthrie Theater, Minneapolis, Minnesota. Sunday, June 8, 1969. *All photos by Mike Barich, the Barich Archive*

The following pictures were taken by Mike Barich at the house of Suzanne Weil, who at the time was producing shows at the Guthrie Theater in Minneapolis. Her guests that night were Tony Glover (who had opened the Who's show with his folk band Koerner, Ray & Glover) and Pete Townshend. Tony was also a rock critic and engaged in a long interview with Pete. The photos here presented show a rare moment of Pete finding in Suzanne Weil's living room Winnie the Pooh's stuffed-toys characters, which were left scattered around the place by Suzanne's daughter. Pete took the opportunity to tell the interesting anecdote about Winnie the Pooh's donkey friend Eeyore inspiring him one night to write "Happy Jack."

Tony Glover, Pete, and "Eeyore." Pete revealed that Winnie the Pooh's famous donkey friend inspired the writing of "Happy Jack." Sunday, June 8, 1969. *Mike Barich, the Barich Archive*

Tony Glover interviews Pete at Suzanne Weil's home in Minneapolis, Minnesota. Sunday, June 8, 1969. *All photos by Mike Barich, the Barich Archive*

Tony Glover interviews
Pete at Suzanne Weil's
home in Minneapolis,
Minnesota. Sunday, June
8, 1969. *All photos by Mike
Barich, the Barich Archive*

Richard Martin Frost

The Who Party on Thursday, June 12, 1969, and the Magic Circus at the Hollywood Palladium on Friday, June 13, 1969

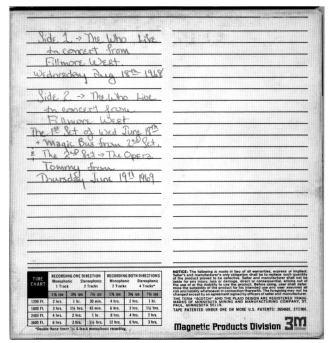

The Night Before

Rock photographer Frank Zinn, Thomas and Richard Frost, and Rodney Bingenheimer threw what turned out to be one of the biggest rock-and-roll parties Hollywood has ever had. Rodney estimated that 500 were in attendance. Devra Di Marco, the sister of famed rock photographer Ed Caraeff, was gracious enough to host the party at her house. The party was in honor of the Who being in town to play the Magic Circus at the Hollywood Palladium the following night. Joining the party was the Who, Bonzo Dog Band, Poco, Jimi Hendrix, the Doors, Sky Saxon, Linda Ronstadt, the Blues Magoos, Lord Sutch, Kim Fowley, Firesign Theater, Burrito Brothers, and the GTOs.

The Following Day

The day following the party was "Clean-the-house day." As we were finishing the cleanup, Frank Zinn discovered a little pill on the floor. Someone must have dropped it at the party the night before. Frank, never one to back down from the crazy, swallowed it. We didn't know what he had taken or what the effects might be, but by the time we drove back to my apartment he was hallucinating. I thought the best thing to do under the circumstances was to take him for a walk to, it was hoped, walk it off.

As we were walking up La Cienega Boulevard to Sunset, Frank was crawling on his hands and knees and barking like a dog. I managed to get him up on his feet, and we proceeded to Sunset. When we finally got there, I decided to cross. When there was a break in the traffic, I told Frank to run. I ran but he didn't. Sunset Boulevard now separated us. I was concerned for his safety and had to wait for traffic to clear again so I could run back across. Before I got the chance, a Volkswagen bus rolled up on Frank. I saw Pete inside. Frank later told me that Keith and John pulled him into the bus. Kidnapped by the Who. As Frank later told me, they were on their way to the Magic Circus for setup and sound check. When they got there, the Lawrence Welk Orchestra was breaking down their show, and hundreds of balloons were everywhere one could step. Kidnapped by the Who—Lawrence Welk—psychedelic indeed.

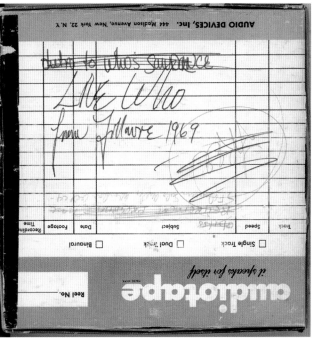

Audience recordings from Fillmore West, June 18 and 19, 1969.
Courtesy of Mark d'Ercole; author's archive

Note from the author on a recently unearthed recording from the Fillmore West, June 18, 1969:
While working on this book, I met a guy named Craig Patterson, who turned out to be the keeper of many of his friends' Who-related music archives. Some of them might sound familiar to hard-core Who fans, such as photographer Steve Caraway; some of them have passed unnoticed . . . until now. People like Jim Sanchez and Gary Pierazzi were

Fillmore West, San Francisco, California. Tuesday, June 17, 1969. *Photos by Steve Caraway, courtesy of Craig Patterson*

Fillmore West, San Francisco, California. Tuesday, June 17, 1969. *Photo by Paul Sommer*

two ordinary Who fans except for one thing: they possessed an intuitive ability to grasp the historical importance of the shows they attended, having the foresight and wiliness to bring a tape recorder with them to immortalize what was happening. Sanchez and Pierazzi recorded on cassette part of the early show and the full late show of June 18, 1969, at the Fillmore West in San Francisco, which Craig unearthed after fifty years and sent to me.

After close and careful listenings, I found out something that contradicts the alleged truth behind one particular recording: the bootleg recording of the show that circulates as "Fillmore West, August 13, 1968."

I received the master source of that recording in 2018 by the original taper, Mark d'Ercole, who could not remember from which Fillmore West concert that recording dated back to. Common knowledge stated it was from August 13, 1968, so I stuck with it until recently, when I received the Sanchez/Pierazzi recording from Craig Patterson. Mark d'Ercole's recording was believed to belong to the Who's August 1968 show, because it missed *Tommy* and the song list was similar to what they were playing during that American summer tour, but I realized it is in fact a partial recording of a much-longer concert that was recorded in its full length by Jim Sanchez and Gary Pierazzi.

The fact that the songs Mark d'Ercole captured on tape match with Sanchez/Pierazzi's recording leads to the conclusion that the d'Ercole recording is in fact from the late show at the Fillmore West on June 18, 1969. As for the August 13, 1968, concert at the same San Francisco venue, no recording has yet surfaced.

Here is the complete set list from the late show of June 18, 1969, at the Fillmore West, as derived from the two recordings. The song order is given by the Sanchez/Pierazzi recording, while in bold are marked the songs from the d'Ercole recording—the alleged "August 13, 1968 Fillmore West recording": "**Heaven & Hell**," "**I Can't Explain**," "Fortune Teller" / "Tattoo," "**I'm a Boy**," "**Happy Jack**," "**A Quick One**," "**My Generation**," "**Shakin' All Over**," "It's a Boy, 1921," "Amazing Journey" / "Sparks," "Eyesight to the Blind," "Christmas," "Acid Queen," "Pinball Wizard," "Uncle Ernie," "There's a Doctor I've Found," "Go to the Mirror," "I'm Free," "Welcome to the Camp," "We're Not Gonna Take It," "Summertime Blues," and "**Magic Bus**."

Fillmore West, San Francisco, California. Thursday, June 19, 1969. *Photo by Paul Sommer*

Fillmore West, San Francisco, California. Thursday, June 19, 1969. *All photos by Paul Sommer*

Fillmore West, San Francisco, California. Thursday, June 19, 1969. *All photos by Paul Sommer*

John Peden

Fillmore West, San Francisco, California, on Thursday, June 19, 1969

I grew up in North Carolina, which is East Coast, and when I was a freshman in college, which would have been 1964, there was a bunch of design students, architecture students, and we built a coffeehouse. Coffeehouses were pretty common primarily for folk music, and in North Carolina there was traditional music: Doc Watson, bluegrass, etc. So we started going to the folk music festivals, and the big one, of course, was Newport in Rhode Island. There was the popular music for people who were "thinking" about music, or people for whom music meant something to them, and folk music very much was "that" music. Rock and roll, which started with Little Richard and Elvis, had fizzled out by the late 1950s: Elvis had gone into the army, Chuck Berry was in jail, Little Richard had gone into the ministry, Jerry Lee Lewis was disgraced, Buddy Holly had died, and along came folk music, which seemed to have a vibrancy and a wit and an intelligence. It was obviously musically simple, which of course was part of the appeal, and it made all of this thing "We can be musicians" and we could be folk musicians, but that was about it! But nonetheless, that was kind of the hip music until along came the songwriters, and Dylan was definitely in the full front.

Then in 1964, in February, the Beatles played Ed Sullivan, and that clearly was a demarcation that reinvigorated American popular music. The Beatles were still doing the kind of music people like Little Richard, Buddy Holly, and the Everly Brothers used to make before they were pushed off the stage, and what the Fab Four did was reacquainting everybody with how good that music was. So, people like Dylan and others realized that folk music needed to go electric. So it did. I was at the Newport Folk Festival in 1965, which is when Bob Dylan came out with a Stratocaster. Musically, perhaps, that wasn't the best concert I've ever been to, but you had a true sense that time will be measured before this event and after this event. Things were changing.

I had formed a blues band in the wake of Dylan going electric and the Beatles and the Butterfield Blues Band and the Kweskin Jug Band—all of this was swirling around my head in North Carolina, and I formed this band called Heavenly Blues Band. The coffeehouse had to close, and I sold all the fixtures. I had a little bit of money, and everyone that had helped build it had all graduated from architecture school, and they had all gone to San Francisco.

The phrase they used was "San Francisco is for design and architecture as much as Hollywood is for acting." San Francisco is unique, and it was unique in the middle 1960s as a sort of a liberal, sophisticated small town, and it had a history of North Beach, the Beatniks, intellectuals, poetry readings, coffeehouses, and so it was a beacon for people that didn't fit in elsewhere. So I took the funds from the selling of the fixtures and went out to San Francisco right after Christmas, in 1965. These guys were out there and they all had jobs, but we were sampling the cultural life of San Francisco, which of course was fantastic. Live music in San Francisco those days was like running water. You just took it for granted. It was special, but you had no sense that it was as unique as it was.

There were a couple of events that I attended where there was a palpable sense of things shifting. I remember getting on a cable car the first night there, which are open to the outside, literally hanging on the side of the cable car and going to North Beach and just walking into a club and seeing Thelonious Monk! It was like going to heaven. In heaven they have cable cars and they have Thelonious Monk playing in a club! They also had a thing there called the Trips Festival at an auditorium at Fisherman's Wharf; I think it was called Longshoremen's Hall. I went there with a couple of friends, and it may sound as a cliché now, but it was really mind-blowing. I was not taking psychedelic drugs, but you went into this thing and all the people were walking around, there was a light show, there was a rock-and-roll band, and it was great!

When my funds went out, I went back to North Carolina, and I told all the members of the band, "Screw this! We gotta go to San Francisco! San Francisco is where it's gonna happen!" I was the only one who wasn't in school at that time. Everyone else was in school, the Vietnam War was cranking up at this point, and everyone was extremely careful about their student deferment. I had been subjected to the recruiting medical doctors, and they had decided I would not make a good soldier. I was the one that was free, so our band played a few gigs in North Carolina, we went up to Chapel Hill, which is a college town 20 miles away, we put together some tapes and pictures, and I moved to San Francisco and began to explore what could be done.

At that point there was the Avalon Ballroom, there was the Family Dog, there were six or eight of these ballrooms, and there were what we would call "loving hands at home," San Francisco bands: Sons of Champlin, Quicksilver Messenger Service, Great Society, Jefferson Airplane, the Grateful Dead, and of course when you say these names now, you think about the institutions that they have become, but at that point, early 1966, these bands were pretty fluid; members would come and go.

I talked to people and everybody said, "The guy you should go talk to is Bill Graham. He is the most together." There was a guy named Chet Helms and other ballroom managers, and Bill Graham was just a guy of fun, so I called him up and he asked me to come over. I brought him the tapes, I had the pictures, and Bill told me, "I like you guys.

I have got this new place I'm gonna be starting here in a month on Fillmore Street; I'd like to book you in there. Which of these dates do you want?" I said, "Well, everybody else in the band is still in North Carolina, they're all in school, but as soon as they finish up, they will all be coming here." So we picked a date, which I think it was the fourth Fillmore gig ever, and he put us on with the Jefferson Airplane and the Great Society, and we were the Heavenly Blues Band. At that point, Grace Slick was still with the Great Society. Unfortunately, for us, our lead guitar player, as it turned out, while taking exams, was taken to a hospital very sick and did not come out for a month or two, so we spent the summer trying to replace him. We used to rehearse at 1090 Page, which was the Grateful Dead's house, and we could never find anybody who was interested in playing the songs to the arrangements that we had. All the San Francisco musicians were very into free form, and we would go, "We are gonna do 'Born in Chicago' in the key of E," and the guys would go, "I don't know from keys, man, I just blow!" It was very frustrating for us, because we wanted to be tight!

By the end of the summer, the notion of going to the ballrooms to see the bands was a routine; you didn't think much more about it than going to the corner to get a newspaper. You went, "Oh, who's playing tonight?" It was

so easy to go the Fillmore in those days completely relaxed and just walk in with a camera. There was no security, nobody searching bags. It was plenty of people in there, there were no seats, and if you got there early you could just go right up to the front. I used the edge to the stage to steady my camera. I was a beginning photographer.

We were very aware that the record shops there very much had the English imports, because we all knew that the English imports had more songs on and generally were pressed better than the American counterparts. There was even an article that talked about the hippies, which of course was the media title for the alternative lifestyle in San Francisco, and it talked about how even the most down-and-out, cooking-over-an-open-fire, living-in-a-tepee hippie would have a decent stereo system! Everybody had a decent turntable and a pair of speakers! And what you would do was to sit on the floor, roll joints, and listen to music! No one would have the patience for that today, but in those days that was the evening entertainment. Nobody had a TV; there was nothing on TV worth watching!

The one other event that—just to contextualize the scene—where I felt that the plates shifted was another group. In the summer of 1966, we were listening to *Blonde on Blonde*, Frank Zappa and the Mothers, *Freak Out*, *Fresh Cream*, and the Who. The Who brought something to San

Fillmore West, San Francisco, California. Thursday, June 19, 1969. *All photos by John Peden*

Francisco. We were certainly seeing bands all the time, and the local bands like the Grateful Dead and the Jefferson Airplane, the Sons of Champlin, Steve Miller, Quicksilver Messenger Service, but no one combined the intensity and that showmanship—showmanship put at the service of the music, not showmanship like Elvis or any kind of cheap showbiz thing. The Who put on a show that was almost borderline religious! Those guys had a message, and that was through the music, and people were taken aback. First of all, they were loud, but they were never brittle. They had great tone. And of course Daltrey was so much a better singer than any other band that I could think of. And they had a tight show. I probably saw them live as much as anybody just because I enjoyed them so much.

By the time *Tommy* came out, that was cinematic. I mean, that was a rock opera! You would just sit there with four, five, six people—you would get together, you would have a nice little dinner, and then you would put on your record! And the Who were one of the ones that went right out to the corners; they filled it all up. They didn't leave any parts of the sonic spectrum unexamined. They were just great.

The English scene brought a certain polish, a certain showmanship, but not just showmanship. The English mastered it in a way that the San Francisco groups never did. In any event, it seemed to me that the audience had a hunger for as much soloing as they could convince Cream to give them. When Cream came, that was another band like the Who where you definitely made a pilgrimage to the Fillmore. I did go with anticipation to see Cream. When Cream played, there was a palpable exchange of energy between the band and the audience. And I think Cream had the same sort of showmanship the Who had, which was obviously part of the London music scene, which was sort of a bath that Jimi Hendrix bathed in and that slicked him up a little bit, and the slickness was just a visual metaphor for the music.

Eric just seemed to go on and on, with Bruce and Ginger Baker. That was another concert where I felt, "Okay, we have gone

to another plateau." The Who did as well, in a different way of course. The Who just put on such a great show. I probably saw more live shows of the Who than anybody else. It was such a complete performance.

When I went to the Fillmore, I went early so that I could be at the front, because that was the only way I knew how to take pictures. That night I photographed the Who, as I entered I realized the room was pretty empty, but what they were playing on the sound system was the tape that I had given Bill Graham of the Heavenly Blues Band a long way back! That was pretty creepy!

Fillmore West, San Francisco, California. Thursday, June 19, 1969. *All photos by John Peden*

Fillmore West, San Francisco, California. Thursday, June 19, 1969. *Photo by Dennis McCoy, copyright of Brad Rodgers, www. whocollection.com*

Fillmore West, San Francisco, California. Wednesday, June 18, 1969. *Photo by Dennis McCoy, copyright of Brad Rodgers, www.whocollection.com*

Fillmore West, San Francisco,
California. Thursday, June 19, 1969.
All photos by John S. Tilson

Fillmore West, San Francisco, California. Thursday, June 19, 1969.
All photos by John S. Tilson

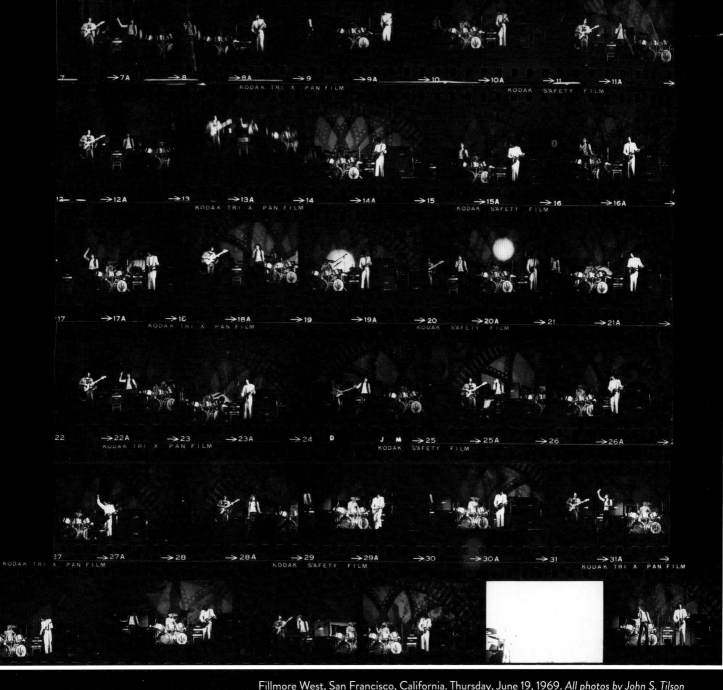

Fillmore West, San Francisco, California. Thursday, June 19, 1969. *All photos by John S. Tilson*

Fillmore West, San Francisco, California. Tuesday, June 17 and 19, 1969. *All photos by Rich Pacini*

Fillmore West, San Francisco, California. Tuesday, June 17, 1969. *Frank M. Stapleton*

Fillmore West, San Francisco, California. Wednesday, June 18, 1969. *All photos by Frank M. Stapleton*

Fillmore West, San Francisco, California. Wednesday, June 18, 1969. *All photos by Frank M. Stapleton*

Fillmore West, San Francisco, California. Thursday, June 19, 1969. *All photos by Frank M. Stapleton*

Fillmore West, San Francisco, California. Thursday, June 19, 1969. *All photos by Frank M. Stapleton*

Image © Dave Seabury, restoration by Jonathan Lyerly

→ 3   → 3A   →

Fillmore West, San
Francisco, California.
Thursday, June 19, 1969. *All
photos © Dave Seabury,
restoration by Jonathan Lyerly*

Image © Dave Seabury, restoration by Jonathan Lyerly

Fillmore West, San Francisco, California. Thursday, June 19, 1969. *All photos by Mark d'Ercole*

Fillmore West, San Francisco, California. Thursday, June 19, 1969. At the end of the set, Pete comes back onstage and says to the audience: "When we were last at the Fillmore in New York, we had a bit of a problem with an alleged police officer, and tomorrow morning at nine o' clock we've got to be in court in New York. . . . We've got to catch a plane at 11:30; we've really got to go. But thanks very much." *All photos by Paul Sommer*

Tanglewood Music Shed, Lenox, Massachusetts. Tuesday, August 12, 1969. *All photos courtesy of Dawn Hall of Douglas Kent Hall estate, thanks to Princeton University Library*

Albert Cooke

Woodstock Music & Art Fair, White Lake, New York, on Friday–Monday, August 15–18, 1969

The posters went up and the newspaper ads started to appear early in the summer of 1969. They listed the bands that were going to play at the festival. It was an incredible list. It seemed like everybody who was anybody was listed. How could a musician and concertgoer like myself resist? Five of us, my guitarist and drummer at the time and two of the guitarist's friends, bought tickets through the mail. We had our tickets. We were ready to go.

It was me, Jack, Peter, Sal, and Phil. We were all either seventeen or eighteen years of age.

Phil borrowed his father's big boat of a car and decided that we should leave on Wednesday night, for a festival that was scheduled to start on Friday night. Phil was either psychic or a genius to make that decision, because it obviously turned out to be critical to our successful journey and arrival upstate. Any later than that, and we might not have been able to get close to it. It was an approximately two-hour drive from Stamford, Connecticut.

We left at 9:00 p.m. and arrived at Monticello Raceway, just off the Route 17 highway, about two hours later, which put us 5 miles from White Lake, where Yasgur's Farm was located. Now on a skinny local road, we immediately found ourselves in traffic that was crawling, so slow that we were able to lean out our windows and talk to people in other cars. One interesting fact of our journey is that we had music in the car, other than a radio. Few if any cars had that in 1969, and I don't remember if it was a tape system or if he had a turntable in the trunk, but as we drove there we listened to *Electric Ladyland* by Jimi Hendrix and *Truth* by the Jeff Beck Group, who had been advertised to appear at the festival but did not.

Upon finally arriving at the entrance to Yasgur's Farm, we drove past it for approximately a mile and found a parking spot in a field, and that and other nearby fields were filling up quickly. Again, this was forty-eight hours before the scheduled start. Because it was now past midnight, we decided to do nothing but set up camp with our sleeping bags and call it a night.

The next morning, we arose and proceeded to walk to the hill. We walked back to the farm entrance on the main road, and the driveway to the hill was a half mile long. Now here's something few remember and nobody ever mentions. Just before reaching the top of the hill, a traveling carnival had set up some rides on the right-hand side, including a Ferris wheel. I never went on any of them.[1] As we were arriving at the hill, many workers were still working on the stage, and others were erecting a fence around the hill. That's right—they were going to collect tickets for entry once the festival started. Or so they thought. So we just sat down on the hill, all nice and grassy on a beautiful August day, and relaxed for hours. We then walked around the area all day, heading back to the car periodically to eat food that we'd packed. I mostly ate food from cans that needed no cooking, although cooking would have helped. As the day wore on, it seemed more and more people were arriving. When the day was over, we went back to the car, each of us now taking turns; some of us sleeping in the car and some sleeping next to it on the ground.

Let me pause here for some observations. What was so impressive to me at this point was the people. Long haired, hippie-looking clothes, vans and trucks and buses painted in the psychedelic style of the time. Guys with hair down to their waists. But the sheer numbers of them were amazing. Where had all these people been hiding? I'd been to many concerts in New York, but I'd never seen anything like this. It was like we'd all been living in secret, and none of us knew how many of us existed until we all arrived at the same destination, something later to be called Woodstock Nation. It felt empowering. Look at our numbers. We were all surprised, perhaps shocked, while recognizing that we were now a force through sheer numbers. We'd had no idea it was this big. It was a revelation. We had just been kids growing up in a Connecticut town with a few hippie-looking kids hanging out in the town park, but we didn't really know what was going on beyond our town. And as I later sat on that hill for the three days, I would keep looking behind me at the sea of humanity that seemed to go on forever, and really had a profound revelation about our generation and what we had done and what we had become at that moment. It permanently changed the way I look at life and society to this day. I thought we were going to take over and change the world. I thought everybody was going to evolve like us to our way of thinking and living. The world had changed before my eyes, all in one weekend. Would it be successful? Would it be permanent? I was subsequently disappointed when Altamont crashed and burned three months later and we were returned to the ugly realities of the world. And some said the Death of Hippie. "Fuck them," I thought. But they might have been right to a certain extent. But you could never kill the spirit for those who had it. I should also mention that this was my first introduction to drugs. No, I didn't take any; that would happen a year later. But my guitarist's two friends had some hash and a hash pipe. I was sort of freaked out by it. I knew nothing about drugs, and I thought they were smoking opium, because that was the extent of my knowledge. I wanted no part of it.

On Friday morning we essentially did the same thing as the morning before. Upon getting back to the hill, we decided that we should now stake out a good spot on the hill and stay put for the beginning of the concert. But the problem was, the workers still hadn't finished the fencing. And once they did, late in the day, the festival MCs attempted to ask all the people on the hill to leave and go back outside the fence, so they could reenter properly with their tickets. Well, nobody was moving. And the fencing looked pretty flimsy anyway. At that point, the management saw the writing on the wall . . . the whole ticket thing wasn't going to work. Turned out people were just going to parts of the fence away from the ticket takers and pushed down parts of it and walked over it. That is shown in the movie, as is the announcement that it was now a free festival. They had no choice.

Now, the Friday night lineup was essentially folk night; mostly acoustic and solo artists. At approximately 6:00 p.m., Richie Havens hit the stage to start the music. At approximately 9:30–10:00 p.m. a light rain started, although it was nothing compared to what happened on Sunday afternoon. At that point, we decided to head back to the car and call it a night, as we weren't really that interested in the remaining Friday artists.

Saturday morning it was the same drill: get up and go back to the hill. But the hill was starting to get muddy, with some puddles here and there from the light rain the night before. The hill was pretty full of people, but we were determined to get as close as possible. We drilled down to the right side of the right light tower and found an open spot, because it was a bit of a muddy puddle, but we sat down there anyway. And we stayed right in that spot for the next nineteen hours. We saw every band on Saturday, starting with a solo spot by John Sebastian. After an entire day of bands like Santana, Creedence, Mountain, Canned Heat, the Grateful Dead, Janis Joplin, and others, I'll cut to the highlight of the night, which was Sly & the Family Stone. They put on a show for the ages. Sly was the master showman. The movie gives you a sense of it, but suffice to say the crowd lost its shit during his performance. He had the entire hill in the palm of his hand. He grabbed the crowd and turned it into a jumping and screaming party.

And next up after Sly? The Who. The only band capable of following what Sly had just done. It was now about 3:00 a.m. They came out and did their entire set, including *Tommy*. The sound was a bit insufficient, and they were not having their best performance, but the enormity of the gig made up for any shortcomings. The movie cuts it to make it seem great, but for the Who it was a C– performance. Yet, it was historic, thanks in large part to the movie. Halfway into their set, between songs, activist Abbie Hoffman ran onstage and up to Townshend's mic and started to give a political speech about how John Sinclair, the manager of the MC5 (who were not there), had been jailed illegally and that we shouldn't be sitting on our asses listening to music, but rather we should be doing something about it. Well, it's common knowledge that Pete Townshend was not in a

good mood that night. He felt they weren't getting enough money to play—they wanted to be paid in cash, and it was a bit of a dustup before the band hit the stage. Plus, they were probably going on six or seven hours later than they had hoped, as schedules at Woodstock were pretty flimsy. And he wasn't feeling the whole hippie festival thing. So, when Abbie commandeered his space, he snapped. He walked up behind him and hit him in the head with his Gibson, knocking him right off the stage. Pete then spit into the mic that if anybody else invaded the stage, he'd "fucking kill them." An exact quote. Pete wasn't big on the peace-and-love vibe. And I've seen his temper on several occasions. But the show must go on. As they approached the end of the set and began "My Generation," the sun started to rise. That was way cool. In fact, it was glorious.

At the end of their set, I was understandably exhausted. I'd just seen my favorite band, and I was done. So as Jefferson Airplane took the stage, now in early-morning daylight and the last band of the Saturday lineup, Grace Slick said, "It's a new dawn," and they launched into "Volunteers," which just seemed like the perfect song for that moment and that festival. And that's what I listened to as I trudged back up the hill and walked the mile and a half back to the car.

Sunday morning it's the same drill; back to the hill. Now the hill was even more crowded than the previous day, and we saw no hope of getting close, so we sat down at the top of the hill. First band of the day was Joe Cocker and the Grease Band. They played a great set, and just as they finished, as you see in the movie, very dark threatening clouds were moving in from the west. The movie documents this well. There was mild panic as the wind started to sway the light towers. And the rain hit, and it was heavy, and it went on for about an hour. And when it was over, everybody was soaked to the bone and a bit delirious, and there was mud everywhere. Although when I say mud, I should remind everyone that the hill had been a cow pasture, so the ground was dirt with a generous sprinkling of cow poop, now rising to the surface. It was bad. The music stopped for several hours, so at that point we headed over to a pond behind the stage, featured in the movie, and pulled off our wet, muddy clothes and went swimming in the nude. I can't tell you how good that felt after four days without a bathroom.

At that point I was about done. I'd seen all the bands I'd wanted to see, even though there were still plenty of great bands scheduled for the rest of Sunday. So I split off from my friends and went back to the car. When I got there, the car was locked, and I noticed an empty house across the street from the field. So I decided to investigate and seek some shelter. I go inside and there were about thirty people inside the house, just hanging out. And that's where I stayed the rest of Sunday, into Monday morning, hanging out with a bunch of Woodstock hippies. My buddies eventually caught up with me there. Early Monday morning, my guitarist asked me to go back to the hill with him to see Jimi Hendrix. I declined. I'd had enough. I totally regret not going back with him to this day, although I could hear Jimi's guitar in the distance, coming from over the horizon. Must have been the "Star Spangled Banner," Jimi style. Once Jimi was done, we all met back at the car, and we were stuck in the mud. But local farmers got their tractors out and were towing cars back out to the road for $10 a pop. We made our way back to the highway and headed home. As we made the drive and passed so many people in other cars also leaving the festival, something extraordinary happened. Without fail, everybody in their cars would flash the peace sign at each other as our cars passed. It happened time and time again, without fail, all the way home. The magic lingered; the magic continued. For a time.

The following summer, in 1970, my drummer and I along with our girlfriends drove back to White Lake and back to the hill so I could show the girls, and to see how it looked a year later and to pay my respects. Perhaps it was a bit of a religious pilgrimage for myself. The entire area looked like nothing had ever happened, although the hill itself still looked a little ragged and pockmarked.

You probably know that they have now built a museum and an outdoor concert stage at the top of the hill. I returned there once again in 2009 and thoroughly enjoyed the museum, with its displays and a movie theater, where they show a movie of scenes from the festival, totally different from the *Woodstock* movie we've watched all these years. I plan to return there again this summer with a musician friend, twenty years my junior, and then again for special events in 2019, the fiftieth anniversary of the event. That will be a big blast! They have yet to announce the activities, but I'm sure it will be a big deal. I'm in. The last hurrah of hippie nation, before we all croak.

Peace and love.

Albert Cooke
2018, Norwalk, Connecticut

Glenn Coleman

Woodstock Music & Art Fair, White Lake, New York, on Friday–Monday, August 15–18, 1969

I was at Woodstock, right at the front for the Who's performance. At Woodstock the crowd was always moving, and you just walked down to the front; it took a while, but if you walked the perimeter and got up front, you just stopped and backed up a couple of feet and you were there.

I did take a few pictures, and if Pete's guitar would have made it past the photo pit they had, it would have landed right in front of me.

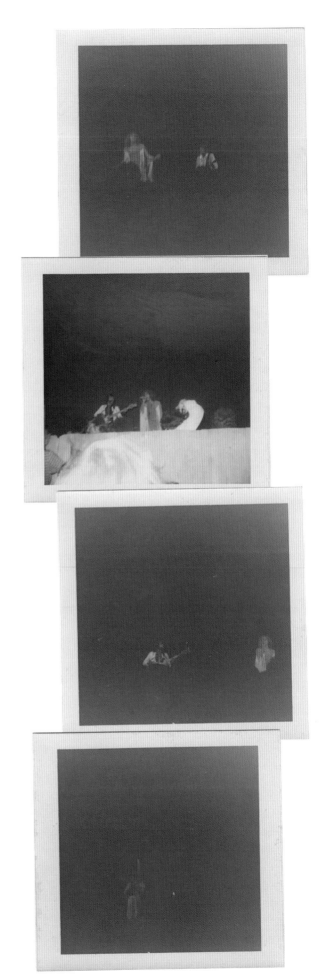

The Who at Woodstock. *All photos by Glenn Coleman, Coleman Audio*

Rick FitzRandolph
Woodstock Music & Art Fair, White Lake, New York, on Sunday, August 17, 1969

Tommy came out May of 1969, and it was fantastic. Around June, I heard about a concert weekend called Woodstock in downstate New York, about 350 miles away, and it had the Who on Saturday on the itinerary. If the Who weren't on the ticket, I wouldn't have been interested. But they were, and I knew I had to go (sort of like Richard Dreyfuss in *Close Encounters*). I convinced three of my buddies to go, and I mailed away for the whole weekend pass for the four of us. The tickets never came. So, I said we have to go anyways; they may have a will call (so naive) or we purchase tickets at the door.

A few days before we left for Woodstock, my parents wanted me to get a haircut. I wanted to keep my Pete Townshend medium shag hairstyle, so I just stayed at my buddy's house for the next three days to avoid my parents and go the concert with my Townshend haircut. My three friends and I left after work (4:00 p.m.) on Friday afternoon and drove the 350 miles to Woodstock. About 20 miles from the site, the traffic started to build up, and by 10 miles away it was a 3 mph crawl. At 5 miles away, we gave up, found a spot to pull off the road, and parked. Arlo Guthrie was bragging about the Thruway being shut down, but we had come on a different, southern route. So, what should have been a six-hour drive turned into ten, and we went to sleep in the car about 2:00 a.m. and got up around 7:00 a.m.

I, as our fearless leader, said let's get going to the concert. I was the ace face, but I was not the driver. Mike, our driver, had just gotten a brand-new 1968 Dodge Dart and didn't want to leave his car in the midst of thousands of hippies, so he just never left the parked car. Never saw the concert. Craig and John and I headed out for the 5-mile trudge. We carried sleeping bags and a little food, and I carried 20 pounds of camera equipment. I had upgraded to a 35 mm camera with a 300 mm telephoto lens and tripod, along with other lenses. When we got to concert field, it was an incredulous site. It was a hillside bowl with a huge stage, with a high wooden fence in front of it and light towers and so many people. The fences and gates were gone; there was no ticket booth, just one big sea of people sitting or lying in a field of mud.

My only purpose in going was to see the Who and get some good photographs of them. So, I said we needed to get close to the stage. And to do that, we needed to circumnavigate the crowd, come in from the side, get down to the front, and push our way back. The wall in front of the stage was about 10 feet high, so you had to be back about 40 feet to see anything. We pushed back through the mud and sleeping people who had been up all Friday night,

and got to stage-left spot, where I knew Pete would set up. This was about 10:00 in the morning.

About noon, my friend Craig said he was hungry and was going back to the car to get something to eat and drink and would be back later. He never came back, never saw any music, but at least he saw the stage. About 1:30, my friend John did the same thing, and I never saw him at the concert. At least he saw a couple of bands. So, I am there for the duration by myself. Not really, because everyone around me was friendly and sharing food and hash and dope and wine. I always declined the dope because we were so close to the stage and TV cameras would be pointing out at the crowd. I was afraid my parents would see me smoking pot on TV, and I would be in trouble when I got home.

During Country Joe's set, a city kid (what us upstate kids called people from NYC) said, "You gotta see this next band, Santana." I had never heard of them, and he was correct—Santana was really good. Up next was John Sebastian, whom I knew and really liked from the Lovin' Spoonful. I liked most of the following bands, but by 3:30 a.m. I could no longer stay awake, so I lay down on my muddy sleeping bag and went to sleep. I was awakened by the entire hill of people shouting "HIGHER" back to Sly and the Family Stone, singing "I Want to Take You Higher." Now I'm awake, and the Who will be on within an hour.

By this time, the crowd had been pushing forward and tighter and were all standing, so there was no room for a tripod. But I felt in my glory, in position to catch a great concert by my band and hopefully get some good pictures. I just wished my buddies had been there with me to experience a Who concert. At the end of their set, and now it is dawn on Sunday, I gather up my camera bag and tripod and leave the muddy sleeping bag stuck in the mud. I start my trudge back to the car, 5 miles away, and I can hear Jefferson Airplane starting their set. I liked them, but I had come to see the Who, and I had seen them close-up in front of 500 thousand others, I got my photos, and I was spent. I got back to the car and told the guys they missed an awesome day of music, and let's get back home. At the time, I had no idea it would be an iconic cultural event. To me, it was just an opportunity to see my favorite band, with the bonus of seeing and hearing some other good music as well.

We got home on Sunday afternoon and said our goodbyes, and they dropped me off at my parents' house. My father tells me we are going straight to the barber in the morning. He takes me there, and I undergo a severely short haircut with 2-inch whitewalls around my ears (actually popular these days, like Bernard Sumner), and I have to go to Stony Brook College as a freshman in two weeks, where everyone else on campus has hippie-length hair. Grrrr.

"Sparks" at Woodstock. *Photo by Rick FitzRandolph*

Bob Grunditz

Woodstock Music & Art Fair, White Lake, New York, on Friday–Monday, August 15–18, 1969

The summer of 1969 will always remain in my mind as a definitive time of my life. I was a registered conscious objector with a religious deferment from the US military draft. I would be required to perform an alternative service in civilian life. I'd been working as a painter/artist for an amusement park at the North Shore Shopping Center in Massachusetts; I'd been working there for about five seasons.

Upon hearing about the Wallkill, later named Woodstock, festival of music and art, I knew I'd be going. I'd already been listening to the renaissance of modern rock groups, and folk and blues music, for several years. I purchased my tickets in Boston and gave notice at work. When it came time to make the trip from Massachusetts to upstate New York, I hitchhiked and arrived after only two rides and 217 miles. The first ride was from a young married couple in a late-model Mercedes-Benz. The last ride was in a much-older Caddie hearse. It was evening, and the growing crowd was setting up camp, milling about, socializing, and enjoying the atmosphere of so many other music lovers. I slept in somebody's tent that night with a few people. The next day, the amount of people had grown enormously. I found a place and sat down to listen to the opening of the festival by Richie Havens, a folk singer whose LP I had. His was a very energetic and moving performance that led the way for the others due to play, often quite emotionally, the music we all came to hear. There were so many happenings and experiences I lived through, and to record them all, of course, would take a small volume. Apart from pauses during rainstorms, to avoid electrical problems and electrocution of artists, the music lasted as a wave over the people, punctuated by announcements and humorous stage banter delivered by Chip Monck and Hugh Romney (a.k.a. "Wavy Gravy"). I answered a request for volunteers to counsel those of the gathering dealing with emotional problems relating to drugs. Up the hill from the stage area were the tepees set up by the Hog Farm, people and their cohorts they'd aligned with from Santa Fe, New Mexico. The Hog Farmers were from Southern California. I'd seen Hugh Romney at free concerts and other music and comedy events in California. It was only natural for me to want to assist with this group of people who'd been enlisted as "security" for the festival. Members like Lisa and Tom Law certainly were dedicated to ensuring the welfare of the people, feeding them nutritious food. Tom gave wonderful yoga and meditation classes. I met a person who'd come with the Santa Fe family group during the emotional rescue of a girl who'd been dosed with an amphetamine. Eighteen years later, the same guy pressured me to go skiing here in Alaska, where I am living now.

The Who were astonishing in their performance. I'd listened to their relatively mild first American LP release a couple of years earlier and was amazed by the volatile performance at their Woodstock set. Of course it was a spectacle for everyone there. As I found out, this was something they were consistently doing in their live performances. The Who's playing was stellar, and the way they held the stage was equally amazing, individually and as a whole. Unforgettable.

Alan Watters

Second Isle of Wight Festival of Music, Woodside Bay, Isle of Wight, on Saturday, August 30, 1969; Kinema Ballroom, Dunfermline, Fifeshire, Scotland, on Saturday, September 6, 1969

When I was nineteen and twenty, I hitchhiked down from Dunfermline in Fife, Scotland, to both Isle of Wight festivals (1969 and 1970), and on the first trip I was standing with my thumb out just on the outskirts of London when I was picked up in Roger Daltrey's Rolls-Royce and given a lift all the way down to the ferry port at Southampton. The Who's road manager was driving, and he told me lots of things about the band that people generally wouldn't know. Like how one of his jobs was to take apart every one of Pete Townshend's new guitars, then strategically bolt them back together, so that when Pete smashed his guitars up onstage, the guys could bolt the good bits from several guitars back together afterward to make a usable guitar again, and that way they could save a bit of money.

I was working part time in the Kinema Ballroom in Dunfermline at the time and was privileged to then meet the band one week after, on September 6, 1969, when my mate Bob Smith and I helped set up their equipment before they played there.

John B. Brown

Grande Riviera Ballroom, Detroit, Michigan, on Sunday, October 12, 1969

My good friend Clark and I, both about eighteen years old, had just attended a Who concert at the Grande Riviera Theater, not the Grande Ballroom, in Detroit, Michigan. After the band finished an incredibly lengthy concert including their hits and *Tommy*, we drove over to the London Inn, on Woodward Avenue, just north of downtown Detroit, where the band was staying. It was a relatively small two-story motel, and I grabbed a can of Coke from a vending machine and we started roaming the halls in search of an after-show party. It wasn't long before we heard some laughing and talking, and Keith Moon was chatting with some people in the hallway while drinking from a half-empty quart bottle of Smirnoff vodka. We joined the conversation and told him how much we enjoyed the show and were amazed at how long and hard he could play his kit the entire set. He just laughed and started pouring vodka into the opening on the top of my Coke can. He proposed a toast and yelled, "Let's drink up, mates," laughing all the while. We told him we'd seen the band whenever they'd previously come to the Detroit area, several times already. He realized we lived nearby, and asked us if we could get some "birds" to come down to party with us. It took us a moment to realize he was asking for us to bring high school girls to downtown Detroit on a Sunday night . . . we declined for about a million reasons. Keith Moon was about twenty-two years old at the time and was the first adult to offer me an adult beverage while I was well underage . . . and for that, I'm forever grateful.

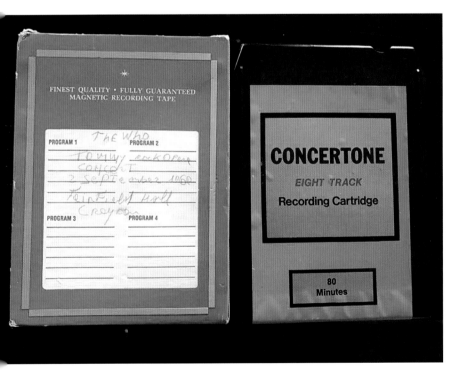

Master 8 track recording of the Fairfield Hall concert, Croydon, UK. September 21, 1969. In a 1971 *Zigzag* interview, Pete rated this show as perhaps the best performance of *Tommy*. *Courtesy of Genero Alberto*

Electric Factory, Philadelphia, Pennsylvania. Sunday, October 19, 1969. *All photos by Will Vogt*

Paul "Paco" Prior

Fillmore East, New York, on Saturday, October 25, 1969

I'm a drummer. I've played drums since I was eleven. Keith Moon was one of my idols.

I think seeing The Who perform on the Smothers Brothers show, and seeing the Monterey Pop movie right around the same time, made quite an impression.

To this day, I maintain that The Who performing *Tommy* at the Fillmore was the best rock concert I've seen in my entire life. I'm sixty-two and have been close to a thousand concerts.

At that time I was I'd say around fifteen or sixteen. My friends and I were probably the youngest ones there.

Greenwich Village (where Fillmore East was located) was, and still is, a mecca for the "Bohemian" types. My friends and I used to go in via bus from New Jersey and just wander around the stores and stuff. But like I said, I don't think there were that many fourteen or fifteen year olds at the Fillmore in those days. My gift from my parents for making the Honor Roll (good grades, all As and Bs) was a trip to the Fillmore East. June 1969. The bill was Buddy Miles Express, Savoy Brown Blues Band, and headlined by the Grateful Dead. How's that for a classic rock wet dream. All bands had the original members. And especially in the case of Savoy Brown, that's pretty amazing. I may be one of only one in a couple thousand that saw that first line up in the US.

I saw The Who at the Fillmore East on Saturday night, October 25, 1969. The final night of the week long run. I remember Townshend commenting specifically that they had been entertained completely during their NYC stay, because "There was just do much to do after the show."

I forgot to mention I met Pete Townshend a couple of years ago. He was doing a book signing near my home. I stood in line three hours. When my turn came, I did not just meekly hand him my book and stand silently while he autographed it. Here's how it went: I said, "Would you mind if I shook your hand?" Pete, "Not at all." As I shook his hand, I said, "I just want to thank you for all the great music you've made over the years. It's made a huge impact on my life." He thanked me, and I moved on. I'm glad I opened up my mouth.

Fillmore East, New York. October 20–25, 1969.
All photos courtesy of Dawn Hall of Douglas Kent Hall estate, thanks to Princeton University Library

Joshua White

Fillmore East, New York. October 20–25, 1969

Half a century later, I still consider the Who to be the best band that ever performed at Fillmore East. The Joshua Light Show was always behind them on the big screen. We had many important bands, but those were upcoming artists. The Who already enjoyed major success as part of the English Invasion at the start of the 1960s. Just for the record, the "sixties" actually began officially in 1964, when the Beatles came to America and appeared on *The Ed Sullivan Show*. By 1968, the Who were very tight and enjoyed playing four shows every weekend. Their set was disciplined and perfect for our light show, familiar and yet full of surprises and tempo changes. Because they had already released major hits, the audience loved them. Perhaps more important, they were without pretention. Unlike many contemporary bands, especially some from the Bay Area, they had no problem singing "Magic Bus" and "My Generation" repeatedly. It's worth noting that everyone was in their midtwenties. We all enjoyed the energy of the Who.

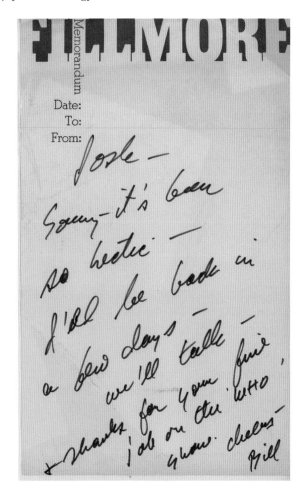

A note Bill Graham left to Joshua White after a whole week of *Tommy* performances: "Josh—sorry—it's been so hectic—I'll be back in a few days—we'll talk—Thanks for your job on the 'WHO' shows. Cheers, Bill."

The album *Tommy* was released in spring 1969. By then, the Fillmore had been open for more than a year. From a production standpoint, we hit our stride. Given support and a little money, there was nothing we couldn't do. When Bill Graham announced a week of performances by the Who performing their rock opera *Tommy*, we were prepared.

All our light-show members were college graduates with extensive experience in all types of production. Most of the stage crew had come out of New York University's Tisch School of the Arts, which was next door. In discussing our approach, we all agreed that *Tommy* was not really an opera in the traditional form. It was in fact a great cantata that didn't always make sense. There was no reason to take the lyrics literally. We would honor the music and text but not try to mirror it.

We did use our skills to make visual markers such as pinballs, patriotic symbols, and World War I barbed-wire imagery, but the bulk of the light show would continue to be our beautiful liquid abstract imagery.

The Fillmore staff made changes to the overall presentation. At the Fillmore, Joshua Light Show appeared behind the bands on a 20-by-30-foot, high-quality, rear-projection screen. The theater's technical director, Chris Langhart, and our light-show filmmaker, Amalie Rothschild, designed a new curved screen that was built in-house and increased our canvas to 40 feet.

In reality, the light-show performances were not significantly different from what we usually created. However, the simple addition of concrete imagery working with the audience's receptivity made the work look totally integrated and synchronous. This is an old, open secret of successful analog light shows. The audience wants to make the visual connections. A good light show gives them material to work with.

Part of our great success was because I received a copy of *Tommy*, copied the lyrics, and made what was essentially a script. For the one and only time, I stood onstage left and actually "called" the cues. This was more like gentle warnings to everyone about what would happen next. It worked. Furthermore, we enjoyed a week of performances, which meant the entire presentation as well as the Who themselves only got better as the run progressed.

My favorite memory of the time, aside from the brilliance of the artists themselves, was the fact that the run sold out completely. I'd never had that experience. Another pleasure was reading the reviews, which were ecstatic. The success of course belonged to the Who, but we were praised by association.

The most perfect musical moment came each night after they finished singing *Tommy*. Naturally, the audience demanded an encore. They got one. The Who came back and sang every hit they had—amazing!

I need to keep reminding myself we were all twenty-five.

Fillmore East, New York. Monday, October 20, 1969. First of
six nights in a row of the Who performing *Tommy* at the
Fillmore East. *Photo by Thom Lukas*

Fillmore East, New York. Monday, October 20, 1969. First of six nights
in a row of the Who performing *Tommy* at the Fillmore East. *Photo by
Thom Lukas*

Photographer Thom Lukas's pass
for the first Who show at the
Fillmore East performing *Tommy*
in its entirety, October 20, 1969.
Courtesy of Thom Lukas

Fillmore East, New York. October
20–25, 1969. *Photo by Thom Lukas*

Fillmore East, New York. October 20–25, 1969. *All photos courtesy of Dawn Hall of Douglas Kent Hall estate, thanks to Princeton University Library*

Fillmore East, New York. October 20–25, 1969. *All photos courtesy of Dawn Hall of Douglas Kent Hall estate, thanks to Princeton University Library*

Kinetic Playground, Chicago, Illinois. Friday, October 31, 1969. *Photo by Gary W. Hodgett, courtesy of Aaron M. Hodgett*

Kinetic Playground, Chicago, Illinois. Friday, October 31, 1969. *Photo by Mike Barich, the Barich Archive*

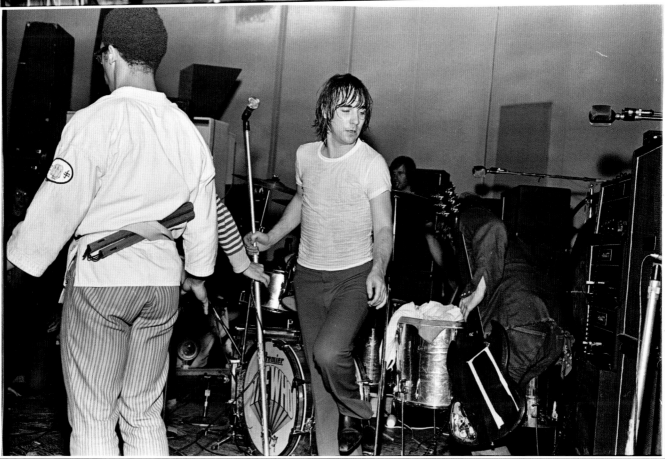

Kinetic Playground, Chicago, Illinois. Friday, October 31, 1969. *All photos by Mike Barich, the Barich Archive*

Pete with Aaron Russo, promoter of the Kinetic Playground. Friday, October 31, 1969. *Mike Barich, the Barich Archive*

Kinetic Playground, Chicago, Illinois. Friday, October 31, 1969. *Photo by Mike Barich, the Barich Archive*

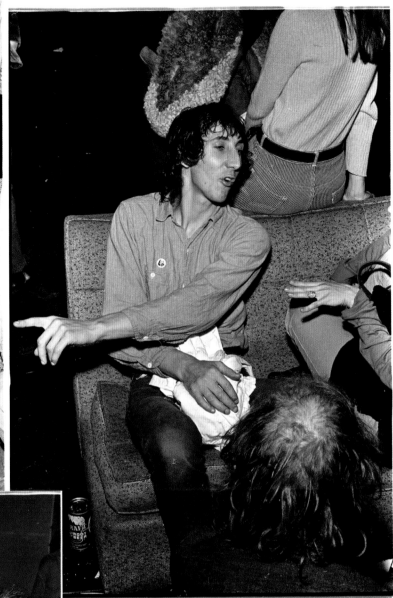

Kinetic Playground, Chicago, Illinois. Friday, October 31, 1969. *All photos by Mike Barich, the Barich Archive*

CHAPTER 9

1970

It All Looks Fine to the Naked Eye . . .

The year 1970 stands in Who history as their peak of expressivity. The band was back from a one-year tour, having played the UK's, US's, and Europe's most renowned and prestigious venues, as well as the most-popular festivals. The Opera Houses tour would continue at the Champs-Élysées Theatre in Paris, moving onto Denmark, Germany, and Holland. At that time, the Who had the reputation of being the best live band in the world. There was an unwritten rule that no one should follow them onstage. They were too good. That, in addition to wanting to show just how their live sound differed from *Tommy*, led the band to record an album that left a definitive mark on music history.

Their previous American tour, which had kicked off in Boston on October 10, 1969, ending in New York on November 16 that same year, had been recorded in stereo by the Who's chief sound engineer, Bob Pridden, described somewhat facetiously and affectionately by Townshend at Fillmore West on August 14, 1968, as their "reliable and faithful roadie." The original plan had been to go through the soundboard recordings of the shows and choose the best takes for a live album. However, Bob Pridden had not proven to be quite his usual self that tour, having forgotten to label the recordings. The missing notes on each reel, which would have helped distinguish one concert from the other, and the sheer amount of work involved trying to correct that, coupled with disagreements as to which take was best for each song, led a weary and frustrated Pete Townshend to order their destruction to avoid the frequent and money-losing phenomenon of bootlegging.

As an alternative, Bob Pridden booked two gigs in the north of England: at Leeds University's refectory on Valentine's Day, February 14, 1970, and in nearby Hull the following day.

Problems, however, with recording John Entwistle's bass channel in Hull made the recording of the band's performance at Leeds the de facto solution that turned out to be a blessing. The near-flawless performance that night, played only two hours after a surprise announcement on the college radio station, with little to no need of overdubbing or manipulation, resulted in a product that quickly became widely considered "the best live rock album ever made."[1] It was in 1970 that the *New York Times* music critic Nik Cohn originally accoladed the work that status, and almost fifty years later, many critics still consider it to be the case.[2]

Flying high on the success of *Live at Leeds* and their latest single, "The Seeker," within less than a year the Who announced another American tour. It was only a month in duration, from June to July, and yet it would turn out to be the most enjoyable one for the band to date, as Pete himself announced at the end of their last set in Tanglewood, Massachusetts, on July 7. The tour started with a double appearance on the same night at the Metropolitan Opera House in New York City. The event was put on by Bill Graham (manager of the two Fillmores, and one of the promoters of Woodstock), focusing on the performance of *Tommy*, an album that had quickly transcended its subcultural dimension and, in throwing off the shroud of its avant-garde status, became an immediately popular and influential classic.

Given the importance of the live event and the needs of its stage act, the Who installed in the Metropolitan Theatre the most powerful indoor PA system ever assembled at the time—4,000 watts—to ensure the best and loudest sound that they could get; it was designed by Pridden and Townshend themselves and was unprecedented for an indoor venue.[3] The Who had already attempted to push the audience's hearing resistance to the limit at the second Isle of Wight Festival on August 30, 1969, blasting over 2,500 watts from one of the biggest PAs available in England, warning people not to stand within 15 feet of the speakers. However, that was quickly exceeded. The *Guinness Book of World Records* staff on May 31, 1976, at the Charlton Athletic Football Ground in London, with a far-over-capacity crowd estimated to be 75,000–80,000, measured and recorded the volume of the Who at 126 decibels at a distance of 100 feet. They could be heard 10 miles away. The Who's PA system had grown to 76,000 watts of peak power and required loud sound monitors onstage, aimed back at the band, so that they could hear themselves. To put this in perspective, the sound of lightning and thunder cracking directly overhead is about 120 decibels, and that of a military jet taking off with afterburners at full thrust is about 130 decibels at 50 feet. The Who were loud! In 1994,

the *Guinness Book of World Records* dropped the category of "loudest band," since several other minor groups later sought to claim (and succeeded in claiming) that crown, making it a clear health hazard.

. . . But It Don't Really Happen That Way at All

Meanwhile, the utopia of a generation was waking up to reality and the demons of show business, with the music festivals at Woodstock, the Isle of Wight, and Altamont all proving to be harbingers of an end to an era. The so-called Flower Power generation—really a small minority of youth and young adults who grabbed the news headlines, making the counterculture appear larger in numbers than it really was—involved so many artists from the East and West Coasts of America and the north and south of England that it was easy to think back then, especially if immersed within it, that society at large would change even more than it did. In fact, it was a genuine watershed period wherein music, literature, civil rights changes, and protestations against the war in Vietnam brought about significant changes in Western culture, albeit more an evolution than a revolution. As far as the three emblematic concerts of decline were concerned, though, the Who and Jimi Hendrix, among others, featured prominently in the first two, the third being primarily the Rolling Stones.

It is rare, if not impossible, to trace back with accuracy the exact origins of a social phenomenon or movement, given the multifaceted nature of historical causes in general, but it is necessary to at least try in order to comprehend such change in historical context. In this case, the third Isle of Wight Festival in 1970 marked a decline, a passage from one era to another. More than Woodstock or other smaller festivals of the same year, such as Goose Lake, Atlanta, or the Festival Express in Canada, the Isle of Wight Festival seemed to unfold a fracture in the collective awareness of the hippie ideology and culture, something most shockingly experienced at Altamont, California.

The Isle of Wight festival alternated between high and low moments on and off the stage. Joni Mitchell's set became emblematic for this reason. The Canadian folk singer gave a seesawing performance before a sometimes rowdy and polemic audience forced to pay a £3 a ticket to attend the festival, a lot for that time (the minimum wage in America was then $1.60 an hour, about 10 percent of the $11.10 of 2017). The "Lady of the Canyon" first struggled to handle the situation and eventually broke down in tears.

The Isle of Wight episode was merely an epiphenomenon of a deeper discomfort that led Bill Graham, careful witness of that historical and cultural shift, to close the Fillmores:

The public changed, and most of the groups wanted to play bigger places, and I didn't want to take them. Other producers took them. I don't like Madison Square Garden. I think it's for Ben Hur and chariot races and idiot wrestlers; it's not for me. . . . There was a particular situation in New York where I and the Fillmore organization had done a show at the Metropolitan Opera House with the Who, and they were very pleased. We did *Tommy* there, and it was the first time that a contemporary event took place there. I was negotiating with Mr. Hurok to bring in a month of contemporary music so that other buildings in other towns would allow rock and roll in. It was very important to me that our music is accepted by America and by the world. The Metropolitan Opera House agreed and started calling groups that I thought should play there. . . . The budget of the Opera House was $50,000 for the week for any artist. By 1971 . . . , this business had gotten so that a lot of these groups made that one night, while years before $5,000 was a lot of money. But by that time, a lot of these groups were making 40–50,000. I started to speak with these and said, "This is the MET, this is what the budget is, I'm not going to make that much money, but it's important to play there not just for the money, but to show the other parts of Cultura Americana who we are." That we're not just some freaks who pop pills and get stoned all the time. I was having some success, and I called the manager of this particular group, who called me back in my office at 3:00 in the morning. I said, "Hello, this is Bill Graham and I want your group to play there." He said, "What about the money?" I said, "Well, it's six shows—five night shows and one afternoon show—and it's the MET." He said, "Yeah, yeah . . . but what about the bread; what's the pay?," and I said, "If you sell out, you can make $50,000," which a few years ago was immense. It is not what he said, it was the way he said it that in one moment told me that I had to get out. . . . I can't do exactly the way he did, but it was something like, when I said, "You would make $50,000 for the week," his reply was "Bill, do you expect my group to play for $50,000 a week?" That was it.[4]

It is quite significant that the two shows Bill Graham produced for the Who at Berkeley Community Theater on June 16 and 17 that year are among the last intimate concerts the band would play in it's career.

As Pete commented to *Rolling Stone*:

The show at Berkeley . . . was the best we did in the States that tour. The sound was great, if a little loud for such a small place, and the crowd just super-aware and alive. I could smell a lot of dope, but I think a good many people are beginning to realize that it is a bit of a risk getting high to watch The Who.[5]

Somehow, the verse "It don't really happen that way at all," as the Who sang prophetically at the Isle of Wight in their song "Naked Eye," at the end of their set between the Doors and Sly & The Family Stone, sums up the cultural shift of that time. "Naked Eye" is a song that perfectly captures the feeling of disenchantment within that historical and cultural shift (as did the Who's 1971 anthem, "Won't Get Fooled Again"). The song "Naked Eye" had a slow and spontaneous development. It first appeared as a guitar riff played in the long codas of "Magic Bus" at the end of the incendiary sets of the first *Tommy* tour, in mid-1969. At every show, Townshend explored the F6/9–Caug9–G chord progression in different ways, as can be heard in bootleg recordings of that time. The most-memorable early versions of this song, although still embryonic, were played at the Merriweather Post Pavilion on May 25, 1969, when the Who shared the bill with Led Zeppelin; at the Fillmore West on June 19, 1969; and, of course, at the Woodstock festival, under the first rays of light at dawn. Within a year of touring, the suggestive guitar riff had matured, as had the song's structure, and while not yet the definitive version, it was played in all of its grandiosity at the Isle of Wight Festival before 600,000 people, lit up and exposed by the huge and powerful World War II air force bomber searchlights brought onto the island a few miles off the coast of England by the Who.

Nevertheless, the constant introduction of new songs at concerts and the maturing sound of the Who demonstrated that the band did not wish to live on a winning formula defined by their rock opera's success. Their creativity had by no means run out. The band left 1970 with the title Most Exciting Live Act in the World, with over a million dollars in their pockets, mostly thanks to *Tommy*, which had by that time gone platinum:

Tommy had become a bit of a monster for The Who, but it was also a monster success and that isn't too hard to live with.[6]

Yet, in viewing this retrospectively, all of the Who's subsequent albums, however influential, would appear in many ways to free themselves of the ghost of Tommy, that deaf, dumb, and blind boy.

CHAPTER 10

1970

Anyway Anyhow Anywhere

Jeremy Goodwin

Out in the Street: Substitute

Pete Townshend, Ronnie Wood, and Ronnie Lane were about to play their guitars in the living room of Mike and Katie McKinnerney's home, Mike being the artist behind the Who's *Tommy* album cover. I was so excited. But then disaster struck. My mother decided she needed to go home. It was 11:30 p.m. and she had work the next day. Work? What is that compared to this? But at twelve years old, one has very little say about such things.

I fought and argued all the way to the car. What madness! Just as we were about to get into the car, the three musicians came into view, each carrying a guitar picked up from Ronnie Lane's place around the corner. Pete acknowledged that we were leaving with some disappointment, albeit he understood my mother's concern. Once again, I loudly protested the absurdity of such an idea, which brought out Pete's kind side. He asked me to pick a tune. I chose "Substitute." He played the first few bars of it right then and there, with Ronnie Wood and Ronnie Lane waiting patiently for him with smiles on their "Faces." But now that I think of it, "My Generation" might have been the more appropriate choice of song.

Linda Allen (as told by Dermot Bassett)

Refectory, Leeds University, on Saturday, February 14, 1970

Dermot, Loraine, and I used to go and see the Who a lot together at this time; well, we still do, but for some reason Dermot wasn't with us this time. I think it was because Loraine and I decided to go to Leeds only that morning. Anyway, we went up on the train but had no tickets for the show or, to be honest, any idea where we were going when we got there! We started walking in what we had been told was the direction of the university when a car pulled up. Through the now-open window came, "Do you want a lift?" It was Pete. This wasn't completely random, as he knew who we were as we used to go to the fan club offices and had also called at his house, but this was still a big surprise! In fact, my friend Lesley and I had also gone to Pete's wedding. We intended to just stand outside, but as Pete ran up the steps, he looked at us and said, "You comin'?" In his autobiography, *Who I Am*, Pete tells this story as we gate-crashed the wedding! Bloody cheek!!

Anyway, back to Leeds: Loraine and I got in the car, straight to the venue (the no-tickets problem was now solved!!) and into the hall, straight to the front! Of course, we had no idea it was to be such a historic event. There's no point in telling the set list, because anyone who's interested already knows. It was an electric night, but then it always was at that time. The thing that really stands out is that not only did they play an encore, but that encore came after a solid fifteen minutes of calling them back. Pete came to the microphone and said, "That's the nicest thing that's ever happened to us." Now I have a secret (shhh!): I had a battery cassette recorder with me that night and recorded the whole thing, so I had the first recording of *Live at Leeds*! No one needs to get excited though, as the distortion caused by the sheer volume means the quality is far short of the album standard!! In fact, Dermot says it's completely unlistenable and that every now and then you can almost tell what they're playing. I'm still glad I have it though. After the show, Loraine and I were walking back to the station, expecting to be sleeping on the platform until the morning, when the same car pulls up, "Oi, do you want a lift?" Pete, of course, and we gratefully accepted, expecting a lift to the station. There was then an unexpected turn, however. Pete drove off and just kept driving, all the way to our homes in South London, over 200 miles away!! As you would expect, our respective parents were mightily impressed!! Pete then presumably drove to his home in West London, then back to Yorkshire the following day for the show in Hull. We saw Pete only occasionally after that, as the Who went on to greater and greater heights, and we hadn't met him for a long, long time until Dermot arranged for us to meet him after one of the shows at the O2 in London in 2015, and that night we spoke about the events of Leeds. He welcomed Loraine and me like old friends and signed my program "To Linda. After far too long."

Rick FitzRandolph

Metropolitan Opera House, Lincoln Center, New York, on Sunday, June 7, 1970

I had finished up my freshman year at Stony Brook University in May and had gotten tickets for the Metropolitan Opera that would be in June. Pete had said it would be the last time they performed *Tommy*. But he also said he hoped he'd die before he got old.

I asked a freshman girl whom I had dated in the spring if she wanted to go with me, and she said sure. I didn't own a car yet, so I hitchhiked the 460 miles back to Stony Brook to use my friend's car to pick her up, but she stood me up. I can see standing me up, but how do you pass up a Who concert at the Metropolitan Opera for the last performance of *Tommy*? So, my buddy with the car and I drive into NYC to catch the second show. The audience was supposed to have reverence for the opera house, but they didn't. All sorts of people were standing on the crushed velvet seats. I was about twenty-five rows back and occasionally stood up on my seat to take some photos. After the second two-hour set and encore, people were booing and Pete came back out and said, "After two fucking hours, boo to you too." So, we got up to leave; I took the 35 mm roll out of the camera and, in the jostling crowd, dropped it beneath my seat. I couldn't find it and we walked out. After a few minutes outside, with the crowd still filing out, I decided to go back in and look for it without people in there. So, I tell my friend to wait for me, and I go back and walk in backward like I'm walking out, and now there is no one in the place. Never did find the roll of film.

Jerry Pompili

Berkeley Community Theater, California, on Monday–Tuesday, June 15–16, 1970

I didn't have much of a relationship with the Who at the time of the Fillmore fire on May 16 1969; Bill did because they were handled by Frank Barselona, and Bill and Frank were very tight. When we got out to California in 1970, when the Who played the Berkeley Community Theater, this was part of the *Tommy* tour, so they had already played

Anaheim Stadium, California. Sunday, June 14, 1970. *Photo by Frank Zinn, Richard Martin Frost archive*

at the Met in New York, and at this time in the concert production stuff, very little was done in the way of production for acts. I mean, the most production that was ever done was at the Fillmore East in New York, with people like the Joshua Light Show and Chip Monck, very creative people, and most of the ideas I got I stole from them.

The Who at that time were the only band that carried their own sound. No one carried everything. I was kind of obsessed with *Tommy*, and I would go home every night after work when I didn't have a show and listen to it at this giant stereo set. I would listen to *Tommy* over and over and over again, trying to say, "What can I do for the Who?" And then it hit me one night. It was like . . . This is about someone who is sense-deprived. So you go to a Who concert, and what happens when you're numb for the sound—the only thing you still have going for you is you can see. So I got together with my light guy and said, "What's the biggest lights we can rent?," and he told me "Well, 10Ks." And at that time, 10Ks—God, they were huge, probably 3 or 4 feet across—I mean they were huge lights. They're much smaller nowadays. You can get more power into a smaller box. But then they were huge. We rented three of them, and Townshend got it wrong in his book, because he said that

after the show, Bill gave them the lights, which is impossible because we didn't own the lights; we rented them. We hung three 10Ks on a pipe at the rear of the stage, and when you looked at it it looked like the engine from a 747. We hung a screen in front of it and then lit the screen with some scoops on the floor with color gels. To operate those lights, you needed one of those like Frankenstein switchers. And right at the end of *Tommy*, as Daltrey is doing his "See me, feel me, touch me, heal me" thing, we flipped these switches on and it was like an atomic bomb going off inside this 350-seat theater! Townshend told me later it was so bright he could see the dust and the cracks in the wall at the back of the balcony. That's how bright was it. And when we flipped the lights on, Townshend turns around and looks at the lights, looks at the audience, looks at the lights, looks at the audience, back and forth! As soon as the show was over, John Wolff, their road manager, comes up to me and says, "Okay, so what was that?!," and I explained to him what we did. And they used it, I think, for the next five years as part of the show. I formed a friendship with Townshend; I would see him over the years, and he always remembered that. He used to call me Geraldine for some reason I don't know!

Berkeley Community Theater, Berkeley, California. Monday, June 15, 1970. *All photos by Steven J. Epstein*

Berkeley Community Theater, Berkeley, California. Monday, June 15, 1970. *All photos by Steven J. Epstein*

Berkeley Community Theater, Berkeley, California. Tuesday, June 16, 1970. *Photo by Steven J. Epstein*

Berkeley Community Theater, California. Tuesday, June 16, 1970. *Photos by Dennis McCoy, copyright of Brad Rodgers, www.whocollection.com*

An audience recording made by Mark d'Ercole from Berkeley Community Theater, Tuesday June 16, 1970. *Author's archive*

Berkeley Community Theater, California. Monday, June 15, 1970. *Photo by Dennis McCoy, copyright of Brad Rodgers, www.whocollection.com*

Al Pethel

Cincinnati Music Hall, Ohio, on Thursday–Friday, June 25–26, 1970

A lot of people associate the Who with their destructive finales. They were awed by guitars swinging into speaker cabinets, and drums flying off the platform, with pieces flying into the crowd for the lucky souvenir collector. But times changed.

During the summer of 1970, the so-called *Tommy* tour, with *Live at Leeds* pounding the airwaves, they were booked at the Cincinnati Music Hall for two sold-out performances. The opening band was the James Gang, with Joe Walsh. I was his roadie.

Townshend is one of the most animated guitarists in rock history, to put it mildly. He is powerful onstage, and it was not unusual for him to accidently jump down too hard on his Fuzz Tone and smash it. Bobby Pridden, the head roadie and soundman, kept three of them in-line onstage just for such an occurrence. He'd swap it out midsong, and Pete would keep on going. As the show reached its crescendo, Daltrey's microphone flew in an arc above the crowd and stage, Moon was a flurry of riffs, Entwistle's fingers were flying over his bass, and Pete's red Gibson SG flew into the air! When it all comes together, it's like a wave pounding the shore. The microphone landed in Daltrey's hand, Entwistle hit his final note and snapped to attention, Moon pounded his last beat, and Townshend, usually, caught the guitar and flailed the final chord. This time he missed the guitar!

It landed on its headstock and broke the bottom three tuning pegs completely off! Whoa! The look on Pete's face was hard to describe. That guitar was his favorite, and, even though there were others stacked onstage, he was completely bummed. That was the conclusion of the first performance.

Bobby grabbed the guitar and put it in its case, and we headed back to the hotel. That's when he showed me how important that guitar was to Pete. He set it on the table in his room and proceeded to go into emergency status. He showed me how he was going to fix that guitar, 'cause Pete needs it. He had clamps and glue in his toolbox and put it together right there. It was pretty amazing to see him work. So, while the glue was drying, we joined everyone at the party that was already going on, as you might imagine. That's another story. The next evening at the Music

Hall, Bobby had the SG sitting onstage, ready for Pete to play. The smile on Pete's face was priceless, and, the show was, again, fantastic!

Those two Cincinnati shows opened the door for more shenanigans, Moon style. He loved to vent, and hotel rooms were often the most-convenient targets. While the group's destructive displays onstage had been curtailed, the offstage antics still carried the band's signature.

Moonie decided his room was not personalized to his taste, so he ordered two dozen cream puffs, two dozen dinner rolls, and a number of pounds of butter. He decided that the mirror needed revision (pun intended), and the dinner rolls would do nicely. He smeared the butter on the mirror and stuck the rolls to it. A work of art! Next, the cream puffs found residence on the wall next to the spare bed. They stuck there nicely after being hurled like a pitcher going for a no-hitter. Of course, some didn't stick, and landed on the shag carpet for future reference.

That night after the final show, Moonie decided that the TV wasn't working properly. So, after collecting some empty whiskey and champagne bottles, he returned to his room

and proceeded to have target practice. The bottles found their way into the TV screen, and the corner of the room it occupied. Problem solved.

The next morning at checkout, both the Who and the James Gang met in the lobby. Now, Townshend was paying the room charges, while everyone talked on the couches, etc. He paid cash. As he was getting the receipts, a desk clerk came up to the counter with another paper in his hand. I was standing next to Pete and could see that the man's hand was shaking a bit. Pete asked him, "And what might this be?" The man answered, "It's a bill for room damage for Mr. Moon." Townshend looked at it and saw it was for $1,000!

The hotel estimated that the room was a total wreck: TV, carpet, wallpaper, on and on. Definitely a total redo.

Pete turned around toward the lobby and said, "Ay, Moonie! You 'ave a good time?" And Moon answered, "It was a'right." Pete then turned to the clerk and said, "Could I 'ave a receipt, please?"

Auditorium Theater, Chicago, Illinois. Wednesday, July 1, 1970. *All photos by Jack Perno*

Minneapolis Auditorium, Minnesota. Friday, July 3, 1970. *All photos by Mike Barich, the Barich Archive*

Joshua White

Tanglewood Music Shed, Lenox, Massachusetts, on Tuesday, July 7, 1970

The Who performed at Tanglewood in 1969 as part of a show presented by Bill Graham.

The event was spectacular, and Bill was invited back the following summer to present three different evenings. By that time, 1970, I'd retired from light shows and began developing live video projection. Tanglewood was perfect for my new venture, and the Fillmore hired Joshua Television.

Tanglewood has a music shed that holds 3,000 people. An additional 6,000 can sit on the surrounding lawn. We placed three cameras inside and one small screen outside on the lawn. The idea was very successful, and my career in television started there. At the last minute Bill wanted us to record everyone, which we did.

John Visnaskas

Tanglewood Music Shed, Lenox, Massachusetts, on Tuesday, July 7, 1970

It's July 1970. My friend Mike and yours truly are driving down the Mass Pike in his Mustang to see the Who at Tanglewood. We're both enjoying a few "crotch-warm" brews during the ride (this was before having a beer while driving was a crime against humanity). Granted, these 1969 *Tommy* shows were getting to be a bit redundant, but a recent *New York Times* review of the Met show had mentioned that there were a couple of new songs in the set, including one called "Water," so the promise of some new material made it worth the long journey. We arrive at Tanglewood and snap up our tickets. It's a long wait until the show tomorrow, so we scoot on over the border to Albany, New York, where the drinking age is eighteen, and I take in my first nude strip show and some "legal" beers. Back to Tanglewood before dark and find out we can't sleep on the lawn and are kicked out.

We end up sleeping in a field across the street with a bunch of other kids that are there for the show. During the night we overhear a conversation and find out that the guys are staying at the Tanglewood Motor Inn, so of course we plan on making that a stop tomorrow before the show. As dawn breaks, we are

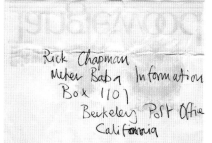

Courtesy of John Visnaskas

awakened by a herd of pigs running down the hill at us, led by an angry farmer who apparently wasn't too keen on a bunch of damn hippies sleeping on his land.

Around noontime we arrived at the motel and walked out to the pool, where Mr. Daltrey in cutoff jeans was tanning and hanging out with two ladies who apparently were friends of Bill Graham, and someone's St. Bernard named "Lily." The convenient bit of luck for us was that Bill Graham's people thought we were with the Who, and Rog thought we were with Bill Graham, so we were all apparently part of one big happy Who family and were treated with respect by all. One funny bit I do remember about that day was that Rog was a bit pissed off over a bad review he had recently gotten but praised Al Aronowitz for his review of the Met concert in *Life* magazine and encouraged us to read it. I already had.

A groupie gal came over and tried to join the conversation. I vaguely remember a collective silent sigh of irritation fell upon all of us, but Rog quickly dispatched her to his motel room in two shakes of a lamb's tail, did his "duty" (I presume), and sent her on her way. I don't remember if she actually knew who he was though.

The discussion moved on to the upcoming Isle of Wight concert, and Rog was pretty excited about his new costume that one of his friends made for him. He ran into his motel room and brought out the colorful tassled outfit that you are all familiar with from the Isle of Wight video. He told me and Mike to go ahead and try it on. Of course I wanted to strike a pose and pretend to swing a Shure, but I didn't get too far because I couldn't get my shoulders all the way in it without ripping it. But still . . . yeah, *I did wear it!* (so now you can all bow before me, the king!). Later he got dressed in that blue blouse and jeans (the 1970 uniform that we're all familiar with now) and took off to the store to pick up a few things with, I think, Bobby. It was funny as hell watching him jump into a giant American Detroit iron, a Chrysler station wagon, and peel off with the tires screeching and barely able to see over the steering wheel. Years later I always thought how odd it was that he went out shopping in what was essentially his Who stage "costume."

Later in the afternoon, Moonie got up but wasn't in the best of moods. Pete woke up next, and I helped him and Joe Walsh push one of Joe's motorcycles up a ramp into a small Ryder/U-Haul trailer.

Pete then came over and chatted a bit. I had heard some of the first Baba LP on WBCN-Boston ("Mary-Jane" was big), and I was trying to get my hands on a copy. Pete wrote out the name and address of Ric Chapman, a West Coast Baba lover, on the back of a Tanglewood schedule and told me I could get the LP from him. I tried to chat Pete up a bit on his new sci-fi opera, *Bobby*, but we were interrupted as they had to leave for the show. We said our goodbyes, and Mike and myself took off for the show ourselves.

Tanglewood Music Shed, Lenox, Massachusetts. Tuesday, July 7, 1970. © *Steve Richards*

The show was memorable to me because of the two new songs, "Water" and "I Don't Even Know Myself" (which as previously mentioned is really why I trekked way out there), that and the geeky guy in a funny plaid sport jacket in front of me that kept trying to explain to his girlfriend Muffy or Buffy (swear to God!) how *Tommy* was an opera just like *Jesus Christ Superstar* [GROAN] . . . That's when I realized that these guys suddenly belonged to the world and not just to a tight band of informed and loyal "Who freaks."

They were very well rehearsed and seemed even more professionally choreographed than ever. That, and the recent appearance in the *Woodstock* movie, made me realize that they were going to go on and become *very, very, very* big.

Robert Lipson (Gracious)

Isle of Wight Festival of Music, on Wednesday–Sunday, August 26–30, 1970

My band, Gracious, closed Thursday night at the 1970 Isle of Wight Festival. We had a long relationship with the Who. Our first professional gigs were supporting the Who on a UK tour. Pete really took a shining to us and gave us great advice. Actually, when we played the Isle of Wight, they let us use their PA. It was made by a company called WEM, and the owner of that company, Charlie Watkins, was mixing the sound. It was the first time we had ever heard ourselves live onstage! An amazing moment. Townshend has always been very complimentary about us—to this day!

Third Isle of Wight Festival of Music. Sunday, August 30, 1970. *All photos by Paul Brewer*

Third Isle of Wight Festival of Music. Sunday, August 30, 1970. *All photos by Paul Brewer*

CHAPTER 11

The House That Bill Built: Bill Graham and the Fillmore Scene

It may seem odd to find a chapter on Bill Graham and his venues in a Who book. One might think that giving such space to an American ballroom scene instead of an English one, with the Goldhawk Social or Marquee clubs in mind, is a mistake. There is a specific reason for this. It has to do with loss of innocence in the evolution from ballroom music to arena rock.

The Fillmore scene in San Francisco gave bands a context within which they could better express themselves and grow creatively through being subjected to unusual conditions. On a nightly basis, every band booked to play at San Francisco's Fillmore Auditorium, the Fillmore West, or New York City's Fillmore East would share the bill with totally different acts and were often spurred to play longer and more-challenging sets than they were used to. Bill Graham created this tension, and the changes occurred from there. The Who would never again sound as ferociously inspired and poignant as they did in February, April, and August of 1968, when they played the Fillmore Auditorium, Fillmore East, or the Fillmore West, respectively. They sounded and looked as though they were playing for their lives, confronting boundaries and exploring the very limits of their skills. The resultant change was suddenly there, and it was palpable if short lived. It was a time and place never repeated.

The Fillmore scene is a fascinating observatory through which to witness the shift of many bands from being exponents of the 1960s underground sound to the media-glitzed rock arena pinnacles of the 1970s. From a wider perspective, it mirrored the growth and evolution of the entertainment industry to how we now know it today. The key question is, did reaching those mountain tops make it any better? Many would say no.

The Who, Cream, and the Yardbirds were just a few of the English bands that shared the same concert bills and stages with bands such as the Woody Herman Orchestra, Cecil Taylor, Paul Butterfield Blues Band, or It's a Beautiful Day, along with many others. It was an era when experimentation and blend were the dominant modus operandi within the culture of music.

This was possible only in the 1960s, an era, as Bob Weir of the Grateful Dead said, "when promoters were actually talking to musicians about what would make a good show," and "an era when the agent and the manager and the artist did not know that they could dictate who else should be on the show."[1]

These venues were the laboratories in which the blending of ideas and styles took place, playing a major role in the development of music at that time. These iconic buildings or venues in that landscape of contemporary music both drove and became representative of the 1960s youth culture. What were once skating rinks, such as the Fillmore Auditorium and Winterland, or what was once the swing-era and postswing-era dance hall El Patio (later Carousel Ballroom and Fillmore West), or the Colin Traver Academy of Dance (later the Avalon Ballroom) would be given a second life by promoters Bill Graham and Chet Helms, the latter most notably with his Family Dog production company. Graham's operation in particular was radical, groundbreaking, and unprecedented: he caught the essence and needs of a newborn culture and nourished it, helping it grow, and in the process made it the heartbeat of a modern era. Not only was he in large part responsible for the changing face of the modern music scene—he is the one, as some would have it, who started it:

> I don't think we are in the ballroom business only; we're in the business of changing the taste of the public.[2]

Bill Graham—born Volodia Wolfgang Grajonca—was the son of two Russian Jews who had moved to Germany before Nazism spread across Europe. When World War II broke out and the youth enrollment Hitlerjugend was spreading, Bill was placed by his mother at a *Kinderheim* in Berlin, where Jewish children were taken care of and received a good education. When the place was closed down, Bill was sent to Chaumont, in France, and for three months he traveled through Lyon, Marseille, and Toulouse as the country was invaded. From there he escaped to Madrid and Lisbon, Casablanca, Dakar, and Bermuda, eventually traveling by ship to the States.

Bill turned out to be one of only four of the original sixty-four children from that school to survive.

He settled and grew up in the Bronx and would tirelessly commute back and forth between New York and San Francisco, after he found out that his sister Rita was alive and living in the Bay Area. Bill showed the restless attitude of a life adventurer, working here and there trying to fit in and to find a place in life. His adaptable attitude and his interest in acting led him to join the San Francisco Mime Troupe in 1965. What drew Bill to the mime troupe was the radical intent behind the acting, the political involvement of people who weren't just actors, but people "using theatre

as a public platform to make a statement about what was going on in the world,"[3] be it the Vietnam War or the violation of civil rights. The aim to shake the sleepy and hypocritical policies of the city led the mime troupe to expose itself at its own risk. The gritty and provocative edge of a particular play in Lafayette Park led to the arrest for profanity of troupe member Ronny Davis. Soon, Bill would realize that this particular bust represented a callout for the artistic community to come together in unity. The charity shows he organized to raise funds set a precedent that changed and expanded the role of cultural-events management.

The first charity show was held in the mime troupe's South-of-Market loft, where all kinds of intellectual, artistic, and cultural personalities gathered to bring their own thing, but mostly, and financially, where thousands of people came to attend.

"This is the business of the future," Bill told his troupe partner Robert Scheer while staring at the horde trying to get into the party.

He had identified the audience; now he needed a suitable place or platform from which to act. Mime troupe partner Ronny Davis pointed out the Fillmore Auditorium. At that time, Chet Helms was presenting local acts there and took Graham under his wing. The two started promoting shows together.

The image of lysergic San Francisco that would go down in history as the home of the psychedelic sound spread all over the US, from Bay Area "rock temples" such as the Fillmore Auditorium, Fillmore West, Avalon Ballroom, and Winterland to New York City's Fillmore East; these did not suddenly appear like a flower in the middle of the desert. On the contrary, it had deep musical roots extending decades back. For example, the San Francisco of the 1940s and 1950s was known by jazz aficionados as the "Harlem of the West."[4] Businessman and music promoter Charles Sullivan had helped foster this identity by organizing concerts that reflected the tastes of a growing community of more than 42,000 black citizens. Before the Fillmore Auditorium became associated with such names as the Jefferson Airplane, Quicksilver Messenger Service, or even Bill Graham himself, it was associated with jazz greats such as Billie Holiday, Dizzy Gillespie, Lionel Hampton, Charlie Parker, and John Coltrane, all of whom played there and in the clubs then extant under other names.

Bill approached Charles Sullivan to rent the Fillmore for the second San Francisco Mime Troupe benefit concert. The deal was eventually agreed to, and Bill was allowed to use Sullivan's permit to run his place for that event. The handbill of the second charity show at the Fillmore, on December 10, 1965, would read "For continued artistic freedom in the parks." The lineup of that night was, to say the least, emblematic: the bill featured jazz artists such as the John Handy Quintet, Sam Thomas, and the Gentlemen

Band, with emerging rock groups such as the Jefferson Airplane (with Signe Anderson on vocals). Joining them was Great Society, featuring vocalist Grace Slick, who would later join the Airplane. It looked like a perfect picture of the changes undergoing the San Francisco music scene.

The third benefit concert, on January 14, 1966, featured Great Society, Mystery Trend, Gentlemen's Band, and, perhaps most significantly, the Warlocks, before they became the Grateful Dead.

Bill realized that what he really wanted to do was "Living Theater: taking music and the newborn visual arts and making all of that available in a comfortable surrounding so it would be conductive to open expression."[5] He also realized that in order to do so, he had to confront his competitors.

Graham started promoting shows of his own at the Fillmore, going head to head with Chet Helms, who had a completely different and much-looser approach to business than Bill's. Their styles clashed as the laid-back Helms and the aggressive, competitive Graham failed to mesh. Helms eventually ended up promoting shows at the Avalon Ballroom, on Sutter Street. The SF Mime Troupe, on the other hand, was becoming a burden for Graham, given that it was too tied to the older conception of art as a political statement and a tool of protest. "Politics have to do with people and what their problems are. And what the problem is right now is that people want a new culture," said Bill.[6] He saw a new market and he wanted to go all the way. He eventually made the decision to burn all his bridges and start walking his own path.

The Trips Festival, performances of music and light-show screenings at the Longshoremen's Hall, further broadened Bill's view of what the public would respond to: "The key element was the public."[7] These get-togethers had generated from "acid tests" that author Ken Kesey, a vocal advocate of LSD, used to hold at his place in La Honda in 1965, challenging the partyers with "Can you pass the acid test?" The Warlocks was a folk band that cut its teeth playing long, improvised sets at these "happenings" and eventually turned electric under the influence of LSD, becoming the Grateful Dead. LSD remained legal until October 6, 1966. Such events, applied with Bill Graham's business model, helped change the face of San Francisco's counterculture.

Bill's new activity at the Fillmore, however, was less than welcomed by the local community, from the synagogue next door to the police force in general. No one liked the idea of so many hippies congregating en masse. The fact that Bill had to rely on Charles Sullivan's permits made it all the more difficult. Regardless, change seemed unstoppable. The sudden death of Sullivan on August 2, 1966, spurred the passage of property of the Fillmore Auditorium to Bill Graham. From then on, Bill's booking business branched out, reaching another San Francisco structure, Winterland. It was becoming harder and harder to keep up with the growing number of

people visiting the Fillmore, so Winterland ended up working well for Friday and Saturday, and sometimes Sunday night concerts, while the Fillmore covered Thursdays.

No one could possibly have figured that one of the greatest revolutions in modern music was being triggered by someone who did not know anything of the music scene of that time. But that was exactly what was happening. Bill did not have the slightest idea of who the bands really were that he called from time to time, but he couldn't have been more successful in doing that. As his colleague Paul Baratta would say, "What we did was keep our ears to the ground. We booked some bands by osmosis."[8]

What he was doing went far beyond mere concert organization. Bill was creating the musical taste of the general public, helping create an unprecedented cultural divulgation.

Simply by mixing musical eras together in concerts, in a way no one had ever thought of before, demand for his shows grew. And rapidly. By making concert bills heterogeneous, the audience was pushed into widening its knowledge, leaving behind preconceptions wrought from older musical tastes and times. Nowhere else in the world then or before that time would the Who have been put on the same bill as jazz musician Cannonball Adderley, as happened February 22–24, 1968, at the Fillmore Auditorium and at Winterland. There are many other such examples, but suffice it to say here that San Francisco gave the US a new show business format for musical performances, on the basis of two aspects: heterogeneous lineups of featured artists previously unseen together on the same bill, and an unprecedented involvement of the audience in those shows: performers "on stage interacting with the audience to form a unit. Not just somebody performing at an audience. If ever there was a unit like that it was the Fillmore Auditorium."[9]

Yet, adversity was around the corner. Martin Luther King's assassination on April 4, 1968, forced Bill to start thinking seriously about moving out of the Fillmore district. The event incited numerous riots by the Black community, and white kids were afraid to come into the area. Attendance was going down.

Bill moved the Fillmore experience to Market Street and South Van Ness Avenue, to the Carousel Ballroom, "a more desirable hall, larger and more attractive and more accessible by public transportation."[10] The Carousel was at that time run by Ron Rakow and his Headstone Productions, a corporation financed by a series of dances given by the Grateful Dead, Quicksilver Messenger Service, Big Brother and the Holding Company, and the Jefferson Airplane. This management team had been in operation for a few months but eventually ran into debt. Graham took advantage of the situation and took over the venue, renaming it Fillmore West to complement his recently opened New York operation, the Fillmore East. With the Fillmore West, Graham gave birth to a new "rock and roll church" (or, as Frank Zappa would later say on a 1970 show in his usual and ironical way, "rock and roll dungeon"!).

The burgeoning success of Bill Graham Presents in San Francisco encouraged novice promoters countrywide to take risks opening similar venues. For example, teacher Russ Gibb, a DJ famous for his part in the "Paul is dead" rumour, reopened the Grande Ballroom, Detroit, in 1966 as a rock and roll venue almost thirty years after it had closed as a jazz and big-band sound hall. There were a number of such openings all over the US, such as the Electric Theater (later renamed Kinetic Playground) in Chicago, owned by Aaron Russo, or the Electric Factory in Philadelphia, owned by Larry Magid. The resonance of San Francisco's music scene around the country was described well by Jann Wenner, director of the newly born music magazine *Rolling Stone*:

> The important thing about San Francisco is that it's a scene; it's a warm, supportive, friendly city that's historical for the bohemians, the Beats, poetry, jazz, and seemingly today it supports rock and roll.[11]

Little did Bill Graham know that his innovative attitude and contribution to the world of show business would also bring about its collapse, at least in terms of its newfound ideals. Here are two theories of how that happened: first, the freedom that the Fillmores gave their artists over the years progressively produced even more exclusive demands both from musicians and audience. This inevitably and paradoxically led to bigger performances in increasingly bigger spaces, creating further distance between bands and their audience. Another theory derives from an Owsley Stanley statement: "Bill started it as a business and offering bigger and bigger money and charging bigger money on the door. As soon as it started being as much money as a movie, the whole character of the thing changed. Instead of people just having a good time . . . they stood around mesmerized. It became like watching a movie. Eventually they even started sitting down and staring at 'em."[12]

It is also possible that Bill's decision to branch out to the other coast with the Fillmore East represented a definitive and somewhat unexpected turn in show business. The decision to take the Fillmore Auditorium experience to a *theater* created a significant change in the audience's behavior: they no longer had an empty ballroom in which to dance to the music, and the seats kept them more focused and well behaved, while watching the artists from a "bottom-up" perspective. The band and audience were no longer influencing one another. It was a one-way, top-down show. And from there, theaters became indoor arenas and huge outdoor concerts (ironically, one of the Woodstock promoters being Bill Graham) and yearlong tours of international football stadiums. The money was huge but intimacy was lost.

And thus we can see that same progression and loss from a different perspective as we return to the story of the Who.

Winterland

Sally Mann Romano

I have had so many wonderful nights at Winterland over the years—too many to recount or recall—but apart from dancing onstage with the Airplane, Grateful Dead, and New Riders (especially when Marmaduke and "Honky Tonk Women" or David Torbert sang "Groupie," a song he wrote for me) and kindling my eventual relationship with Alvin Lee of Ten Years After—the most-memorable nights always took place at the annual New Year's Eve extravaganza with the Grateful Dead and New Riders on the bill. Bill Graham, dressed as Father Time, would fly from the back of the house to the stage, high over the heads of the audience on a pulley device, and the packed-in crowd was beyond electric. As with all of his productions, Bill really did New Year's Eve up right, and the experience was always overwhelming—exhausting, but overwhelming.

As you know, my husband, Spencer Dryden, was drummer for Jefferson Airplane and then the New Riders. One New Year's Eve, after the New Riders of the Purple Sage had played their opening set, the Grateful Dead and all their camp followers and roadies took the stage to a hyped-up, sold-out crowd and began their set. At some point—I can't remember how many songs had been played or how long they had been performing—we became aware (from the side of the stage) that something was off: the crowd was yelling, but not the usual clamor, and pointing frantically to the rafters of the building. Looking up, I saw that one of the (many) presumed acid casualties had somehow managed to crawl out onto a very narrow metal beam—many, many feet above the stage—and was in terrible, terrifying, immediate danger of falling to his death or severe injury, right at the feet of Jerry Garcia. As the band slowly became aware of what was happening, each musician stopped playing, with no one exactly sure what to do or how to intervene without making

things worse. Folks on acid and other drugs can be a little unpredictable, as you may or may not know, and we did not want to do anything to exacerbate an already dangerous situation—whether he crawled backward or forward, it didn't look like this would end well. The fun of New Year's Eve at Winterland had suddenly dissipated and dissolved into something quite different.

Unfortunately, but not surprisingly, the crowd had started to scream, "Jump!," and other unhelpful epithets as soon as most everyone became aware of the man's presence, and the situation quickly became grave. As usual, though, Bill Graham is a very resourceful man, and the person I would most want with me when things go south. Someone had alerted him—probably Jerry Pompili, the greatest manager who ever lived—that something was very, very wrong, and Bill took command of the stage and the problem as only he could. He shouted to the audience to shut the fuck up (when Bill Graham screams, people who want to live tend to listen) and somehow enlisted one of his foolhardy gaffers or other circus-type stagehands to get as close to the crazy man as possible without scaring him or causing him to lose his balance and plunge to the stage. I can't remember how they eventually talked him down, only that a rope was somehow secured around his waist, but his life and limbs were spared—probably by the sheer force of Bill Graham's will. After the dazed amateur acrobat was escorted away to an ambulance, Garcia said a few benevolent words of gratitude, the band began to play with the most amazing joy and relief, and the audience went absolutely insane.

All in all, just another night with the Grateful Dead and the New Riders of the Purple Sage at Winterland—what could possibly go wrong?

©2017 Sally Mann Romano

All photos by Mark d'Ercole

Photo by Mark d'Ercole

Mark d'Ercole

Winterland was originally an ice rink primarily to house the "Ice Follies." That's how big it was. There was a little refreshment stand in the lobby that had beverages and typical food stuff, but other than that, it was made for local events, including boxing. It was made for very modest crowds. I believe its seating capacity was about 2,500. When Bill started to do his concerts there, instead of them being at one end of the narrow, rectangular floor plan, they were held on a stage that was on one side of the seating area. This resulted in the seats in the balcony directly out from the stage being only about five to seven rows, if my memory serves me correctly. Diminishing the seating even more was the fact that in spite of only a few rows for seats, that was where the light show would set up their equipment, which was the kind of projectors used back then for business meetings to show slides (before the age of PowerPoint). They would take glass dishes filled with liquids and oils, which used the projector light under the flat area to produce the fluid images you would see projected by the upper section of the device, but also they had movie cameras simultaneously playing things like antiwar news reels and silent films. Somehow it all worked. The stage faced west, which left a large, rising balcony-seating area to the south that rose for something like thirty rows, and only at that one end. So when they had the light show, it stretched all around the upper deck, and they didn't even have people standing in their seats, obscured by the light-show backdrop sheets. The bands that played, including local musicians

who weren't playing that night but just visiting, used to go sit in seats behind the stage, so if you wanted to talk to the Who, you just went behind the stage, and they were all there smoking pot and doing stuff, and the most amazing thing, though, was you would go back and be respectful, and they would be respectful, and they would be happy to have you sit down to smoke a cigarette and find out what's going on in your life.

Photo by Janice Burnham

Fillmore Auditorium and Fillmore West

Fillmore Auditorium (now the Fillmore) on Fillmore and Geary Boulevard in San Francisco. September 2019. *Edoardo Genzolini*

Mark d'Ercole

The original old Fillmore is located at the intersection of Fillmore and Geary Boulevard. It was really small, and you had kind of everything typical of concert venues in the front, and then you went into the playroom, which was the size of the common basketball court. In its later manifestation, especially after the British bands rose to prominence, "the Fillmore" moved to Market Street and was renamed Fillmore West; it was originally the World War II dance hall Carousel Ballroom, and it was set up so that, as a ballroom, there were places to socialize as well as the ballroom itself. A 3-foot-high wall limited the playroom itself, but there were many comfy couches and chairs in the area outside the playroom. The playroom was also roughly the size of a basketball court. Not the entire arena itself, just the basketball court. I know that because Bill used to play in basketball games with a "court" set up literally in the performance room, and the Fillmore guys would play against the road crew of the groups that came in. Bill Graham was pretty good at playing basketball; Bill was insane

Fillmore West, formerly Carousel Ballroom, on Market Street and South Van Ness Avenue, San Francisco. June 12–14, 1969. *Joe Leatherman*

for his age. He had more energy than any other ten people you'll ever meet. When you would go to a party at Bill's, he had this enormous house and its property, which he called Masada, an enormous-size ranch home with three or four bedrooms or something like that. But it wasn't a sprawly thing like you see today with celebrities. He had a lot of land, so all around the home itself he had a basketball court, a horseshoe pit; he had a swimming pool, he had a place where you could picnic, and as you ate your food a huge sound system would be playing recordings from the concerts Bill had thrown. It was like this park all around his house. When he had a party going on, all the doors of his house were open and all the rooms were set up for joints, drinks, and conversation; he had a museum-like glass cabinet of things that were given to him by artists; if there was a barbecue going on, it would last all day, and Bill would go around and spend time with every single group in every single area of that house for the whole day. It would be like if some final thing was going on, and he would lead that. This guy was in his fifties and he would play basketball, volleyball; he would make me play a one on one, three or four times, and we would get other guys and do that for like two hours. Just when you thought he was done, he would play ping-pong for another hour. His company was very esoteric; it was really like a family. You would see him every single concert selling popcorn and Coke, so he could allow for people to complain about anything to him directly. He wanted to be here for people. It was the postwar ethic interaction between human beings.

Paul Sommer

When Bill Graham felt that the original Fillmore Auditorium on Geary Street was too small, he moved it to the corner of Market and Van Ness, into what was the Carousel Ballroom. He renamed the venue Fillmore West. At that time, Bill Graham's staff had a basketball team called the "Fillmore Fingers" that would play once a week. There would be a basketball game and a jam session every Tuesday night for $1.00. Bill Graham, from the very beginning, had three bands play for every show. At the old Fillmore Auditorium, the only chairs were in the front, about four rows of chairs about 6 feet in front of the stage. You could sit on the floor in front of the chairs or stand up on the big wooden dance floor. The old Fillmore had two-story-high white screens on two walls, including behind the stage. The light show also had billing on the posters and projected an ever-changing selection of psychedelic images and videos on the walls. Each band played two sets, and unlike at Fillmore East or other concert venues, everyone stayed for all the shows. As you entered the Fillmore, up a couple of flights of stairs there were two big galvanized garbage cans. One had lollipops and the other had apples, each for everyone to take. There were black lights to show off the fluorescent paint some people wore for the occasion. When everything moved to Fillmore West, the vibe changed too. The ceiling was much lower, so the light shows were gone. Gone were the fluorescent lights too. The seating was similar, with only a few rows of folding chairs near the front of the stage.

Bruce Campbell

In the mid- to late 1960s, San Francisco was ground zero for the entire world of rock and roll. Bill Graham was the man responsible for presenting the best bands, in the best productions for the lowest prices. He was an intense personality, and it carried over to another passion: playing basketball. He organized a team made up of his employees and played games on Tuesday nights. He set up a court and backboards on the dance floor at his fabled Fillmore West and scheduled games against radio stations, music stores, and bands, with band auditions after the games. Two bucks! He called them the Fillmore Fingers in honor of a famous picture of him giving a photographer the middle digit. I worked for Peninsula Music Center in the Hillsdale Mall, owned by the Lane family. Chet Lane III and I were the only players on the payroll, so we recruited some friends, including my good buddy Mark Wilson, all-league center for Hillsdale High. Chet produced some equal talent. We got to Fillmore West at around 7:00, tired from a day's work, while Graham's people were fresh and ready to go. It didn't matter. We ended up winning by twenty, and, to coin the old joke, we could have left the court with three minutes left and still won. THAT'S when it got interesting. I dove for a loose ball and banged heads with Graham's wild point guard. He was seeing birdies, but I got my glass lens pushed against my eyebrow area and started some steady bleeding. I was in a bit of shock from the collision, so Graham, no doubt concerned about a lawsuit, took me and my fiancé Jan into his private office and offered me some of his prized cognac. Brother, that was good! As I perused the wall with autographed pics of Grace, Janis, Eric, and many others, I started giving Bill a hard time about not booking the Kinks and Small Faces. Graham smiled and enjoyed my rants and said he was going to look into it. We got extra posters, and Patrick, the stage manager / power forward and Vietnam MASH vet, patched up my wound and bought me a drink on my next visit. My doctor gave me eleven stitches. About twenty-plus years later, I wrote a piece about the game for the sports section of the old *San Mateo Times* and called Graham for a quote or two. "What do you want to write about that for? That's old news!" Seems I caught Bill in one of his busy moments, but I explained my involvement in that game and he slowly mellowed into a reflection of a game against Chicago where he psyched out James Pankow and won the game. All in all, it was a memorable evening playing the Fingers, but sadly, not long after that 1990 interview, Graham's helicopter crashed and he was gone. At the end of that interview I apologized to Bill for bringing in ringers on my team. "That's OK; we just were having fun" were his final words to me. That we were, Bill, that we were.

Donald Groves

Bill Graham ran a pretty tight ship at the Fillmore. I had encounters with him, all positive except for one! I was dancing in the back, in the dark at the Fillmore, when some guy attacked me because he said I was dancing with his girlfriend! The way you danced back then was twirling around on drugs. I had a ponytail, and the guy dragged me to the ground, hitting me, and I had my camera around my neck and he smashed it on the floor. Pretty soon, Bill's guards came and hauled us back into Bill's office. We stood in the bright lights of his office, these two guards behind us waiting for Bill Graham to come, who was the judge, the jury, and the executioner! He came in and said, "Okay, what's going on here?," and the guards said, "Well, this guy attacked this guy . . ." Then Bill said, "Okay, I've heard enough of it." He grabbed the guy by his shirt, put him against the wall, and was digging his fingers into his chest, yelling at the top of his voice, "If I ever see you here again, I'll call the police." Then he took a polaroid picture of him, because he had a book where he kept pictures of troublemakers. Before the doors opened, Bill would always walk the line and he would look at every single person all way down the line! After that night, he profusely apologized to me and gave a couple of free passes to future concerts of my choice, which was great because I didn't have any money! In stark contrast, you had the Avalon Ballroom, which was a Chet Helms / Family Dog production, and they ran a total-opposite operation. They had the Hell's Angels as security. That was a nightmare; they actually robbed me of a jacket one night. I had a

fringe jacket and one of the Angels took a liking to it, so he made me take it off. I was pretty intimidated by these big biker guys. He offered me a Hell's Angels' vest in return, but I said, "I don't want your vest." My great fear was that he was going to take my camera, because I was taking pictures of Buddy Guy that night. Later, the Rolling Stones came into town and they hired Hell's Angels as security at Altamont, and as soon as I heard it I said, "I ain't going!"

Fillmore West, San Francisco. Thursday, June 19, 1969. *Photo by Donald Groves, grovesgallery.com*

Fillmore West, San Francisco. Thursday, June 19, 1969. *Photo by Donald Groves, grovesgallery.com*

CHAPTER 12

1971

Behind Blue Eyes

The success of *Tommy* amazed even the Who. In 1971, the band faced one of the toughest hurdles of their career: trying to at least match and, they hoped, exceed the impact of *Tommy* not only musically and creatively speaking, but also as the linchpin of their live performances. It is said that "Mater artium necessitas" ("Necessity is the mother of invention"), and it was from that almost primal drive that the *Who's Next* album came to be, albeit in a roundabout way: a very multilayered roundabout. Since its inception, *Who's Next* remains arguably the band's finest work, and for five decades it has established itself as a musical milestone. Yet, unlike other influential projects by the Who, and despite it being yet another conception of Pete Townshend's, the sound created was for the first time a truly balanced reflection of the combined talents and skills of each member of the band. By 1971, all four were—in almost all polls—considered by the public and critics alike to be among the top five musicians and performers of their genre, with Townshend having breached the elite group of songwriters and composers such as Lennon and McCartney, Jagger and Richards, and Bob Dylan. With the breaking up of the Beatles, the Who and the Rolling Stones—the remaining two of the "Holy Trinity"—generally vied for the title of the World's Greatest Rock and roll Band. And live, the Who were simply unrivaled.

Between 1969 and 1973, *Who's Next* was the third of four sequential Who albums that significantly influenced the direction rock music would take. Just as the song "My Generation" presaged punk rock a decade later, "Won't Get Fooled Again" helped further define what was becoming known by then as "hard rock," in addition to adding itself to the short list of great rock anthems. It is therefore almost paradoxical that behind the elaborate studio production and what is widely considered to be the first use of the synthesizer as a major instrument in recorded music, with many of the tracks becoming staples on music radio for years to come, that *Who's Next* was, in fact, nothing but the casting out of "leftovers" of a much more ambitious if ultimately aborted project called *Lifehouse*. That endeavor tortured Townshend for years, even if, ultimately, the obstacle in the way became part of the way.

Lifehouse was a work originally intended as a cinematographic and musical chef d'oeuvre, a film and a double album depicting a futuristic tale of a world coming apart at the seams, repressively controlled by institutions, and finally saved by the collective power of rock and roll. However, few, if anyone, seemed to understand Pete Townshend's concept, which delved deeply into philosophical, spiritual, and social themes theretofore as yet largely ignored by modern music. And on a technological level alone, it would be another five years or so before such an expression of these themes could be adequately realized in the studio or on "playback" technology and, importantly, live onstage. It foresaw the use of synchronized multimedia that wasn't really fully developed for another decade or two. And as such it became a powerful source of frustration for the now twenty-six-year-old composer, who felt increasingly alone in his world of new ideas and creativity.

None of the ideas behind *Lifehouse* or any reference to it would appear on the *Who's Next* album, not even in the album sleeve credits, except, perhaps allusively, on the front cover: the "Kubrickian" monolith on which the band looks as if it has just urinated, thus symbolizing a great idea ultimately aborted.[1]

The symbolism of that picture actually served two purposes, the second more concretely related to that descriptor, "Kubrickian." During this time of escape from the almost repressive weight of the commercial success of *Tommy*, the *Who's Next* cover picture was also said to be representative of the irritation felt by the Who toward Stanley Kubrick, the Oscar-winning and enormously respected film director, screenwriter, and producer, who had turned down the opportunity to direct the film version of *Tommy*, an endeavor eventually taken up by the highly eccentric film director Ken Russell. Why choose something resembling the squared-off obelisk from the film *2001: A Space Odyssey* to pee on? What was the significance of that

monolith anyway? According to film critic Roger Ebert several years earlier, on April 21, 1968, the huge block or pillar was a recurrent symbol of unexplainable presence, "a monolith without explanation. It's the fact that man can't explain it that makes it interesting," he wrote. What better representation of the concept of *Lifehouse* as seen by the music industry at that time? And better yet, it was the creative, visual masterpiece of the very man against whom the Who's frustration would be directed for turning them down. And to add yet another layer of irony to these interwoven creation-frustration crests and troughs, the Who were both trying to rid themselves of the shackles of *Tommy* while seeking ways to make even more money from it! This is not so much hypocrisy as an example of multilayered tensions that, consciously or unconsciously and through paradoxical juxtaposition, lead to history-making creative output. It is the chemistry behind the explosion. But from the rubble left behind, would progress actually arise? Perhaps the answer lies in "Meet the new boss, same as the old boss," a metaphorical punctuation from "Won't Get Fooled Again," which is, importantly, the final track on *Who's Next*.

To more fully understand this process of conflict, resolution, and creativity leading to a relative failure to progress—something that seems to have tortured Townshend throughout his career thus rendering him a sort of musical Sisyphus, the king in Greek mythology whose punishment by the gods for his self-aggrandizement was to push an immense boulder up a hill only for it to roll down again, every time and for all eternity—it is worth taking a closer look at the *Lifehouse* project and the personal philosophy of the man behind it.

The Phases of Lifehouse

The end of the 1960s and the reinvention of the "ritual"

The idea of *Lifehouse* probably derived from Pete's personal experience at the Woodstock and Isle of Wight music festivals. At both events, he witnessed—firsthand and by example of his peers and the audience's response to their work—the evolution of rock in real time:

> The Next Big Thing can only be a variation on the most recent big thing.[2]

Pete acknowledged that during the 1960s, rock "began to liberate itself from the strings of mighty business control, . . . with rock and roll stars being little more than glossy consumer products."[3] He observed that in the previous decade, rock had matured as a genre, reaching a level of artistic dignity and authenticity, moving it beyond a mere youth branch of show business, to something able to "liberate the soul" of a generation. However, and also according to Townshend, this process now stood suspended in limbo, the path ahead being obscured by fog, the direction unclear. Yet, rock music in its wide appeal had become a sort of "youth Esperanto," a common language of communication among the young and rock stars that had an extraordinary influence on millions of people, even their politics. And yet, despite all of that and in what people saw as a goal for rock music, Pete saw stagnation, conflict, and frustration. He felt deeply the unspoken uncertainties in the future of rock—a genre of music that seemed to have promised many answers yet had not actually asked of itself essential questions. For example, how could it apply its ability to liberate in general, in a much-wider context? That is to say, when would rock leave that "centuries-old scenario of a mass audience clamouring at the feet of stars and heroes leading to a radical change in the attitudes both rock musicians and audiences—a new way of involving people in a rock situation?"[4] It is likely that Pete was paraphrasing a passage in Homer's *Ulysses and the Sirens* as depicted in the *Dialectic of Enlightenment* by Max Horkheimer and Theodor W. Adorno.[5] In that passage, the "revolutionary" and liberating potential of music becomes socially controlled and transformed into applause at the end of the performance:

> At rock concerts you can achieve those rare moments where both group and audience completely forget themselves and become completely ego-less. The most precious moments of my life are those moments on the stage when all is one. I've seen moments in Who concerts where the vibrations were becoming so pure that I thought the world was just going to stop, the whole thing was just becoming so unified. But you could never reach that state because in the back of their minds everybody knew that the group was going to have to stop soon, or they'd got to get home, or catch the last bus or something—it's a ridiculous situation.[6]

Pete wanted to move beyond the usual process of an artist's "message" being transmitted as a finished product to the audience only to be passively reflected back in appreciation. He wanted the audiences via their reactions to help *shape* his work. And that could be achieved though live performances. The ideal music event that he envisioned for this to take place was one of musician and audience being on the same level as both authors and readers of the same experience, a concept perhaps influenced by his many times working with Bill Graham:

Musicians and the people who come to hear them would be able to meet and live together and work together in terms of music for as long as it took to achieve something lasting.[7]

Yet, Townshend, years later in a filmed interview, self-described as a control freak explaining his refusal to collaborate with others in songwriting, decided to reinvent what had become the standard ritual of rock through several ultimately "Sisyphean" steps.

First, it would be achieved through communicating intellectual thoughts and ideas to his audience via the written word. Through a section called "The Pete Townshend Page," featured in the music magazine *Melody Maker*, he focused not on the writing *of* music, but on writing *about* music. In 1969, he had already written a number of times for *Melody Maker*, including reviewing new album releases such as the debut albums of King Crimson and Mott the Hoople. But in 1970 and 1971, his articles for the magazine would reveal purposes other than merely spreading awareness of new music; there was a distinct aim to directly involve the readers in that awareness by involving them in its creativity. "The Pete Townshend Page" became a forum in which the guitarist expressed his ideas about music, ideas that were in part based on the written replies and reactions of his fans to earlier pieces.[8] This process, called "creative feedback experiment," was one that he had learned in his Ealing Art College days about a decade earlier. Back then, Pete was struck by Roy Ascott's lectures on the creative potential of the feedback that artists receive from their audiences. Specifically, the public was able to influence the creative or artistic process by showing its reactions directly to the artist. The audience's reaction might suggest artistic solutions previously not thought of by the artist, at least not consciously so. In addition to forging new philosophical underpinnings of the experience of music, in some ways it forced recognition that seemingly opposing forces of the creative process, such as the business and politics of music and the need to creatively innovate, both considered driving forces behind commercial art, were not, in fact, mutually exclusive. They could be compounded, separated, or used for or against one another. So here, once again, tension is seen as an essential part of the creative process. And to fully appreciate freedom, one must experience the feeling of restriction or repression. To be brave, one must feel afraid.

So, on September 19, 1970, Pete revealed his *Lifehouse* idea:

> Here's the idea, there's a note, a musical note that forms the basis of existence somehow. Mystics would say it is "OM," but I am talking about a MUSICAL note. . . . Do you hear it? I think you must, particularly the allegedly musical lot who read *Melody Maker*. Probably all musicians or music lovers, i.e.: people with trained ears

waggle waggle. They all hear it. Musicians have to learn to listen before they can begin to learn to play. I think it's the hardest part, the listening part.[9]

Inspired by Hazrat Inayat Kahn's *The Mysticism of Sound and Music* (i.e., "Everything in life is speaking in spite of its apparent silence," and, "I have seen all souls as my soul, and realized my soul as the soul of all"), Pete used the concept or idea of a musical note as a point of infinitude at the very origin of the universe, a metaphor for the acme or highest-level ideal that artist and audience can try to reach or experience together as One. This single cosmic note reflects the individual and collective consciousness—a primordial "One"—an awareness or consciousness able to comprehend and reflect plurality within the same experience.

On this philosophical, even spiritual platform, Townshend composed a tale set in the vaguely postwar-postatomic scenery of the annihilation of individuality. The setting was Great Britain, shattered by a nuclear-ecological disaster. Entertainment, especially music, had been banned by the government. The population lived through "experience suits" wired to a net called the Grid from which the government fed programmed and false or manufactured experiences to each individual. A young dissident called Bobby hacks the Grid, offering free music for all to experience both individually and as One through a concert called Lifehouse. Music would thus free them of bondage and allow them to come together through a higher awareness. The concert's slogan was "Come to the Lifehouse; your song is here."

Pete wanted this work to be a sort of Ray Bradbury–like, "modern retelling of Aldous Huxley's *Brave New World*."[11] Nonetheless, however clear Pete's conception about his project might have been to himself, he was unable to successfully sell the concept to his band or even his friends, in part due to its conceptual, technical, and narrative complexity and in part due to them being on totally different intellectual wavelengths.

For the first time, Pete found himself alone at elaborating a project he had written for the band. His mentor and producer Kit Lambert was still keen on a *Tommy* film, but Pete's disagreement with him about the form of its realization or even whether or not it was a good idea led the manager to a state of frustration and depression. Lambert moved away to decadent Venice and then to pulsating New York, leaving Townshend to his own devices and individual management of his ideas for the new Who project. Although skeptical of his idea and not fully comprehending it, the band showed confidence in Pete's intuition by recording the songs he had recently composed, with the *Tommy* film now long on the back burner.

Reproducing the Lifehouse Project in Real Life: The Who at the Young Vic

After the "creative feedback experience" via *Melody Maker*, Pete's second step toward the reformulation of the rock ritual consisted of reproducing the Lifehouse concert onstage.

He chose the Young Vic Theatre in London as a lab in which to create a "total work of art" made of music and images. In this experiment, "The Who would cease to be The Who and the audience would cease to be the audience,"[12] and both would engage to achieve the "Note." The experiment would consist of a series of live performances by the Who, precisely "three shows at the theatre, starting in February, . . . about 400 people will be involved with us and we aim to play music which represents them,"[13] "which will enable each person present to get a better understanding of the fundamentals of their own personality."[14] "Each participant is both blueprint and inspiration for a unique piece of music or song,"[15] and, consequently, "we shall not be giving the usual kind of Who rock show. . . . The audience will be completely involved in the music, which is designed to reflect peoples' personalities. We shall try to induce mental and spiritual harmony through the medium of rock music."[16] The music created at the Young Vic would then serve for a movie: "If you don't make a film of it and show to people that it can be done, it is going to remain a very isolated and private thing for 500 people."[17]

Pete, in his seventh article for *Melody Maker*, made his definitive statement about this project:

The idea is to make the first real superstar. The first real star who can really stand and say that he deserves the name. The start would be us all. The Young Vic becomes the "Lifehouse," The Who become musicians and the audience become part of a fantasy. We have invented the fantasy in our minds, the ideal, and now we want to make it happen for real. We want to hear the music we have dreamed about, see the harmony we have experienced temporarily in rock become permanent, and feel the things we are doing CHANGE the face of rock and then maybe even people.[18]

Pete planned to introduce synthesizers in this work. He remembered a lecture at Winchester Art College, where he learned how the synthesizer could be the ideal medium between the artist and his audience. It had the potential to be an instrument allowing even those with limited musical training to express their artistic individuality.

As Pete got on with the project, however, he was faced with more and more problems:

We originally wanted the Young Vic for six weeks, and this was to be a trial period in which we were going to make the film, but the Young Vic is a government sponsored bloody organization, and it turned out that we could only have it every Monday—I could never see it like that, I always figured it would be something where you woke up and went to bed with it; either that or you came and went every day. But it failed, more I think because we, The Who, couldn't really find the energy to cope with the technical problems, and by the time it came to doing it we couldn't fully identify with the idea. We proved that it was all possible, but by the time we'd done that, we just didn't have it in us to do it. We'd had so much of it, I mean I was getting slightly . . . hallucinogenic I think is the word, and the whole thing eventually just fell apart.[19]

The modest reaction from the public and the weak motivation among the other three members of the band made the *Lifehouse* project fall apart.[20] Chris Stamp saw it as an involuted creative process, incapable of creating proper synergy.

In 1999, Pete would look back at that frustrating time and remember himself as

a jungle explorer who had stumbled upon an Inca temple of solid gold and become impeded by roots and vines in a knot of undergrowth, only yards from civilization. One day I would emerge crying aloud that I'd discovered

something marvelous, but would be patted on the head and indulged in my triumphant ranting.[21]

The Young Vic experiments subsequently became old-hits performances, and Pete gave up on the film idea too:

I wrote about four different scripts, about forty tunes, got about four hours of experimental tapes, I spent thousands on synthesizers, we bought new lighting systems, we had the acoustics at the Young Vic altered, we developed a quadrophonic PA system, we bought special cartridge type playback machines with very specific logic controls so that as you're playing you can hit the button and get an instant piece of music to play along with you at a given tempo, we went into the production of machines that can alter the tempo of music but without altering the pitch so that the music could play along with us at our tempo rather than the other way around—I mean we went into an incredible number of things. And now we're back on the stage doing the same old things—new numbers of course—but what has gone into the making of the new album you just wouldn't believe.[22]

Pete also suspected that the time was not right for the theoretical and practical implications of the project: "The story contained ideas that were once regarded as overly ambitious."[23]

Record Plant Sessions

A sudden and unexpected call from Kit Lambert saved Pete from frustration. The band was invited to New York to record their new songs at the Record Plant studio, "where all you American groups record all yer heavy things," as Pete later said at a concert in Forest Hills, New York. New York actually opened up new horizons for the Who, and even though the *Lifehouse* film idea was at that time abandoned, Pete still hoped that Kit would help him create a sequence for the songs in a way that the concept behind *Lifehouse* would yet emerge, but his hope quickly died. Kit had started using drugs since moving to New York and had become a heroin addict. His chemical dependence revealed itself in the form of unpredictable, erratic, and destructive behavior. Before flying to New York, Pete had learned that Kit contributed to the failure of the *Lifehouse* film by telling Universal Studios, unbeknown to the band, that *Lifehouse* was the working title for music workshops aimed toward the production of a forthcoming film of *Tommy*. Furthermore, while recording in New York, Kit was enacting ever more destabilizing and awkward attempts to intervene in the format and arrangements that new songs would take. Finally, Pete abandoned the new sessions altogether.

Thereafter, the wall that had organically grown between them would never be torn down.

Olympic Studio Sessions: The *Who's Next* Album

Back in London, the Who turned to legendary sound engineer and producer Glyn Johns in the hope that he could somehow rescue *Lifehouse*. Glyn was the band's old producer and sound engineer from their first sessions with Shel Talmy in 1965, and he had a long history with the Rolling Stones and many others. Pete first tried to get Kit Lambert back by asking Glyn to work on the tracks that the band had recorded with Kit Lambert in New York City. Glyn, instead, suggested that the band start all over again, promising a much-better sound. The Who had enough tracks for a double album, and Pete hoped that he could still give the songs a sequence that would suggest an underlying storyline, but he finally had to settle for a compromise: to pick up a few songs from the whole repertoire and make a really good single album, instead of a double concept album. From the initial twenty tracks, nine would make the final cut. The few credits on the sleeve did not even hint at the bigger project behind the work: thus, *Lifehouse* became *Who's Next*.

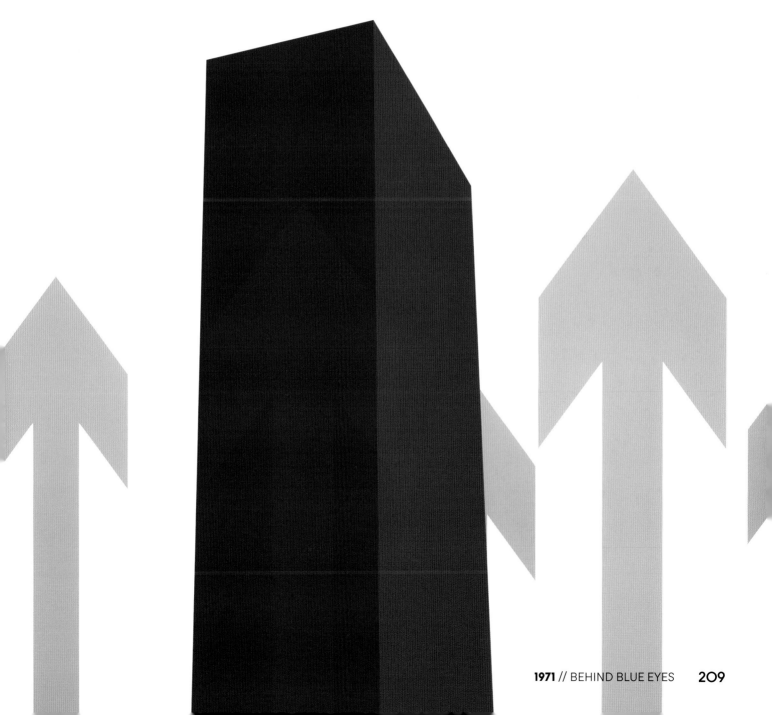

CHAPTER 13

1971
Anyway Anyhow Anywhere

Frank Dunlop, Young Vic Theater Director

Lifehouse rehearsals and concerts, Young Vic Theatre, London, from January to April 1971

Pete and I met often, and for a while he was on the Young Vic board. As he was a kind of genius, I was fascinated by any ideas he had. I trusted him. I could not spend much time with the band and with Stamp at workshops as I was running the theater and directing plays, but I remember thrilling times and incredible audiences. I saw much of Pete outside theater work times. I think the *Lifehouse* project failed to happen possibly because of disagreements within the Who setup.

Jeremy Goodwin

Lifehouse rehearsal and concert, Young Vic Theatre, London, on Sunday, April 25, 1971

I was there. What could have been more thrilling to a thirteen-year-old? People called those shows at the Young Vic workshops, but they were basically two or three dress rehearsals for a tour promoting their new album yet to be released: *Who's Next*. I recall an audience of 150 or so friends of the band in a small actors' theater. I didn't take pictures— it would've been embarrassing to take pictures of someone you know in a setting like that.

The rhythm section stood out. Some of their best work ever. Huge. And while now currently taken for granted, several megahits hits were first played onstage there ("Behind Blue Eyes," "Baba O'Riley," and "Won't Get Fooled Again," among others from *Who's Next*). I still have Keith Moon's drumsticks from the show, and his cushioned stick that he used on the huge bronze gong that always hung behind him. Moon used very heavy drumsticks compared to the much-lighter ones that I was given by Pete when visiting his house and playing the drums, keeping his newborn baby Emma awake.

Over the last few years I have been surprised at how good the recordings from the Young Vic dress rehearsal shows were. The Who were very loud, but, as always, they varied the tempo to provide breaks from the sonic attack, attacks that I loved because my ears would ring for three days. I would have been disappointed if they didn't. In those days, it was only bass, guitar, and drums. They didn't need anything else. And they were so tight compared to the Stones or Zeppelin, both of whom were comparatively sloppy onstage. Almost fifty years later I can't remember much else from that show. I just recall that I loved it. My ears buzzed for two or three days after, as they always did. It was a night to remember.

Larry Gross

Forest Hills Tennis Stadium, New York, on Thursday, July 29, and Saturday, July 31, 1971

I had been to Woodstock two years earlier but was not around the stage area when the Who performed, missing that iconic performance. Having been a frequent attendee of the Fillmore East, I had always wondered what it would be like to work there and get to see and hear all the fabulous music that was performed there. Well, I got that opportunity when I landed a job at the Forest Hills Music Festival setting up chairs on the tennis court floor in the summer of 1971.

The show that really caught my attention was the Who. There was a stabbing of a security guard during the first show, so there was a lot of apprehension about going to the second show on Saturday, July 31, 1971. After setting up the chairs in the afternoon, we left and came back for the show. There was a solid fence put up between the audience and the stage, leaving a space for photographers and people who were working the show to sit on the floor. I sat at the base of the stage right in front between Pete Townshend. What I remember was the sheer power and force of the music that was created by only one guitar, a bass, and drums, with Daltrey's solid, strong voice cutting through the evening air. There was also a lot of twirling. Daltrey twirling his microphone, Keith Moon twirling his drumsticks, and Townshend windmilling his arm, strumming his guitar. I probably wasn't the only one anticipating a repeat of their Woodstock performance with numbers from *Tommy*. And while we did get a number of *Tommy* songs, including the amazing "See Me, Feel Me," most of the songs were from *Who's Next*, which would be released two weeks later. So most of the crowd was not familiar with the songs. Nevertheless, the performance was strong, and we were treated to some oldies such as "My Generation," "I Can't Explain," and "Magic Bus." And then Bo Diddley's "Road Runner" for the finale. At the end of the song, Townshend tossed his guitar into the air and slammed it to the stage, breaking it into pieces. He flung pieces of his guitar into the crowd. Townshend took the broken guitar neck, picked up the body of the broken guitar, and batted it into the crowd like a baseball and bat. Part of the neck of the guitar was thrown into the pit, and I caught it. No doubt, a prized concert souvenir. I believe I recall that John Entwistle also smashed his bass and Keith Moon tossed over his drum set. Eventually, the chaos stopped and they exited the stage, and the crowd went home. It was then time for us to break down the seats. Having seen a number of famous concerts, such as Woodstock and the Doors riot concert at the Singer Bowl, which by the way the Who opened, this concert took its place among my most-memorable concerts to this day.

Forest Hills Tennis Stadium, New York. Thursday, July 29, and Saturday, July 31, 1971.
Photo by Steve Richards

John Visnaskas

Music Hall, Boston, Massachusetts, on Wednesday–Saturday, August 4–7, 1971

I remember going all three nights. With our Bill Eberline connection, we had access and got to we see a lot of bands at the Music Hall. I remember the Who, the Allman Brothers, and the Grateful Dead. I watched the Who unload the trailer trucks in the afternoon, I counted twenty-something SG hard-shell guitar cases and asked the roadie about it. He said they started the tour with thirty something. Remember watching the sound guys wrapping Daltrey's mic with duct tape and stretching the cords out. Also preparing Townshend's guitar straps. Just before the band went on, I was stage left, right in the wings behind the curtain, and Roger came up right next to me and was in the midst of an argument with a beautiful blonde. I was surprised that he seemed to be about the same height as me.

We went the next two nights. The third night was when Rod Stewart showed up and wanted to come onstage, but Roger Daltrey had left the stage, supposedly because he was pissed because Pete had knocked over one of the speakers and it split a sound guy's head open. I forget if it was night two or three, but they had a Three Stooges–style pie fight backstage. "Won't Get Fooled Again" ripped the roof off that hall.

Boston Music Hall, Massachusetts. Wednesday–Saturday, August 4–7, 1971. *All photos by John Visnaskas*

Boston Music Hall, Massachusetts. Saturday, August 7, 1971. *All photos by Phil Lorenzo*

Public Music Hall, Cleveland, Ohio. Thursday, August 12, 1971. *All photos by Robert Kavc*

Super 8 film frame. Public Music Hall, Cleveland, Ohio. Thursday, August 12, 1971. *All photos courtesy of Charlie Andrew*

Super 8 film frames. Public Music Hall, Cleveland, Ohio. Thursday, August 12, 1971. *All photos courtesy of Charlie Andrew*

Jim Gustafson

Public Music Hall and after-party at the Agora, Cleveland, Ohio, on Thursday, August 12, 1971

I got to play for the Who at their after-show party in Cleveland with my old band. This was my band right before Poobah, called Biggy Rat. I started Poobah about nine months later. One of my albums is produced by Jimi Hendrix's bassist Billy Cox.

It was Wednesday, August 11, when John Entwistle and Keith Moon came walking into the Cleveland Agora, watched us play, and then invited us backstage the next night at Public Hall. The owner of the Agora said he was usually closed on Thursday but opened after the Who's concert to have the after-show party. It was so much fun! John was very friendly and talked to us for hours. After the show, he played my bass player's bass and showed him how to play the bass solo in "My Generation"! It was his idea to invite us to the Who's show on Thursday, after hearing us on Wednesday in Cleveland. It was so cool to see the Who in the audience, watching me play!

Courtesy of Jim Gustafson

Courtesy of Jim Gustafson and Sherry Rockney

Cheryl Prati

Hara Arena, Dayton, Ohio, on Friday, August 13, 1971

It was the *Who's Next* tour. Friday, August 13. I had just turned eighteen the day before. My girlfriends bought me tickets for my birthday. That night I noticed an older man on the side of the stage. He was eyeballing me and winking at me through the entire show. We had third-row seats. What a show! They were at their best! The show ended, and my friends and I made our way to the car. We were parked in the back of Hara Arena in Dayton, Ohio. I was literally picked up and thrown over the shoulder of that man on the side of the stage. He tossed me into the back of a limo. He called out for my friends to join me. He said, "Don't you want to party with the Who?" I was young and frankly a bit scared. Then Keith Moon dove on our laps! We were all shaking with excitement! Then Pete got in the front seat, with hundreds of fans screaming outside the car. One was my best friend with her boyfriend. The witness to the extravaganza! Turns out the guy that picked me up was Chris Stamp. We went on to a Holiday Inn. How posh?! The antics in the room followed with Keith. He tore the room apart, threw food all over the walls, TV out the window, etc. The rest of the band sat in silence, observing. I questioned Pete about his behavior because I was frightened. He said, "Just Keith being Keith." There were hours of conversations between all of us. I hesitate to reveal what else happened that night. I will say this: I was scared by Chris Stamp, but Pete intervened and took me under his wing for the rest of the night. I still love him for his warmth and kindness to me. Pete did get me safety pins to put my hippie halter dress back together. As my friends went back to the arena to get the car, I did spend some alone time with Pete in his room until they came back to get me.

Jeremy Goodwin

"Goodbye Summer," the Oval Cricket Ground, London, on Saturday, September 18, 1971

"Maggie May" was huge that year, as was the album *Every Picture Tells a Story*. That single and album were promoted as Rod Stewart solo efforts, but really it was the Faces. Par for the course for Rod. And both entered the record charts at #1 on both sides of the Atlantic, and on the same day. It was the first such feat in music history. Onstage, the Faces proved themselves to be fantastic live, almost as good as the Who. Rod wore a leopard skin outfit, almost knocking my head off twirling and throwing his mic stand around. It was dangerous up there. I wondered if the Who would actually top that performance—it was *that* good! But when the boys from Shepherd's Bush came on with the stage maximally expanded, all of us having been pushed farther back and to the sides, and with the full volume of that huge sound system turned up to 11, there was no doubt that the

Auditorium Theater, Chicago, Illinois. Tuesday–Thursday, August 17–19, 1971. *Photo by John Denk*

Who ruled. Pete needed a lot more room than Rod. He windmilled and wrung into submission the neck of his poor, terrified-sounding guitar, again and again. It was almost cruel. John's bass pounded my chest, Roger sang brilliantly, viciously throwing his mic around the stage, while Keith crashed his drums and cymbals into oblivion. Yes, it could be dangerous up there; but the 'Oo lose their crown as the greatest live band on Earth?

Never. Had I really wondered that?

Only briefly. Won't Get Fooled Again.

Pete Minall

"Goodbye Summer," the Oval Cricket Ground, London, on Saturday, September 18, 1971

This daylong gig had been marred by sound problems; the Who had insisted on using their own system, which was a great improvement. On the rest of the day, unfortunately, some of the microphones had been moved during the setup, and the event's somewhat overzealous security staff refused stage access to the sound team to reposition some of the microphones.

The Who performed a blistering set. So many jaw-dropping moments. They really were at their peak.

The band had two mammoth searchlights behind them, which at various times were aimed into the crowd, producing a dazzling effect. We were lucky enough to have witnessed them from a stage perspective.

After the Who's appearances at Monterey and Woodstock, their position as the world's greatest live band was secured. Yes, Pete Townshend did smash his guitar onstage, and yes,

Moonie did destroy his drum kit. As an aside (I was lucky enough to have been in the dressing room, which if my memory serves me was one of the Cricket Grounds' team dressing rooms), before the Faces set I saw Townshend struggling to tune his guitar, and in a rage of fury he smashed it to bits against the dressing-room wall. So, not just part of the act then! I did not deem it wise to attempt to take any photographs while backstage!

This concert was held six weeks after George Harrison's fundraising gig, the "Concert for Bangladesh," happened in Madison Square Garden. The first in a long line of charitable events culminating in Live Aid.

This was the English version of the above concert. This concert was massive at the time.

Although not guest-listed, my photographic partner John White and I decided to go to London from our homes in Somerset and try to get in with our *NME* press card. This we managed to do with ease even though we were only nineteen.

The photographers were in a sunken, private enclosure at the front of the stage. A perfect view. At some point, John thought he would get better shots by being onstage. No other photographers that we could see were allowed onstage during the sets. Although he made it for the Who's set! He told the security people he was there as a photographer working on behalf of the WHO, meaning the World Health Organization. Miraculously, he was allowed onstage. We will never know if the security people thought it was for the band or the organization.

Although it was recorded live by the Pye Mobile studio, no recording has been deemed worthy of release. Such a shame.

It is amazing to think that the band has sold more than 100,000,000 records in their career.

"Goodbye Summer," the Oval Cricket Ground, London. Saturday, September 18, 1971. *All photos © Pete Minall*

"Goodbye Summer," the Oval Cricket Ground, London. Saturday, September 18, 1971. *All photos © Pete Minall*

Dermot Bassett

Rainbow Theatre, Finsbury Park, London, on Thursday–Saturday, November 4–6, 1971

The Who were the first band to perform at the Rainbow, formerly Finsbury Park's Astoria. They brought over Joe's Lights from the Fillmore. Linda, Loraine (they come up a lot in my Who histories!), and I queued out all night for tickets. I can't remember the details, but there was a limit on how many tickets you could buy, which wasn't enough to cover us all going to all three nights. Luckily, when we got to the front of the queue, they were only letting in a small number at a time to queue at the various ticket windows, of which there were maybe six. So we were buying at one window, and then, rather than leaving, dodging onto the back of the queue at another window until we had enough! Great shows!

Pete: "It may not be much, but it's all we've got, so let's get some sweat in these fucking seats!"

Oh, we did, Pete, we did.

Guildhall, Southampton, UK. Monday, October 18, 1971. *All photos by David St. John*

ABC Cinema, Hull, UK. Friday, October 29,
1971. *All photos by Charles Swann*

Jeremy Goodwin

Pete Townshend and Geoff Gilbert walking on Myrtle Beach, South Carolina: "You Can Cover Up Your Guts but When You Cover Up Your Nuts, You're Admitting That There Must Be Something Wrong!"

Several decades ago, my friend Geoff Gilbert was walking on the beach with Pete Townshend near the Meher Baba center, in Myrtle Beach, South Carolina. Pete was saying that he wished at times that people didn't know who he was, because it always affected the way he could interact with them. And so, by synchronicity or mere coincidence, a man walked up and asked them what they were doing there. I don't quite know quite what they answered, but they ended up talking music. He loved classical. When Townshend started speaking, the man asked, "You're a musician?," to which he replied, "Yes, I play guitar, some piano, and a few other instruments." To which the man continued, "Professional or amateur?" Pete said, "I'm a professional—a singer-songwriter with the group the Who." And the man said, "The Who? Is it a popular band?" Pete seemed to go blank. Geoff said it was really funny because Pete for once really didn't know what to say! He was quite taken aback, almost confused. It certainly wasn't unusual for someone to not recognize his face—he's not as immediately recognizable as Elvis, Mick, or Michael Jackson—but when "I'm with the Who" elicits a genuinely blank response, that really was unusual, or so it was back then. Geoff's eyes shone as laughed, recounting it to be the best part of the weekend; Townshend got his wish and had no idea what to do with it.

Municipal Auditorium, Atlanta, Georgia. Tuesday, November 23, 1971. *Photo by Gerard K. Nass*

Municipal Auditorium, Atlanta, Georgia. Tuesday, November 23, 1971. *All photos by Gerard K. Nass*

San Diego Sports Arena, California. Wednesday, December 8, 1971. *All photos by Steven J. Epstein*

Jonathan Pearl

The Forum, Los Angeles, California, on Thursday, December 9, 1971

The sound that night was not consistent. When Pete played at his highest volume, his power chords and feedback effects drowned out the other three. It may have sounded different to them on the stage. When the balance was optimal, they were in great form, not quite at the *Live at Leeds* peak, but close to it. Pete berated the audience at one point. And did so also in Long Beach, California, at around the same time. People were tossing beach balls around and other things. It annoyed him. He did his act of pretending to act drunk but seemed completely in control the rest of the time. His adrenal level when performing must be very high, causing emotional outbursts like that, which still occurs sometimes even now. *Who's Next* songs were received very well. *Tommy* got a huge response though. Pete was very loud on "Naked Eye," all but drowned out Roger. We had good floor-level seats. It may have sounded different elsewhere in the arena. There were no tensions, but they started tossing beach balls and frisbee saucers, and Pete became angry and cursed loudly at the crowd.

The Forum, Los Angeles, California. Thursday, December 9, 1971. *Photo by Frank Zinn, Richard Martin Frost archive*

Civic Auditorium, San Francisco, California. December 12, 1971. *Photos by Dennis McCoy, copyright of Brad Rodgers, www.whocollection.com*

Civic Auditorium, San Francisco, California. December 12–13, 1971. *Photo by Leonard Bisgrove*

Civic Auditorium, San Francisco, California. December 12–13, 1971. *Photo by Paul Sommer*

Civic Auditorium, San Francisco, California. December 12–13, 1971. *All photos by Paul Sommer*

Civic Auditorium, San Francisco, California. December 12–13, 1971. *All photos by Paul Sommer*

Center Coliseum,
Seattle, Washington.
Wednesday, December
15, 1971. *All photos by
Shawn Crowley*

CHAPTER 14

1972

Rock Is Dead—Long Live Rock

"The year 1972 was the quietest in Who history, at least until that point. They did nothing (together) until August, when the leisurely eighteen-date European tour began in Germany. It was spread over two months and concluded in Rome on September 14."[1]

What we can grasp from *Melody Maker* journalist Chris Charlesworth is that as far as the Who's history is concerned, 1972 might reasonably be viewed an extended tail to the end of 1971 and as a mere preview to 1973, partly because the band spent little time together. In effect, 1972 was a Who "leap year," where February 29 came and went quickly, vanishing almost as if it had never really happened:

No schedule, no gig [in America], there's a rumor that we might play in Moscow one day. We're not planning to come back to America until 1973, and that's about it.[2]

In 1971, the Who had reached a musical peak from where they could almost see the future of their career. It was a long way down, and something new was needed in order for the band to stay aloft and enjoy the view. In July 1971, at the beginning of the *Who's Next* tour, Pete tried to envisage the band's creative development through 1974:

I still feel that the group should be making a film. . . . At the moment, we are leaning heavily on the fact that we are good experienced musicians and can put on a good stage act but . . . and I hate to rub it in . . . what we really need is a film.[3]

The bitter end to the *Lifehouse* project had not deterred Pete from producing a film that would take "two or three years to make."[4] It was Chris Stamp, the second Who manager, and music critic Nik Cohn who convinced Pete to make a film about something that would revive the band, to bring Kit Lambert back with the Who, and ultimately to create something that would become their greatest legacy. "I felt The Who were in trouble at the time, and so was their management team," said Pete many years later.[5]

The *Lifehouse* experience had led the group to the precipice of a split, held off only because of its success and, perhaps, because of the break it afforded the group, which seemed always to be under tension. Each one of the Who, in fact, decided to privately enjoy the immense success both of album and tour: Keith turned his Tara House in Surrey into a twenty-four-hour party area in which he broke from reality more so every day:

People often say to me: "Keith, you're crazy." Well, maybe I am, but I live my life and I live out all my fantasies, thereby getting them all out of my system. Fortunately, I'm in a position where financially I'm able to do it.[6]

Roger enjoyed his private life with his wife, Heather, while John put out his second solo album, *Whistle Rhymes*, after *Smash Your Head against the Wall*, the latter released just before *Who's Next*. Meanwhile, Pete flew to India to visit Meher Baba's grave. His stay there would inspire the soon-to-be-released *Who Came First* solo album, made of scraps from *Lifehouse*, demos that had never made it onto a Who record, and material initially featured on the Meher Baba Organisation albums *Happy Birthday* and *I Am*, both privately circulated earlier in 1970 and 1972. There was also a singular collaboration with Ronnie Lane, the bass guitarist for the Small Faces and the Faces, also a follower of Meher Baba, as well as "Forever's No Time at All," written and recorded by his friend Billy Nichols, who would later become his and the Who's musical stage director. On the "universal prayer" track "O Parvardigar," and on Ronnie Lane's nod to reincarnation, "Evolution," Townshend's beautifully played acoustic guitar, both twelve-string and six-string, stands out as some of his finest playing ever. His sense of rhythm, musical harmonics, finger-picking skill, and ability to play quietly or commandingly at different tempos with perfectly placed crescendos are well demonstrated on those tracks. In fact, while Dylan had electrified folk music by recording and playing with the Band, Townshend was overdubbing acoustic guitar into even his loudest hard-rock songs, such as "Won't Get Fooled Again," adding a texture that is experienced almost unconsciously, with much being added in doing so. Decades later he would sometimes have his brother, Simon Townshend, play acoustic guitar off to the side of the stage to add that same intangible quality to his own much-louder live electric guitar.

Back to our story: Several brainstorming sessions took place among Pete, Chris Stamp, and Nik Cohn from September to December 1971, in Wardour Street, London, and between one gig or another toward the end of the Who's North American tour that year. What Pete had in mind was an album with the title "Rock Is Dead—Long Live Rock," while Chris and Nik vied for a film script with the title "Rock Is Dead (Rock Lives)."

Nik wrote down the introductory notes to the project:

The Who have now worked together longer and harder than any other major group; have played to more people on more nights in more places under more pressures than anyone, until they have to come to encapsulate almost all of rock, past, present and future, within themselves. So, if one catches their development, that isn't simply a story about four kids growing up and getting rich. Partly, yes, but it also becomes a metaphor of rock in general—their public, and their context, and their time. That, in the simplest terms, is what *Rock Is Dead* aims for: to catch The Who and, by doing so, catch the essence of rock itself.[7]

Pete wrote new songs for this purpose. Yet, somehow the new work did not progress easily. Pete did not seem too convinced by the material Nik had put together for a different medium, and finally decided to put an end to it, giving up on the idea of a film once again:

We finished an album with Glyn Johns working at Olympic, and we in fact produced songs like "Is It In My Head" and "Love Reign On Me," "Relay" and a few other things, enough for an album. We put a rough assembly together, and it sounded like a shadow, if this is possible, of *Who's Next*. And I thought at the time, and Glyn was courteous enough to agree, although it did mean scrapping all his work, which was pretty amazing—to scrap the album as such and put out odd singles. I also thought it would be better to work in another studio with another engineer and again Glyn was very nice about that. We'd put in a fantastic amount of work together and it was pretty much an exhausted relationship at the time.[8]

It was within this context that Pete came to terms with his role in the band: he realized just how much the Who depended on him. *Lifehouse* had essentially proved to be an egomaniac, "Sisyphean" endeavor, and part of its failure as a Who project was at least in part due to a lack of synergy with the rest the other members. Pete also realized then that his spiritual inclination could not work as the main source of inspiration for the Who any longer. He understood that in order to reunify the band, he needed to focus on the aspect that had made the Who unique and different from any other band: Its heterogeneity and chemistry provided by four completely different and unique personalities. This aspect had been brought up by Nik Cohn in his sketches for the new project but had been completely ignored by Pete at the time.

So, 1972 may not have been very productive for the Who in terms of completed projects, but it was a pivotal year that saw the band almost disintegrate and then rejuvenate mostly because Pete Townshend finally woke up to his role and raison d'être within the group. And in addition to the mini tour of August and September 1972 amid almost a year off, two new singles were released in June and November: "Join Together" and "Relay," the only material Glyn Johns had produced for the Who before parting ways. The songs were only modestly successful, though perhaps because they sound strangely isolated, as if plucked from a bigger storyline and performed out of context, which indeed was the case (material considered for "Rock Is Dead—Long Live Rock"). Yet, something far more significant was to come, a brew based on the realization that the Who were in fact four as much as they were one.

The new work, for the time being, would have the name of "Four Faces."[9]

It is noteworthy that during the preparation of the new work needed to increase the Who's velocity of escape from *Tommy*, which had been started by the *Live at Leeds* album and accelerated on by *Who's Next*, that the Who was "visited" once again by the ever-looming specter of Tommy. American producer Lou Reizner managed to involve Pete in a theatrical/classical version of *Tommy* to be performed live and also formally recorded in the studio by the London Symphony Orchestra, sung in part by the Royal Chamber Choir. The major solo voice parts were to be played and sung by Roger Daltrey, Pete Townshend, Ringo Starr, Richard Harris, Stevie Winwood, Sandy Denny (of Fairport Convention), Rod Stewart, Richie Havens, and Maggie Bell. The deaf, dumb, and blind boy proved to be more alive than ever! As a matter of fact, he would keep the Who more alive than ever: as Kit Lambert would tell film director and friend Tony Palmer, it was only after the LP release of the orchestral version of *Tommy* in 1972 that the band *really* started to make money and definitively left their massive debts behind.[10] Furthermore, it was a huge honor. It was the first time that a world-renowned symphony orchestra was to tackle a work of modern popular music.

And Pete was terrified.

CHAPTER 15

1972

Anyway Anyhow Anywhere

Alex Kipfer

Mehrzweckhalle, Wetzikon, Zürich, on Tuesday, September 5, 1972

All photos by Alex Kipfer, except photo of Keith and Alex by Pete; photo of Pete and Alex by Keith

It was in the summer of 1972 when I learned that the Who would come to play Switzerland for the first time in their career and, obviously, for the first time ever for me. It was either Track Records, London, that gave me the news, or it was a press article. I was twenty years of age at that time, and I was excited like a little child at Christmas. The news broke like a lightning strike. It had been some five years since I started to follow the Who, after having seen them on German TV (*Beat Club*) performing "Happy Jack" at the Marquee Club.

I consequently strengthened my already good contact with Track Records, the company that also ran the Who fan club in those days. Closer to the date of the show, I spoke to Track Records' concert manageress Penny on the telephone, and she inquired about the venue hall and asked about directions to go there from the Hotel in Zurich. I offered to join them and bring them to the right place in Wetzikon, near Zurich.

We arrived at the venue hall in Wetzikon, which is about 20 miles from the city center of Zurich, in good time in the late afternoon of a sunny Tuesday. All staff members and roadies were busy with preconcert work, and I tried to lend a hand to the works onstage, handing out tools to the roadies. After that, I never left the stage area for obvious reasons, even when all preparations for the big show were finished and the lights were tested.

Doors for the public opened at 6:30 p.m., and the band was due by 7:30. They arrived about two hours late for reasons beyond their control, as on the previous day, while the Olympic Games in Munich were on, a fatal terrorist attack on the Israeli sports team occurred and led to a temporary closure of all road, river, and air ways.

I made myself comfortable on John's side of the stage, right behind a piano-sized sound control desk (not Bobby Pridden's one on the left side of the stage). Golden Earring played as a supporting act. They seemed to never finish playing. I was anxious to finally see the Who, and so were thousands of others.

Without warning, all the lights went out in the hall, and I could spot persons running in front of me toward the stage. It was the Who, finally! I grabbed Keith for a second, and he looked back to me; a few seconds later, one could hear some drumbeats, some bass notes, some guitar chords, and silence again. Not a word was spoken.

You could compare this to a bombshell explosion on a battlefield when the Who took off with "I Can't Explain"—such a power, such an energy, such a rocket start, such a sensation.

I forgot to mention that I was more than nervous—this was the night when I could see my idols for the very first time, close to me, only a few feet away. I didn't even use my concert ticket (tickets cost CHF 20, which is approximately EUR 17), as I got admission along with the Track people.

I carried a Meher Baba pin button on my Levi's jacket to show my solidarity with "His" teachings and of course to impress Pete. Right after they finished with the first song, I was foolish enough to speed across the whole stage, in front of a crowd of some 5,000 people; passed John, Keith, and Roger; and stuck my Baba pin onto Pete's white shirt.

Not realizing what was going on—we are talking a matter of a few seconds—Pete immediately pushed me away with the power of his right arm, screaming, "Take off!," and I was forced down the stage (which was only about 3 feet in height). The pin button dropped on the stage floor, and the Who carried on with a hammer-like "Summertime Blues." I was doomed, as I had to give up my first-row seat next to John. I had to watch the remainder of the show from the public area, right next to the stage on John's side. No blood trickled down, but I felt a lot like Sally Simpson. Wondering about my own stupidity on losing control and jumping toward Pete while he was doing his damn job, I stood there and let the magic of the Who's music comfort me. All trouble was gone and forgotten when I realized that Pete had picked up the Baba button and stuck it on his own shirt with his own hand. The button stayed there for the rest of the evening.

In those days, the promoters would hire a gang of Rockers to do the security jobs at the entrance gate and by the stage. They were greasy-haired, ugly, and scary-looking wild ones, and none of the crowd would want to start trouble with them. Only a year later, at the London Lyceum concert in November, the security staff consisted of formally black-dressed gentlemen with neat haircuts and wearing fly ties!

So, after "Going Down" had faded, I made my way directly to the doors of the dressing room. I don't recall how I managed to get there, as I was no longer in the backstage area. What matters was the unbelievable fact that after a few minutes, Pete appeared outside the dressing room with his drink in his hand (in a white plastic cup). I pushed my way to him and confronted him with my dramatic query: "Why did you treat me so badly, Pete?!"

A glimpse in each other's faces, and he wrapped his arms around me and pat-dapped me twice on my shoulder! Now this embrace meant the world to me, and I was invited to join him and the boys in the dressing room.

I met Keith and Roger and John after I had Pete "exclusively for me." Pete recalled me as a "Swiss Baba follower." I think he had heard my name before, as I was in contact with the London Meher Baba Association too. In a later interview he gave me a mention with something like, "A boy in Zurich, for example, became merely interested [in Meher Baba] because of me."[1]

The dressing area was the changing and shower room of the local school's ice hockey or soccer teams. No fancy furniture, no luxurious buffets, nothing, and some Track people hanging round and amid them were the members of the Who. Pete introduced me to Keith, who showed his widest smile.

Photo by Alex Kipfer, courtesy of Swiss Who Archive: www.thewho.ch

All photos courtesy of Alex Kipfer, Swiss Who Archive: www.thewho.ch

I felt like having a most wonderful dream. About an hour passed when the group decided to go to the hotel.

A groupie demanded Roger, but I couldn't care less, as I was asked by Pete to join him and Keith in the black Mercedes limousine (with curtains on the windows!) to go back to Zurich to the hotel. Time flew when I was with them for the transfer, and I shot some more photos. Both Pete and Keith were in the best of mood.

All photos by Alex Kipfer, courtesy of Swiss Who Archive: www.thewho.ch

Now, back in the hotel. I don't really remember whom I joined for a drink at the bar—was it Pete or Keith or John or none of them and some roadies instead? I really don't remember.

I knew that I would be back at this hotel in the early morning, and I went home for a good night's rest—soaring on cloud no. 7!

My brother and I were lucky to meet all of them, also Bobby Pridden and John "Wiggy" Wolff the next day in the hotel lobby. Roger asked me if I could keep an eye on his brown leather bag while he was going to the cashier's desk, John was smoking when he went to the money exchange desk in the hotel, and Pete, Keith, and Bob were, with some interest, going through one of the fan magazines I gave them, and had it signed for me.

After a while the taxis showed up, and one after the other left to go to the airport. Their next show was Paris, France, on the ninth of September.

My job was to fly to the photography-developing shop to have my photos processed. This process took a few days. My photos of the Who are timeless, priceless, and a treasure by all means.

This is the story of my first meeting with my all-time favorite band! My next encounter with Pete Townshend was soon to follow, and after that I was the lucky one to get to meet the boys on some other occasions.

Sports Palais, Lyon, France. Sunday, September 10, 1972. *All photos by Pierrot Mercier*

Sports Palais, Lyon, France. Sunday, September 10, 1972. *All photos by Pierrot Mercier*

Sports Palais, Lyon, France. Sunday, September 10, 1972. *All photos by Pierrot Mercier*

Press conference at Shangri-La Hotel, Rome, Italy. Thursday, September 14, 1972. *All photos courtesy of Genero Alberto*

Genero Alberto

PalaEur, Rome, Italy, on Thursday, September 14, 1972

It is truly a great pleasure that such a book made by a fan for fans gets published, since a similar project was started by me in the early 1990s, but it never came to be.

While working on my book on the Who in Italy, I got the chance to interview various people related to those circumstances in 1967 and 1972, among whom were impresario Leo Wachter, who brought the Who in Italy in 1967, and David Zard, who managed the 1972 concert. The research I made turned out to be useful for Andy Neill and Matt Kent, who contacted me in 1999 to get information about the Who in Italy to publish inside their monumental book *Anyway Anyhow Anywhere*. A nice anecdote on Keith Moon in Rome in 1972 was told to me by David Zard:

It was not easy to accommodate the Who at the Shangri-La Hotel when they arrived in Rome in 1972, since they brought over a group of English journalists that had to be arranged too. There was not enough room in the hotel.

Eventually Keith Moon came to the rescue, saying they could fix another bed or two in his suite. The bellboy added only one bed and was rewarded by Keith with a 200,000-Italian-lire tip, which in 1972 were as much as a monthly salary!

In the end, everyone was settled and happy . . . or, at least, it seemed that way.

Zard came back the next morning, September 14, and guess what he saw in the hotel's swimming pool? A TV set. He looked up and realized Keith Moon's room had a broken window! Zard went up immediately and found Moon lying on the bed, with an astonished look, saying, "David, I don't understand Italian. It seemed logical throwing the TV in the pool: it didn't have a single program in English!"

"However—ended Keith—David you are lucky that we're playing only tonight and then we leave!"

Who knows what he could have gotten up to, if they had to play there another night!

PalaEur, Rome, Italy. Thursday, September 14, 1972. *Photo by Giampiero Evangelista, thanks to Edoardo Evangelista*

CHAPTER 16

1973

Remembering Distant Memories

The live performance of *Tommy* at the Rainbow Theatre by the London Symphony Orchestra and "Special Guests" on December 5, 1972, was a resounding success. And the beautifully embossed, spectacularly packaged album released earlier that year was awarded a Grammy for artistic design. Even the critics who initially lambasted *Tommy* as sick and pretentious at the original album's premiere three and a half years earlier came around. Whether as a moth or a butterfly (a matter of perspective), *Tommy* was clearly here to stay, and yet its continued success created more tension for Townshend and the Who. Inner tension. In effect, it forced the Who's salute as musical representatives of the working class.

It wasn't only a changing of people, social class, or place as audience that marked this progression. It was a shift in time. More precisely, a shift in times. It affected everyone. In four short years, what had been in principle a working-class, largely youthful male following originating in Shepherd's Bush, London, now included males and females all over the country, many of whom had grown up and moved on in life seeking meaning to their existence in a different, more inner-directed way.

It was also that the band's draw had become truly international, and with that and the conquering of America, the band now had the attention of intellectuals, artists, and spiritual seekers, as well as the eye of the more staid if world-market-reaching musical establishment of the United States. Perhaps with this acceptance and the money that came with it, Townshend felt his role changing. Change can be unsettling. There is sometimes within an artist's career a window of time, a doorway through which he or she must jump in order to reach the next level. Above that window, however, hangs a ceiling, and below it a drop. Moving all four of the Who through that gap was never going to be easy.

The Who had made its entrance into the theaters of their followers' lives while "out in the streets," as they sang back in 1965. But that was only the beginning. In the late 1960s and early 1970s, at least in England, the new skinhead generation was growing up and integrating itself into the establishment. New movements and fashion spokesmen among the young were being elected. The Goldhawk Road kids had grown up, some having become "accursed intellectuals," as Pete told music journalist Nick Logan.[1] And he was no exception. It was to the middle classes that Pete's songs were now being aimed and received. The sonic impact of the Who was the same as before; it was the themes of their songs that had changed, and so too had the audience.

If, in 1965, the "Wagnerian" energy Townshend wanted to nail with "My Generation" represented the manifesto of a social revolution for youth, by 1973 this channeling of life through music and art was taking place on a more spiritual, introspective, and intellectual basis.

Yet, according to Pete, the present still felt connected to the past:

Actually, the good thing I'm going through at the moment is a kind of renaissance in songwriting, which is a strange process. It's not a conscious move; it has nothing to do with the way the scene is, or rock revivals, or anything like that. Suddenly I find myself writing songs that sound as if they could have been written in 1965.[2]

Pete would employ this new inspiration in composing "one of the most powerful things that [the Who] have ever managed to organize."[3] The songs he had brushed aside for the aborted *Rock Is Dead—Long Live Rock* project, and the ideas for the embryonic Four Faces concept, converged on Pete's two main priorities: to speak for the new generation but mostly to hold the band together:

I wanted to do an album that would mark The Who's tenth anniversary. I wanted a replacement for Tommy in our stage act. I was also looking for a way to stroke four eccentric egos, generate a sense of optimism and rally us. I believed I had one last chance to do something that might hold us together. My bandmates had almost stopped listening to me.[4]

It would turn out to be even harder than breaking into the American market in 1967.

Why Should I Care?

If by 1972 the Who had reached its peak as a four-piece live band arguably without equal, offstage its members seemed like session men trying to get back to their respective lives after a mammoth, months-long, all-consuming recording session. Pete was worried. All four members of the band were pursuing different goals and traveling in different directions. Both Roger and John had cut solo albums. *Daltrey* was the singer's first solo work, while *Rigor Mortis Sets In* was John's third. Keith, meanwhile, was going through the darkest period of his life. He was close to losing his wife, Kim, and his daughter, Mandy, a situation unbalancing him even more than usual. Apart from being arrested without a license for possession of a shotgun, Keith managed to distract himself from the troubles of his private life by sitting in as a session man for Dave Carlsen with Noel Redding on bass. And Pete? He had learned from Bob Pridden, the Who's soundman, that Eric Clapton had not recorded an album since 1970 and had become a recluse. "Slowhand" was reportedly depressed and addicted to heroin.

Jeremy Goodwin, stepson to the band's unofficial hairdresser and fellow Meher Baba follower Dallas Amos, was only fifteen back then, but living nearby in Richmond and also being a neighbor to a design engineer working on Andrew Loog Oldham's home and Ronnie Wood's new mansion, the Wick (later to become Pete's home). He clearly remembers that

Pete was concerned about Eric's self-imposed seclusion. He wouldn't play music and wouldn't interact with people, so his friends became very worried, and Pete was one of them. It was Pete who was instrumental in getting Eric back on his musical feet.[5]

Pete himself observed that

[Eric] is the kind of guy that unless he's pushed into something or is genuinely fired up, he doesn't really have the burning ambition to sort of get up and go.[6]

And as Jeremy adds:

According to what Dallas had been told by Pete, Pete had managed to get Steve Winwood and the rest of the Traffic together, asking them if they would, along with himself and Ronnie Wood on rhythm guitar, perform a concert where he would get Eric Clapton to front as lead guitarist. Eric was actually resistant to this because he hadn't been out in public for a long time—other than for an appearance at the 1971 Concert for Bangladesh—and this was all still over eighteen months before Dallas had even cut Eric's hair short for his new-look album, his first release since 1970, *461 Ocean Boulevard*. Clapton finally, if under semiprotest, agreed to be the lead guitarist for that group of superstars, and the concert was subsequently held at the Rainbow Theatre on January 13, 1973. The album was released eight months later, having been recorded on Ronnie Lane's Airstream-based mobile recording studio. It ultimately became Eric's way back into the music business.[7]

The initiative turned out to be as revitalizing for Pete as it had been for Eric, an altruistic distraction from his responsibilities with the Who.

The Past Is Calling

Back in his home studio at the Cleeve Lock on the river Thames near Goring, Oxfordshire, on one particularly dark and rainy winter's night, Pete experienced an unexpected attack of melancholy that took him back to another winter's night many years before. His mind went back to his nineteen-year-old self, to a night spent with a girl under the Palace Pier in Brighton after a Who concert had ended with a huge Mods and Rockers beachfront fight. That feeling of pride in being a Mod (or dressing like one anyway) was accompanied by the same uneasiness he was to experience nine years later when facing the uncertainties of his life and work. At that moment, though, he had an epiphany. There was no other choice. To move forward, igniting another spark in the new Who audience while simultaneously rescuing the band, he knew that the new Who album had to entail a leap into the past. It would be set in the early days of the Who. The story would introduce the young Mod Jimmy as the main character. And so it was that over a few minutes, on that very windy and rainy night, Pete wrote down the plot that would be featured inside the cover of the *Quadrophenia* LP, an album considered by many to be the band's last great work.

In a later interview, he would say this:

The theme is a mixture of the history of the group and the story of a kid who's going through adolescence. . . . When he's a child he doesn't suffer from schizophrenia but from quadrophenia. The album will be quadraphonic and each different part of the guy's character will be a reflection of one member of the group. So, one part of his character will be the good part, which is Roger. The other will be insane and abandoned, which is Moon, and the other . . . surprise, surprise . . . romantic, which is John Entwistle. There will be various themes and they will all mix together.[8]

The adolescent Jimmy, who projects onto the Mod ethos his hope of self-realization and his need of "recognition, meaning, redemption, absolution, and freedom,"[9] eventually reconciles these drives in solitude, on a rock, in the middle of a stormy sea. His story is a journey toward self-awareness. His loneliness within a group—the Mods—and his eventual realization of his uniqueness as an individual is the spine of the story.

Quadrophenia also depicts the path taken by Jimmy toward self-acceptance, the rock in the ocean being far from a place of asylum. It is the point where he comes to terms with his inner self, initially unrecognizable, and variable like the sea. The water element metaphorically represents an idea dear to Meher Baba and amplified by Pete:

The ocean is a symbol of universal consciousness . . . the individual [being a] soul trying to find its way back to infinity.[10]

Is It in My Head?

Townshend's success was in framing the deeply philosophical and conceptual nature of *Quadrophenia* into a solid and concrete picture. One of the most interesting aspects of the album is the transversal nature of the quadraphonic aspect. In geometry and mathematics, a transversal is a line crossing two or more other lines that—by the angles created—helps define them. Jimmy is the point of intersection for the four faces of the Who; the point where self-realization manifests as conscious awareness. The experience it offers involves all the senses. While the music and lyrics of *Quadrophenia* project the listener into another dimension—a dimension made of archetypes, symbols, figurative references, and open endings—the story grounds its audience into a specific time and place, offering an almost cinematographic experience of infinitude, the point where one feels connected with all. Perhaps this theme is an echo of *Tommy*, but the narrative of *Quadrophenia* is more direct, and so are the musical arrangements:

It starts with a sort of "Can't Explain" '65 feel and progresses like a reflection of The Who's history . . . there's a story which is really just a caricature of The Who.[11]

Or, like Chris Welch said, "Quadrophenia is a kind of culmination of musical progression and a bow to their roots."[12]

Journalist Charles Shaar Murray further explained that "basically, the early Who classics were straightforward expositions of an attitude, while Quadrophenia is an investigation of what went into constructing that attitude, and of its result."[13]

Jimmy's progression toward a state of self-awareness runs parallel to the evolution of the songs themselves. Some were songs demoed by Pete between late 1970 and mid-1973 for a possible use inside either of the two main projects of the time, *Lifehouse* or *Rock Is Dead—Long Live Rock*; some were sketched during brainstorming sessions for minor projects (such as "Drowned" during the Guitar Farm project in 1970); some songs were written and demoed by Pete without any specific wider "vision" in mind than just trying to get across a particular mood or feeling of the moment. Some of them would remain unused demos, while others, such as "The Real Me," "Is It in My Head?," or "Love Reign o'er Me," initially independent songs, eventually revealed as variations on the same theme. Finally, the nostalgic operation of choosing to set the plot in the early days of the Who was an adaptation of Nick Cohn's idea *Rock Is Dead* (*Rock Lives*), the album/film that would have celebrated the band's career.

Poet André Breton's statement "Only what is dead can be celebrated" would prove to be an ironic truth where *Quadrophenia* was concerned. With its unpredictable tying together of loose ends, what was designed to be the band's ultimate album, revitalizing its raison d'être, would stand instead as its epitaph, the point of no return.

This Can't Be the Scene

Since its earliest conception, *Quadrophenia* was born under a bad sign. Ill omens during its making predicted an imminent requiem, an act of remembrance for the dead.

First of all, there were studio problems. After Pete requested a larger recording room than the one he had at his home, Wiggy suggested the Ramport building. Ramport was once a church hall in Battersea, London, converted to a storage facility for the Who's road crew. Wiggy worked on its conversion to one of London's best-equipped recording studios. It was originally designed with Pete's wish in mind to record a quadraphonic album. Pete soon realized, however, that his ambition (which also entailed the creation of a quadraphonic PA system for live shows) required an amount of money that restricted the guitarist's creative potential.

Second, Keith Moon and Kit Lambert were going through turbulent times. The drummer's private issues had become so overwhelming as to undermine the group's dynamics. He was completely unpredictable, with drugs and alcohol making things worse. Furthermore, Kit's heroin use, which began during the *Lifehouse* recording sessions in New York, had also taken its toll. He would often interfere with sound engineer Ron Nevison's work, usually showing up very late and usually smashed. Chris Stamp, the other half of the Who's management team, was suspected of embezzling money from the band. The heroin addiction of both had led them to neglect the Who's financial assets.

As film director and Kit Lambert's friend Tony Palmer would recall:

Pete was very fond of Kit but realized that something had to be done about his drug habit, because all of their

money—or what he felt was all of their money—was going into feeding Kit's drug habit. And Pete, for obvious reasons, did not want that to happen, but also, because he loved Kit very much, he had to find some way to stop it.[14]

Roger witnessed all of this with foreboding: "We're starting to suffer internally, which really is bad."[15]

Fingers So Clumsy, Voice Too Loud

Although their world seemed to be falling apart, the Who were fine inside Ramport Studios. The recording sessions unfolded successfully.

As Pete recalled:

The real surprise for me was the amount of energy John Entwistle put into it. In the past John's always been as much a quiet one in the studio as he is on stage. The experience he's had in arranging stuff on his own albums, and zest and energy at the recording sessions was incredible. He worked like fourteen hours at a stretch on each number, multi-tracking horns. His attitude to Who music has really matured.[16]

Sooner or later, however, the band would have to step out of its bubble and face reality. Initial enthusiasm had faded into frustration and exhaustion. Track Records had anticipated the album's release on October 19, 1973, and had announced a tour commencing October 28. But the band needed at least another month to complete the quadraphonic mixes, make the master tapes in Los Angeles, and get the tapes ready for stage rehearsals required for the band to play the album onstage. With the tour commencing on October 28 and the album unable to reach the record shops before November 2, a breakdown seemed likely, at least with respect to the tour. The audiences would hear songs they had never listened to on vinyl. And the band would be restricted in terms of improvisation, because in those days the backing tapes of synthesizers and horns, etc., were unforgiving where timing was concerned. Multimedia formats, such as those employed by Pete in his groundbreaking *Psychoderelict* project almost twenty years later, in 1993, required technology unavailable back then. It wasn't the first instance where his musical ideas were years ahead of his time. *Lifehouse* comes to mind. Given that the band had planned to go on tour in the spring of 1974, the workload needed to meet the record company's earlier deadline led to general disarray. A few days before the first concert, Pete arrived late at rehearsals, having had to work on the backing tapes. Roger, annoyed for having waited for hours, simply told everyone he would leave. This would prove to be the straw that broke the camel's back: Pete, in a fit of rage, exhaustion, and frustration, brandished his guitar like an ax toward Roger, who avoided the hit and responded with an uppercut that knocked Pete out.

Nothing Ever Goes as Planned

After a two-year absence, the Who hit the English stage in a bitter mood. The band had been forced to renounce the idea of building three giant film screens as a backdrop, in front of which the group was to have played, because it proved, at that time, another technically unworkable scheme. Today such props are commonplace. Despite the bad omens, though, thousands of people queued up for tickets. For the Who's first appearance performing *Quadrophenia* in London—three concerts at the Lyceum Ballroom in November 1973—20,000 people would gather on the street for the 9,000 available tickets, forming a line that reached all the way to Charing Cross Railway Station. In those days, there was no internet on which to order tickets.

They kicked off their English tour on October 28 in Trentham Gardens, Stoke-on-Trent, the first of a series of dates in venues far too small to allow a quadraphonic sound system. Furthermore, the band struggled to handle situations on- and offstage, making it hard to play through the album. Keith often failed to keep time with the backing tapes, tapes that sometimes started before or after the band began the songs, leading Pete to a state of exasperation. Since this was a relatively new idea in the setting of live concerts, it was perhaps unfair to make it all about the drummer.

During one of the three gigs at the Odeon Cinema in Newcastle, Townshend smashed his guitar in anger, damaged the amplifiers and the backing tapes, and stormed offstage only to return after ten minutes with the rest of the band to play old hits. The audience's unfamiliarity with the new material didn't help either. Pete and Roger tried to make up for it with long-winded introductions between the songs, something that only added to the show's poor flow. In Wolverhampton, during the intro to "Doctor Jimmy," someone from the audience yelled "Magic Bus"! And during the first Lyceum Ballroom concert in London, the huge amount of equipment relative to the venue's small capacity obstructed the audience's view, causing a massive surge from behind that resulted in a dozen people passing out in the front row.

The North American tour that November didn't unfold any more smoothly. The month before, Chris Welch asked Pete about the possible difficulties involved in taking *Quadrophenia* on the road.

Pete answered somewhat sarcastically:

> Well, we're getting Keith Moon rebuilt. We're getting him a nice new pair of legs. Yes, I think he played well on the album, too. It's just that he keeps forgetting . . . how to play the drums.[17]

And yet, on November 20, at the Cow Palace in San Francisco, Keith passed out midway through "Won't Get Fooled Again." His backstage drink had been spiked with elephant tranquilizer. In the 2010s, carfentanyl, an elephant tranquilizer 10,000 times more potent than morphine, was the cause of thousands of unintentional opioid-related deaths. Keith was lucky if that is indeed what he ingested. He was hastily replaced by a lucky fan, nineteen-year-old Scott Halprin, who led the band through the last three songs: "Smokestack Lightning," "Spoonful," and "Naked Eye." It later was rumored that Keith Moon later gave him his gold-plated white Premier drum kit as a means of thanks.

Quadrophenia would also be played live with backing tapes in 1974, in a five-date tour of France that closed February 24 at the Palais de Sport in Lyon. That was the last time the band performed the album in its entirety until it was revived again, years later, in 1996. Despite its commercial and critical success, and a 1979 critically acclaimed film that included a young Sting as the "Ace Face" and bellboy, *Quadrophenia* would essentially be laid to rest onstage for over twenty years, other than for three or four songs that had become live favorites: "5:15," "Drowned," "I'm One," and "Love Reign o'er Me."

Still, this somber background is only a part of the story of *Quadrophenia*. Its release, on the other hand, caused a near-frenzied enthusiasm among many people who identified with the album while crashing through their teenage years. The memories presented in the next chapter show the effect it had.

CHAPTER 17

1973–76

Anyway Anyhow Anywhere

Jeremy Goodwin

I'm One, London, 1973

I was fifteen and walking home from school in Richmond when I passed the record store. I caught the last few bars of an epic song, the last few seconds of carefully titrated chaos. No one else sounded like that. No one. It had to be the Who. I ran in and immediately bought a copy of their new record, a fantastically packaged double album and storybook, all in black and white and shades of gray. My stepfather Dallas Amos' name was on it as their hairstylist. *Quadrophenia* entered the charts that day at #2 both in the US and UK. I rushed it home and had my friends come over. Dallas played it very cool (but he was really quite chuffed to see his name on the sleeve) and agreed to play the album—loud—on his fantastic stereo.

At first, I recoiled in horror. The sound of waves breaking on the shore? Footsteps on a pebbled beach? Distant hints at lines from songs unknown? And then, the little death. I felt an ever-widening grin spreading slowly across my face. From those bombastic opening bass lines, thunderous drumrolls, and crashing guitar on "The Real Me," I was hooked. Drums, bass, and guitar. What else was there? The Who were angry, and so was I. We were connected. They knew it. I knew it. They understood. And that song brought it all home. *Quadrophenia* was all about growing up and fighting for life with life, of pushing away parents while desperately wanting them to be close. It was about the confusion of growing up, of being an individual in a crowd, of surging hormones behind fits of rage and confusion. It was about coming of age, looking inward and outward, finding oneself, and meaning in life. It was music. It was everything. It *was* life. And it felt good to be alive.

Richmond, London, 1973

Fifteen years old and approaching sixteen, I asked Pete to come into my bedroom so that I could play him something important on my stereo. I felt a responsibility to show him something of which I doubted he was aware. It would soon be 1974, and while I loved *Quadrophenia*, I felt that he needed some feedback to stay current. After all, he was almost thirty years old. We lived near him in Richmond, in the countrified outskirts of London in a nearly 300-year-old cottage only walking distance from the river Thames. I had noticed a shift in music that was blurring the lines between soul and rock. I didn't want the Who to get left behind. So, I suggested to Pete that he might try adding a little "soul" to his music. For some reason, he put up with me. He actually seemed to listen. Perhaps few offered such suggestions, and I was young enough for it to be amusing to him? I don't know. It is amazing how teenagers feel that they know everything.

Anyway, I played for him a few tracks of an album by Little Feat, *Feats Don't Fail Me Now*. I especially liked "Rock & Roll Doctor," and I studiously pointed out how Little Feat and the Rolling Stones incorporated a little funk into their sound. I thought that he might do the same, "to stay current." He listened very patiently and clearly knew who guitarist Lowell George was, complimenting the band on its sound. He then told me that he fully agreed and, in fact, loved soul music. However, if he actually tried anything like that in the studio, Keith Moon would literally burst out laughing and fall off the drums, totally unable to play ("Eminence Front" came out a few years after Keith Moon died). At that point in time, Pete's favorite concert had been either Pink Floyd or Stevie Wonder. He then followed up with a comment that completely freaked me out: "Did you know that I hate being the axman of the Who? I don't even know if we'll stay together much longer. I want to pursue other projects besides 'white boy' rock 'n' roll."

Huh? What? I had no idea what to say. My mind went completely blank. At fifteen, I couldn't even conceive of life without the Who. It then seemed to me that *I* was the one trapped in time. I really don't recall how the conversation ended, but I at last understood what was meant by the adage "Be careful of what you ask . . . you might get it."

Georgiana Steele-Waller, Ramport assistant

I have many memories of my time with the Who, both at Ramport and outside it! I lived with Moonie for a while, first at Bywater Street when Chalky was the driver. Then on and off at Tara House. I had originally met them all while working at Monterey Pop. Then when I returned to England in 1969, I ran into Keith at the Revolution Club in Bruton Place, and after I got back from Ibiza I started seeing Keith. We were all sitting in the Speakeasy restaurant one night—Wiggie, Cy, Keith, and Dougal, who had replaced Chalky. Keith, they were talking about the new studio, Ramport, and Moonie leaned in and said to Wiggie, "Give Georgiana a job." So I began and helped not only getting the studio together, but getting *Quadrophenia* launched. I found Chad, a.k.a. Terry Kennett, at the local pub, the Butcher's Arms, Battersea. He became Jimmy in *Quadrophenia*. And the girls, Janey, who I introduced to

Simon Townshend; she later married him, and they are still together. Ethan Russell was the photographer for the *Quad* book in the album. The making of that album had so many anecdotes attached! Both in studio and out! I told of my ear getting blown out on the *Quadrophenia* documentary. Another time, I was tasked to find an anvil, for a cut on the album!

I remember also going to tramp one night with Keith, and in the restaurant he saw George Lazenby, all decked out in a kaftan. Keith walked up to where he was sitting at a table and punched him, his entire chair tipping over. Then he simply said, "There. I always wanted to deck James Bond!" It was a laugh a minute.

How about getting driven back to Chertsey by Dougal, and Keith and I in the back of the Corniche; Keith suddenly leans forward and removes the keys from the ignition and then throws them over to the other side of the motorway! It was about 5:00 a.m., so not much traffic; thank goodness, Dougal was able to find them!

Right offhand, I think of a night out at the German Bierskeller, with Moonie and Viv Stanshall. They were dressed as Hitler and Goebbels! Guess I was Eva Braun! We almost got arrested.

Keith's birthday, August 23, was also my parents' wedding anniversary. Keith would take them out; sometimes I got to go! One night, my dad and Keith kept drinking, and we arrived back to the flat in Sydney Street. The bathroom was small; Dad was getting undressed when Keith barged in and knocked Dad over a chair in there, the door opening inward, and my dad, naked, lying over a chair with his bum against the door . . . Keith pissing and turning around to talk and spraying the walls! It was certainly a scene to remember, and I have over these past fifty years.

These events were rarely planned, and no sooner did you get out of jail that you'd be into something else with Keith!

Courtesy of Georgiana Steele-Waller

In this pic I was waiting on Keith and Dougal to pick me up in Prince's Gate Mews for the premiere of *Stardust*, in 1973, I believe.

Civic Hall, Wolverhampton. Monday, October 29, 1973. *Photo by Howard Pratt*

Ian Hallam

Lyceum, London, on Sunday–Tuesday, November 11–13, 1973

I was sixteen years old and had just started working in a bank. I had loved the band ever since hearing "Pinball Wizard" back in 1969 but had not yet managed to see them. When the 1973 tour was announced, I sent off by post for tickets, as was the custom in those days. When I was unsuccessful with that, I placed a small ad in *NME* requesting a ticket and leaving my phone number. I subsequently received a phone call from a lad with a spare ticket and agreed to pay him the colossal sum of £15! That was a lot of money then, I can tell you.

Come the day of the gig, I caught the train from my hometown of Coventry and got the tube to Westminster Bridge and met the chap with the ticket. We walked along the Strand and into the Lyceum Ballroom, which seemed to me at the time rather a strange venue for a rock concert. The place was absolutely packed solid, but I managed to work my way upstairs and found a seat to stand on at the front of the balcony, which gave me a better view. Down below me on a different level, there seemed to be people sitting at tables with bottles of wine—more like they were attending a cabaret show! A bit out of place, to put it mildly.

I think I must have arrived late, because I have no memory of a support band, although I have since learned that Ian Dury with his band Kilburn and the High Roads had played.

The tension rose as it moved toward showtime and the lights dimmed. I can't convey to you my excitement as they ran onto the stage. But hold on—there's only three of them. Then from stage right came Moon sprinting toward Townshend, whom he rugby-tackles, and they both go crashing into a Marshall stack, which collapses on top of them! Total chaos!! I was buzzing before they had even played a fucking note!!! Having dusted themselves down, Townshend chopped out the glorious opening chords of "I Can't Explain" and we were off. Next up was, I think, "Summertime Blues" and "My Generation." The *Quad* stuff followed, and I don't seem to remember there being too many problems with the tapes as in earlier gigs. They ended up with "See Me, Feel Me" and "Won't Get Fooled Again." I don't remember an encore, but I could be wrong on that.

Other things from that night I remember: Pete Townshend trying a bit too hard describing the plot of *Quadrophenia*, which prompted the usual "Get on with it," and Daltrey complaining about the venue and saying they had received a lot of stick in the music press for choosing to play there.

Subsequently, the band played a few more gigs near to Christmas at the Edmonton Sundown, one of which I attended. This particular concert is a bit hazier, but I do remember the venue being very difficult to get to, and I missed my last train home. I also remember the support group being quite good—Babe Ruth.

I have since gone on to see the Who a total of twenty-nine times, including both Charltons, Hammersmith Odeon, Madison Square Garden, and Radio City Music Hall. However, nothing has ever beaten that first time at the Lyceum.

Lyceum, London. Monday, November 12, 1973. *Photo by Piero Togni, Genero Alberto archive*

Lyceum, London. Tuesday, November 13, 1973. *All photos by Alex Kipfer, courtesy of Swiss Who Archive: www.thewho.ch*

Lyceum, London. Tuesday, November 13, 1973. *All photos by Alex Kipfer, courtesy of Swiss Who Archive: www.thewho.ch*

Guy Perry

Cow Palace, San Francisco, California, on Tuesday, November 20, 1973

I clearly recall that November 20 began as a gloomy, drizzly Tuesday morning in the Bay. Cruising in my dad's gold El Dorado a little after 5:00 a.m. to the Cow Palace with Dave Capper, Craig Saunders, and Du Dixon, we blasted the new eight-track tape release of *Quadrophenia*, en route to get in line for the launch of the Who's North American tour—Fallout Shelter.

We arrived to be greeted by raindrops the size of marbles, fired up to be at the beginning of the line, not caring that within moments we would be soaking wet. It didn't matter, because witnessing Maximum R&B with 14,000 other drenched souls was the only thing that did matter on that fall day in 1973.

As it started raining harder, we took turns in line and seeking refuge in the car. It was nice my father was out of town on business and let us mess up his Cadillac! There, we ate snacks and occupied our time through various means. It was a total Who day: *Sell Out*, *Tommy*, *Live at Leeds*, and *Who's Next*. With *Quadrophenia*, what a solid four-album run the band had.

About 1:00 p.m., Capper and I were in the car (while Sanders and Du were getting poured on) when we noticed a series of huge freight trucks finding their way to the rear of Cow Palace. We decide to have a look, as the last thing we wished to do was to spell Saunders and Du in the rain.

When we arrived at the loading dock, all kinds of equipment, light trusses, monitors, and speakers were being unloaded. We asked if we could help, and with the assistance of a bribe, Dave and I became temporary roadies for the Who. The massive sound system included stacks of speakers to be placed up in the rear corners, facing the stage. We helped with those and stage monitors.

After we were done, the crew directed us to seats on the side of the stage, where we could wait until the gates opened. We were treated to a brief sound check, where the band played "My Wife" and "Roadrunner" (by Bo Diddley), with very little singing. Dave and I couldn't believe the surrealness of the afternoon, like it was scripted especially for us.

By now, Saunders and Du were wondering where in the hell we were. Whoops, I took the keys too. I went to the front gate and caught the disbelieving, intense eyes of Craig Saunders. Both he and Du were trying to process how I could be standing on the inside (dry), looking out to what now appeared to be a parking-lot marsh.

The determined and ultracompetitive Saunders went around back and snuck in, winding up hiding in a bathroom, while Capper and I sat on the side watching preparations take place. When an announcement was made that the doors were opening in five minutes, Dave and I strolled to the very front of the stage, between Roger Daltrey's and Pete Townshend's microphones, and sat down, then watching a sea of frantic fans vie for general seating spots. It was quite a sight. And, what do you know, Saunders and Du were right with us again.

The show was terrific, with a new band named Lynyrd Skynyrd opening the evening. The Who then came out and ripped the place up, performing almost the entire *Quadrophenia* double record.

Bill Graham introducing the Who at the Cow Palace.
Photo by Guy Perry

Then, something went terribly wrong. During "Won't Get Fooled Again," there was no drum solo, no Daltrey scream—just easing into "See Me, Feel Me" with a bass and guitar. Keith Moon had collapsed a first and then a second time moments into "Magic Bus," pressing Townshend to plead for a drummer in the audience to help them finish the show. When Scott Halprin joined the Who onstage, November 20 became a legendary show in the annals of rock and roll lore. Pete Townshend's thirty-plus consecutive windmills during "Naked Eye" to end the show was an astonishing moment.

Though Moon's exit cut short the concert, the Who would return to San Francisco in the spring of 1976 to play two shows at Winterland as a favor to Bill Graham.

The four of us teenagers could not have fathomed or planned the unfolding of such a wild, eventful day . . . but, on the other hand, we were all from a place where unique things occur on a daily basis—Marin County. I remember the day as though it happened a half hour ago.

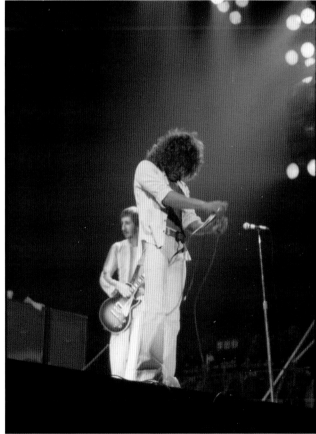

Cow Palace, San Francisco, California. Tuesday, November 20, 1973. *All photos by Dennis McCoy, copyright of Brad Rodgers, www.whocollection.com*

Cow Palace, San Francisco, California. Tuesday, November 20, 1973. *All photos by Dennis McCoy, copyright of Brad Rodgers, www.whocollection.com*

Cow Palace, San Francisco, California. Tuesday, November 20, 1973. *All photos by Dennis McCoy, copyright of Brad Rodgers, www.whocollection.com*

Cow Palace, San Francisco, California. Tuesday, November 20, 1973. *All photos by Dennis McCoy, copyright of Brad Rodgers, www.whocollection.com*

Soundboard recording of the Cow Palace concert. *Courtesy of Nick Schram*

Brian Cady

The Omni, Atlanta, Georgia, on Tuesday, November 27, 1973

I got started on the Who because I was so into movies. At that time (the early 1970s), the big theory on movies was the auteur theory, in which directors etched their personal themes into pop movies. One night I and a friend were watching TV when a commercial came on. It was for UNICEF, but the soundtrack was "Tommy Can You Hear Me?" "What does that song mean? I don't get it," I said to my friend. "You've never heard *Tommy*?" he replied, and the next day he loaned me his copy of the rock opera. After listening to it, I thought, here's someone trying to do the same thing in rock and roll that the great directors are doing in movies. Why haven't I read anything about this Pete Townshend? So I went out and investigated, buying a book on the Who sold by *Rolling Stone* magazine. I got bootlegs and their then-rare early albums. Then one day, the band came to Atlanta. I talked my mother into taking me to Atlanta to see my first rock concert, the Who performing their newest rock opera, *Quadrophenia*.

To this day, I consider Townshend one of the twentieth-century's great artists and don't understand why I can't fill a bookcase with analysis of his music and lyrics.

I do recall Roger and Pete trying to describe the songs of *Quadrophenia* before playing them and being completely inaudible. There were strong primary-colored lights for each of the band members (green for John during his "My Generation" solo), the surround sound of the tape playback of "I Am the Sea" ringing through the arena, and Keith Moon putting umbrellas up over his drum kit during the opening of "Dr. Jimmy." When he brought them down, Pete was standing behind him and soaked him with a pitcher of water.

Considering that you couldn't see the stage by the end of the show for all the marijuana smoke, I'd say the audience had trouble focusing on anything! The inaudible talks by Pete and Roger stopped the work dead between each song, so it never really built up as *Tommy* did.

People here ultimately responded to the album because in the US it was all about a emotionally distraught teenager, a big seller since *Rebel without a Cause*. The Mod stuff was window dressing for those who noticed it at all. I'd say the atmosphere at the Omni was a combination of unfamiliarity with the album (it had just come out) and audiences that were there primarily to hear the well-known hits. As I heard someone in front of me say, "I don't care what they play as long as it's 'Won't Get Fooled Again' and 'Teenage Wasteland'!"

Recording made by Gary Hodgett at the International Amphitheater, Chicago, on November 29, 1973 (mislabeled as 1974). *Courtesy of Aaron W. Hodgett*

John Visnaskas

Boston Garden, Boston, Massachusetts, on Monday, December 3, 1973

It was December 3, 1973, and they were coming into Logan Airport in Boston for a show at the Boston Garden. I picked up a bottle of Courvoisier Napoleon cognac (that's the top-top-top-shelf stuff) for Pete for when they arrived. They didn't get off the plane when they were due, so there was a bit of confusion as to what was going on. Someone told us they were just sprung from jail in Montreal and were going to be late, and it probably wouldn't be a good idea to hang around and greet them, as they would probably be in a nasty mood. We decided to take the chance anyway.

When they finally arrived, they were all in a fine mood, and Roger posed for some pictures with my wife. I presented Pete with the cognac, and he was very appreciative. Keith mugged for a few more photos, and their handlers whisked them off in a limo. It just so happened that the limo had vanity plates with the name of the limousine company (I think it was Abbot). My alter ego, Mr. Phelps (from IMF), stepped into a nearby phone booth and called the limo company. With my best phony English accent, I whined that I was with the Who rock band and the limo left without me, so where did they take them? (Insert *Mission Impossible* theme here). The limo company apologized (LOL) and told me they went to the Colonnade Hotel.

We arrived at the Colonnade, and the lobby was swarming with fans. Once again I went to a phone booth in the hotel and called the front desk. I told them I was a reporter for the *Boston Phoenix* and I was supposed to do an interview with Pete Townshend, and what was his room number? I must have sounded convincing because they gave it to me. I promptly called Pete from the lobby, and he invited us up to the room.

We chatted for a while before the show and drank the Courvoisier in official MCA plastic *Quadrophenia* glasses. Pete went on a bit about the brouhaha in Montreal. When

The Who arrive at Logan Airport, Boston, Massachusetts. Monday, December 3, 1973. *All photos by John Visnaskas*

they arrested him he was so sh*t-faced that he was on his knees cutting up the carpet into neat little squares. I think he said Moonie was making ketchup paintings on the walls of his room (or I could be confusing that with another Moonie story). We talked for quite a while about flying saucers and George Adamski, Lincolns vs. Jags, the new *Quadrophenia* piece, and Baba. As Pete got ready for the show, we loaded up on a bunch of *Quadrophenia* gear-ashtrays, coasters, and party glasses that MCA had whipped up. As we left, Pete asked us if we needed tickets, and I foolishly said no, I already had some, but little did I know how much our seats sucked.

We arrived at the Gardens and mercifully missed the entire Lynyrd Skynyrd set. As I mentioned before, our seats sucked, so we tried to move to the front and were roughed up by security, which was plainly audible on my tape recording, LOL. The band was on fire that night! I swear they put on their best shows when they're angry. "I've got a message for the Montreal Police! F**k their f**king a**holes!"

Sundown Theatre, Edmonton,
London. Saturday, December 22,
1973. *All photos by Piero Togni*

Sundown Theatre, Edmonton, London. Saturday, December 22, 1973. *All photos by Piero Togni*

Olivier Coiffard

Parc des Expositions, Paris, France, on Sunday, February 10, 1974

It was in November 1967 that I heard for the first time in my life a piece of Who: "I Can See for Miles" (B side of the French single "Mary-Ann with the Shaky Hands"); I was then twelve years old. The power of this piece literally transported me.

In January 1968, I was fascinated by the music and visual of the LP *The Who Sell Out*. And since that time, I have never left the world of the Who.

Throughout the summer of 1969, I listened to the double album *Tommy* in a loop on the chain of my parents.

But the most incredible thing that happened to me was that I saw the Who onstage in Paris, for the first time in my life, in the prestigious Champs Élysées theater for the birthday of my fifteen years (Saturday, January 17, 1970). For me it was my very first rock concert, and it remains permanently engraved in my memory.

I saw the Who in concert in 1972, in December 1973 in London, and then when they came to France in 1974, where I attended five of the six concerts of the tour, including the concert in Paris on February 10, 1974.

The Who came into my life at the age of twelve; I am now sixty-three, and they are still part of my life.

Long live rock, and long live the Who.

Parc des Expositions, Paris, France. Sunday, February 10, 1974. *All photos by Olivier Coiffard*

Tony Palmer

I knew Roger had ambitions to be a dramatic actor, long before *Tommy* was "invented." When I joined the BBC in 1966, the first project I was involved in was Ken Russell's film about the dancer Isadora Duncan, an epic to be called *Isadora*. Although I never worked with Ken again, I stayed very close friends with him. I remember when Kit told me they were interested in making a film of *Tommy* and whether I might be interested. I said, "Well, I might be, but a much more appropriate director than me is my friend Ken Russell." I do not think that was the only reason Ken got involved with *Tommy*, but it was certainly one reason. My recommendation with Pete was that Ken was an extraordinary director (and a crazy person!), and he would be just right for *Tommy*. I remember Ken telling me that he found Roger a most interesting actor, so I felt quite responsible for having pushed Roger forward as an actor. About ten years ago I went to a special screening of *Tommy* at the Academy Cinema

in Hollywood. Ken was there, although, sadly, very sick by then and in a wheelchair. I thought then that parts of it remain absolutely astonishing and parts of it were mad, completely mad—typical Ken! The Tina Turner section about the Acid Queen is a breathtaking piece of filmmaking. And I think Oliver Reed, who was one of Ken's favorite actors, is wonderful as the sleazy "Uncle" Frank Hobbs. I cannot think of anybody who could possibly have done it better. Same with Elton John's Pinball Wizard: astonishing! I used that and "The Acid Queen" scene, with Ken's permission, in my seventeen-part series on the history of American popular music, *All You Need Is Love*, in 1975. These were brilliant examples of virtuoso filmmaking by someone who really understood the power of music in film. The important thing about the film *Tommy*, however, and I think this would be generally acknowledged, is that it was absolutely of its time. Even more so than the music, which I think is not particularly characteristic of the late 1960s, early 1970s. But the film definitely stands as a reminder of what was being attempted in English culture at that moment.

Super 8 film frames. Richfield Coliseum, Cleveland, Ohio. Tuesday, December 9, 1975. *All photos courtesy of Charlie Andrew, scans by Michele Patucca Archives*

Super 8 film frames. Richfield Coliseum, Cleveland, Ohio. Tuesday, December 9, 1975. *All photos courtesy of Charlie Andrew, scans by Michele Patucca Archives*

Rick FitzRandolph

Memorial Auditorium, Buffalo, New York, on Wednesday, December 10, 1975

I watched this concert almost the whole time through my recently acquired professional camera and lens, but I was still an amateur. Still, I would put these pictures up against anybody else's at the time. Because to get great pictures, you have to have technique and you have to have the audacity to get to where you need to be. Also, at that time, there was no auto focus, auto exposure, or Photoshop. Of all my rock photographs, these concert photos are my favorite. I have good equipment; I am right up tight to Pete and I didn't screw up the settings. They were doing plenty of songs from *Who's Next*, my favorite Who album, especially "Won't Get Fooled Again" with lasers. I was so close I didn't get the full effect of the laser show. It was the last time I saw Keith Moon.

Back in the day, there was minimal security and only a few ushers. So, it really wasn't too much of a problem to get to the front and take pictures. At Who concerts, nobody sat down after the first song started—they always started with "Heaven & Hell." So, at that time, I would just walk down the aisle and kneel by the stage. From there, I would make sure not to obstruct the view of the front-rowers or risk getting them annoyed. At the end of the concert, I would stand up during encores to get a few better shots.

Memorial Auditorium, Buffalo, New York. Wednesday, December 10, 1975. *All photos by Rick FitzRandolph*

Memorial Auditorium, Buffalo, New York. Wednesday, December 10, 1975. *All photos by Rick FitzRandolph*

Jon Erdahl

Civic Arena, St. Paul, Minnesota, on Sunday, March 14, 1976

It was February 1976 when the ad hit in the *Minneapolis Star Tribune*. Who tickets for their show in March would be on sale Monday morning for purchase through Dayton's department store in Minneapolis, Minnesota. The concert would be on a Saturday, March 13 as I recall, and it would be about the third or fourth show in the tour. The problem was we lived in a very small town about 240 miles away from Minneapolis, in South Dakota no less. No chance of ever getting tickets. In those days, you could dial in randomly for a chance to purchase tickets from Dayton's, but, since they opened the box office on Monday morning, we were all going to be in school. No way to even have a slim chance of purchasing. That's where my friend's mom came to the rescue. She offered to dial long distance when they opened the lines on Monday, and she would keep trying to see if we could secure anything. Now that's love! She tried all morning with a busy dial tone until, finally, she got through and was able to secure tickets! Miracle indeed, as the lines outside Dayton's went around the building. It sold out quickly.

Super 8 film frames. Civic Arena, St. Paul, Minnesota. Sunday, March 14, 1976. *All photos courtesy of Jon Erdahl archives, scans by Michele Patucca Archives*

Now in those pre-internet days, news traveled slowly from coast to coast in the US. Even slower outside the big cities, and in South Dakota we were dead last to hear anything. As the date was near, an unusual note appeared in the *Minneapolis Star Tribune* indicating that the Who show for the upcoming Saturday would need to be moved because the drummer, Keith Moon, had collapsed onstage in Boston due to the "flu." The Minneapolis date would have to shift to Sunday, March 14, to accommodate his recovery and to reschedule Madison Square Garden and Madison, Wisconsin. Boston would have to move to April. It was just lucky that my friend's mom even saw the little reschedule note in the Sunday paper, as we never read the paper as kids and our parents wouldn't even be interested in anything Who related.

Miracle number 2. She was a *great* mom—may she rest in peace.

Well, for the kids in Minneapolis, that was just fine. But for us in South Dakota, hours away before the US interstate travel highway system was finished in our area, that would mean side roads for three hours one way, at least. By the time the show would end on Sunday night, that would put us back home around 4:00 a.m. at the earliest, with school that Monday morning. That is when fate entered again into our favor, as the show, due to conflicts with the Civic Center, would have to shift to an afternoon concert start. Perfect!

Most if not all the shows we attended in the early and mid-1970s were general admission, so you had to get to the venue early to make the stampede to get the good seats or be up front on the floor. Of course that would all change with the Cincinnati Who show years later, but for now, it was fun to hang out with Who fans preshow for hours and buy some bootleg T-shirts from the vendors. Everyone always sat on the concrete outside the venue and passed food and other items around as rumors and news about the band changed hands. The early internet. It was also during this sit-in preshow that we found out about what really happened to Keith in Boston and how he had cut himself the night after in New York, and that had caused all the first few shows to move back a date or so. Street-level news from the early fans. Always the most reliable.

My friend Rick, a budding film student, had one of the only Super 8 cameras around. They were unique and expensive to operate, and few families could afford them at the time. Rick made his own home films, so naturally he wanted to take his filmmaking skills to the next level. The Who would be a perfect chance to capture the band live for our archives (he did this throughout the 1970s). It was also a big risk, since in those days security was cracking down hard on bootleg recordings of any kind, let alone someone with a full Super 8 camera setup. However, that didn't stop Rick from successfully smuggling all that gear and film, within his socks, pants, and coat. Thus, thanks to his skill and fortitude, we now possess a Super 8 film of that show in St. Paul. It is not

a complete show, but about eight minutes or so of all the highlights of that concert. However, what makes the film even more special and memorable is that when you play it back today, you're instantly transported back to those moments, and you can clearly see the sunlight coming through the stage-right doors of the auditorium over John's stage-right setup. It was really weird seeing that show, knowing it was afternoon outside and that omnipresent sunlight streaming through those windows. It permeates the film and gives an eerie feeling to the whole event. A unique experience with a permanent time stamp.

I remember the real draw was to see the Who perform songs from *Who by Numbers*, since that was the new release and we *loved* the album start to finish. We had to wait a long time for it to come out in the US, and now our band, who wasn't that popular in South Dakota, was in the charts with "Squeeze Box." When they did "Dreaming from the Waist," "Slip Kid," and "Squeeze Box," the crowd went wild! They did amazing arrangements live, and both Pete and Roger were in full flight. They always loved playing Minneapolis / Saint Paul, and you could tell they were pulling no stops. Windmills, jumps, and Roger swinging that mic, nonstop in front of Keith's gleaming white drum arsenal, are stuff of legend now. That little band on that big stage with *no* special effects was jaw dropping, and the sound hit you to the core. The symmetry of their setup, clean and sleek, with those personalities in full assault, is contained in images that, even though the film is a bit fuzzy, are clearly coming from only *one* band in the world. The film has preserved those memories forever, and we believe it is the only surviving footage out there today from the only afternoon show the Who did in an auditorium that tour … or any as far as we know. We made it home later that night, but concentrating in school—impossible!

"Gary"

Seattle Center Coliseum, Seattle, Washington, on Thursday, March 25, 1976

Before this and a few other Who concerts I attended, I was not really a big Who fan. I knew and liked a few of their songs, like "Pinball Wizard" and "Won't Get Fooled Again," but hadn't listened to much of their music. The Who concert tickets were very hard to come by, with their huge US following. I happened to be listening to one of the Seattle FM radio stations when they announced that someone had some concert tickets for sale. I called up right away and later that day had four tickets for this concert. I took three friends who were big Who fans. Before the concert, we all ate a few "magic mushrooms." These grow all around the Seattle area, often in fields where cattle graze. We ate them when we got in line outside the Coliseum. We were probably in line for about two hours before the gates opened. I didn't feel much from the mushrooms other than I kept yawning. We had seats about halfway up the side of the Coliseum, just in front of the left side of the stage, where Townshend and his amplifiers were. The Who came onstage in a line, with their arms around each other. Moon and Daltrey were in the middle. As they hit the stage, Moon and Daltrey did somersaults. Moon jumped over some of his drums and sat, ready to play. The Who opened with "I Can't Explain." Townshend had a coiled guitar cord and started dancing in a circle, until he had the cord wrapped around him, from his shoulders to his legs, then he started doing wide jumps sideways, with his legs held together. I had heard that the Who was a great live band, and I was beginning to see why. I'd never even heard "I Can't Explain" before and had to ask one of the people I went with what the name of the song was. We had taken a pair of small binoculars, as we knew we weren't going to be very close to stage, being above and to the left of it. We all took turns looking through them, seeing Moon, with his head tilted to one side, making funny faces at Townshend. I don't exactly remember when the following events happened. I was looking through the binoculars when Townshend looked up directly at me, and it felt like he was looking directly into me. He danced around stage, looking back up in our direction a few more times. The next time he looked up, I felt hypnotized, and out of nowhere a voice said, "Will Keith be alive a year from now?" I had no idea what to think, figuring the mushrooms were having an effect on me. But then, I seemed to answer him, once again coming from where I don't know, and I replied, "No." This exchange really took me by surprise, and I didn't know what to think. Townshend

didn't look up in our direction for some time, but then he did again a few times and he looked angry. He was looking directly at us when this happened a few times. I never considered myself to have any sort of psychic powers, so this whole thing really stuck with me for some time, more after Keith passed soon later. I saw them all play again in October of that year, and of course it was an amazing concert once again. It was Keith's last US performance, and I believe they played in Canada one more date before returning home. I've been blessed to see some amazing performers—Alvin Lee, Stevie Ray Vaughan, Fleetwood Mac, Yes, and others, but the Who is by far the best live band I've ever seen, and I'm so happy that I could see them all play together that year.

Jeremy Goodwin

Winterland, San Francisco, California, on Saturday–Sunday, March 27–28, 1976

It was Saturday and I was wondering how the day would pan out as my friend Brad Vicknair dropped me off at home. I was eighteen. We were going to the concert that night, so it wasn't all that strange to find a limousine outside. I guessed that Pete Townshend had come by to say hello to my parents. We knew one another from Richmond-upon-Thames, on the outskirts of London, having immigrated to the United States a year or so earlier. I invited Brad in. Inside, we all chatted, Brad being surprised to find Pete "a really normal, nice person." Yes, I suppose so. He can be that.

Winterland, San Francisco, California. Saturday, March 27, 1976. *All photos by Janice Burnham*

The Who had wanted to play a more intimate setting following so many shows at football stadiums. Winterland held only around 5,000. Pete asked if we had tickets. For those two performances, there had been an allocation of only two tickets per person, and with only 5,000 seats a night for two nights, the demand was high. Back then, no one attracted bigger crowds than the Who. No one. In the *San Francisco Chronicle*, Bill Graham had said that he had been overwhelmed by a flood of applications for 166,000 tickets. And we were lucky enough to have received two of them. Really, though, we wanted stage passes. Pete said, "Well, I'll give you both backstage passes, as long as you sell your tickets for only what you paid, yes?" He was against ticket scalping.

"Why don't you just follow my limo and we'll go to San Francisco in convoy?" he suggested. So, Brad drove his 1965, 289 high-performance Mustang—a road-racing car souped up by Shelby at the factory—behind Pete's limo, with my stepfather in tow behind us, and others behind him, all of whom now had backstage passes. Seeing San Francisco in the distance was breathtaking. When we got to the Bay Bridge, we had to stop because the traffic was heavy and the toll slow. All the radio stations seemed to be blaring the Who. Just then, a Volkswagen Beetle passed on our right, only to suddenly put on its brakes and roll down its window. I rolled mine down too, and a young, pretty woman looking directly at me said, "Do you know . . . the car in front of you . . . that's Pete Townshend?!," to which I responded, "Yes, we're in convoy!"

We were now at the toll booth. "You don't have any tickets, do you?" she asked. "Well, I have two." "Really? How much?" "$12.50 each," to which she responded, "So what's wrong with them?" I explained. And they were so grateful. They had been hoping to buy five on the street but feared the street prices. She then got out of the car, paid me, and ran up to Pete's limousine, which was still stationary, and knocked on the window. Pete opened it and she put her head in, presumably to give him a kiss. On the way back to her car, she suddenly spun around— her name must've been called—to see a hand extended through the window holding two more backstage passes. One minute the five in that Beetle (which had a Colorado license plate) had no tickets, the next, two for only $12.50 apiece and two free backstage passes with seats. The tickets were selling illegally

outside for ten times or more their retail value, if one was lucky. They were lucky. They now needed to buy only one.

When we got to San Francisco, Pete's car peeled off into the facility, and we looked for homes advertising concert parking at the going rate, which was quite high back then. We found a place that had several. "How much?" we asked. The "attendant" said, "Five dollars, but you don't have to pay." "Why ever not?" I queried. "Because the people in that Volkswagen paid for you."

Sometimes you can just tell that everything will be all right.

Tim Bernardis

My Memories of The Who at Winterland, San Francisco, Saturday, March 27, 1976—the single greatest concert I have ever seen

The lead-up to the show—the tickets to this show were EXTREMELY hard to get. At that time, the Who were as big as any band in the world, and when they announced that they would play the 5,400-seat Winterland venue in San Francisco, the demand was enormous. I had never seen the band before but had liked them for a few years and very much wanted to see them. I had seen the Stones the previous July at the Cow Palace, also in San Francisco.

Due to the ticket demand, the legendary, iconic rock and roll promoter Bill Graham announced there would be a two-ticket limit, and those were available only via a mail-in request from which a lottery would be conducted. I think I sent in more than one request, and several of my friends did as well. One day, I got a notice in the mail that I was one of the lucky few who would be getting a pair. I just plain got lucky! All my other friends got none.

I decided to take my new best friend John Tuvo of San Francisco. I had met him the previous spring at a retreat at the Christian Brothers Retreat House in the Napa Valley, when I woke up the entire dorm by playing the raucous Stones tune "Can't You Hear Me Knocking" over the dorm sound system, totally disrupting the mellow atmosphere of the retreat. Unlike everyone else there, John loved it and, I found out, loved the Who. We were kindred brothers in spirit, in rebellion, much more so than any of my friends from Sacramento. When I called him, the first thing I said was "We're going to see the Who, buster!" He was just ecstatic, overjoyed.

I have a few memories of the day of the show. We probably went to a great Italian deli in the Marina district, which we often did the day of a show, ordering great salami sandwiches and the like on good San Francisco sourdough bread. I know we got to the venue early, in the morning or afternoon, and got our place in line, which wound around the block, around Winterland. My memory is that we were not that far from the front of the line. There were a few hours of waiting before they opened the doors. I used that time well. I had borrowed a high-quality 35 mm camera from someone but had never used a 35 mm camera before. I found a few people nearby me in line who had some, or maybe much, experience in using such cameras. I quizzed them on exactly what to do, kind of went through a number of drills on how to use the camera to get good pictures. This really helped, as it turned out. Thinking back on it, I have no idea why I was allowed inside with such a semiprofessional camera, something that would never happen today.

I don't have a lot of specific memories about the show, but a few things stand out in my mind. The Steve Gibbons Band was the opening act. All tickets were general admission. Winterland was unique in that they had seats behind and above yet very close to the stage. We got seats somewhere about the third to the sixth rows. That was where I got my best photo, the one of Pete and Roger standing together nearly back to back. Yet, I know I also went all around the building, taking pics from several different locations and angles. I can remember the legendary promoter Bill Graham introducing the band as "the greatest fucking rock and roll band in the world," and then they came onstage, Keith Moon doing a somersault.

As for the show itself, words cannot describe it. It was just so powerful and intense, breathtaking, really indescribable; it cannot be described in words. You had to be there. I remember the green light lasers that they used,

Winterland, San Francisco, California. Saturday, March 27, 1976. *All photos by Tim Bernardis, Plexiglass Productions. Large photo restoration on page 275 by Alessandro Prepi Sot*

which were just SOOO cool and powerful. The show had a feel of just rocketing through the night, cruising along, becoming more and more powerful and reaching greater and greater heights to a final crescendo with the green laser lights beaming across Winterland during the finale, "Won't Get Fooled Again." Stunning, majestic. The power and substance were just incredible, take-your-breath-away intense.

And at some point, perhaps at the end of the show, when the house lights came up, seeing the entire roaring audience on the floor in a frenzied mass, all of them with their arms raised straight up into the air as if raised on high. I had NEVER seen, heard, or experienced anything like that before, or since, not even at the Stones concert eight months before. No show has ever matched the experience of that night. There was Pete, leaping high above the stage doing the splits, slashing savagely at his guitar with his iconic windmill strokes.

I should comment here on the nature of the music of the Who and that of the Stones. They were/are both rebellious, but somehow the Who's rebellion was positive and uplifting, appealing to "the better angels of our nature," whereas the Stones were just kind of negative rebellion for rebellion's sake, without any "higher purpose." There was and is a message to the music of the Who not necessarily found in the music of the Stones. It was as if the Who meant to change the world for the better in the best spirit of the 1960s. (That said, the Stones are still my favorite band and channel my rebellious, fuck-you attitude better than any other band. But the Who is a close second. Just wish I could

have seen them in the days when they smashed and destroyed their instruments and equipment.)

I bought a "Who '76" T-shirt at the show. Afterward on the street, I put it on over "The Stones Tour of the Americas '75" shirt that I had worn that day. I can remember John, watching me as I put the shirt on, and will forever remember the look on his face of what I might describe as triumphant, that this was a show greater than the Stones we had seen the summer before. I think he couldn't believe that I was putting on the Who shirt ON TOP OF the Stones shirt. We shared a sense that what we had just witnessed was something amazing, triumphant, powerful beyond our wildest expectations. We both still feel this way about that show, forty-four years later. Nothing before or since has ever equaled what Pete, Roger, Keith, and John gave us that night.

Chris Bradford

Winterland, San Francisco, California, on Saturday–Sunday, March 27–28, 1976

Winterland, in San Francisco at the corner of Post and Steiner, was one of the best concert venues in the Bay Area for years. One could walk around the entire venue, climb up into the balcony, and watch the band from behind the stage, or push your way through to the front. The stage was located in different areas from time to time as well. I love looking at the expressions on the faces of the fans near the front, as well as the hairstyles of the times. I was just glad to have hair in those days.

Winterland, San Francisco, California. Saturday, March 27, 1976. *All photos by Chris Bradford*

Winterland, San Francisco, California. Saturday, March 27, 1976. *All photos by Chris Bradford*

Winterland, San Francisco, California. Saturday, March 27, 1976. *All photos by Chris Bradford*

Jeremy Goodwin

Drama at 20,000 Feet

It was, I think, 1976. I was eighteen and the Who had just played the San Diego Sports Arena. My friend Geoff and I were backstage talking with Pete Townshend when the band's manager, Bill Curbishley, offered us a seat on their chartered plane back to San Francisco. I noticed a pretty sixteen-year-old girl talking with Keith Moon, and she too was given a seat. Bill Graham had arranged for six limousines to take the traveling party to the airport along with a police escort. Each member of the band got into a separate car (security, estate value, and insurance likely being the reasons), along with others. We both were herded into one of the remaining two cars and could hear and feel the fans banging on the doors and windows as we slowly exited the facility. The windows were blacked out so that they couldn't see in. There were no stars in our car. Despite that bit of excitement, we boarded the plane without further incident. The flight, though, was anything but calm, at least for me.

Keith was a couple of rows in front of me, to the left. He was aisle side, with the young woman sitting next to him. He had a bottle of cognac or whiskey in his right hand and had already drunk a third of the bottle. He got up, presumably to go to the bathroom. I took the opportunity to ask her what she thought of the show, but I had to sit down, so I plonked myself into his seat. Suddenly, he was telling me loudly to get out of his seat, calling me "sweet face." I stood up, red faced and embarrassed. He then mocked me, threatening to throw me out of the plane as he had televisions out of hotel windows. He was drunk. Very drunk. I looked to Pete for help (I knew him as a family friend), but he could barely keep his eyes open out of exhaustion. So, I sat down elsewhere, quickly. Bad idea. A 300-pound bouncer growled, "That's my seat!" So, I went to the front of the plane to escape, forgetting where my actual seat was.

At the San Francisco International Airport, we somehow crammed into five limos taking us to the Fairmont Hotel at the top of Russian Hill (the secret service would later evict the band as a threat to President Gerald Ford's security; Ford was in the midst of a presidential campaign). We went into the lobby to say goodbye to Pete. We would take a taxi home. It was 4:30 a.m. and the place was dead.

"Sorry, Jeremy. I was knackered. I know Keith well enough to know he was probably joking." Thanks, Pete, thought I. *Probably?*

Next to come up was Keith, who put his arm around me and said, "Sorry, mate; I recognized you but wasn't sure. Didn't mean any harm. You all right?" I laughed it off and we said goodbye to both of them. I was tired too.

One last memory from that night was that at 4:30 a.m., the Fairmont had no bellboys to help with the luggage; the first ones coming to work that day would be in a bit later. I remember seeing a very weary Pete Townshend and the rest of the group walking up the wide, winding staircase because the elevators were undergoing a maintenance check. He was carrying his own briefcase or carry-on bag. It would have made a fantastic picture on the cover of *Rolling Stone*. It is in my head, but I wish I had it on camera.

Tim Bernardis

My Memories of the "Day on the Green" Show, that October (of 1976)

The band played two shows in the now-iconic and legendary Day on the Green (DOG) series in the Oakland Coliseum Stadium that Bill Graham put on every summer, which extended into the fall. I thought then and still think now that it was an odd pairing with the Grateful Dead opening the show for the boys. Total opposites —the Dead the stoned-out, mellow, psychedelic band of the Summer of Love of 1967, which took place across the bay in the Haight (Ashbury) in San Francisco, contrasted with the frenzied and passionate energy of the Who. I saw the first of the two shows, "Day on the Green" number 8, on October 9.

I have even fewer memories of this show than I do of the Winterland show seven months before. I remember that a bunch of us from Sacramento, where I grew up, drove to Oakland the night before and went straight to the stadium, joining John Tuvo and a friend of his. It must have been 2:00 a.m. or so when we arrived and joined the line. This time, we were REALLY close to the front of the line. When the gates opened, we ran like a bunch of madmen across the green and got in the front row right up against the wooden barrier.

I remember that there were a set of planters with very tall plants right in front of the stage that were interfering with the view of the stage. I don't remember if it was before the Dead or it was before the Who came on, but I happened to see Bill Graham up walking around the stage. He had his back to us. I started yelling at him, "Graham, move the planters!" A few others joined in on this. I kept yelling and yelling it. Suddenly, in a great flash, Graham whirled around, flipping the bird, and yelled, "Hey, FUCK you" at me, with the emphasis on FUCK. I yelled to him, "You've got a lot of class, Graham." But shortly thereafter, the planters were moved out of the way. That was Bill Graham in a nutshell—a flash of his famous temper followed by doing the right thing. He always took care of the fans, made sure they got a good show and that they were happy.

Again, I don't have a lot of specific memories of the show, but I do remember that it was VERY loud. The day of the show was "the Ox's," John Entwistle's, birthday. I made a sign that I brought in that said, "Happy 30th Ox." When the band came onstage, during the first song, I raised the banner high. I was right in front of him. He immediately saw my sign and acknowledged it but flashed three fingers, then two, meaning that it was his thirty-second birthday, not his thirtieth. Somehow, I had gotten the wrong information, but I was ecstatic that he acknowledged me!

Finally, I should note that as we waited for the show to start, or maybe it was between bands, some guy came along between the barrier and the stage, taking photos of people in the crowd, including me. I made a lot of faces, just having fun, but thought no more of it. A few weeks later, I got my issue of *Rolling Stone* in the mail, with a little

headline on the front cover about the Who and the Dead shows. I turned the page to the article, and, lo and behold, there I was in not one, but TWO pictures along with one or two of my buddies!! And on the same page as pictures of Pete Townshend, Roger Daltrey, and Jerry Garcia! I couldn't believe it! I guess I had my fifteen minutes of fame.

It was a great show, but nothing like the small, intimate, and extremely powerful Winterland show of a few months before.

Brief note: I saw this show with John Tuvo, Jim Griffin (John's friend from San Francisco and a high school classmate of his at Sacred Heart High School), Steve Artz, and Mike and Jim Leonard.

"Day on the Green," Alameda County Stadium, Oakland, California. Saturday, October 9, 1976. *All photos by Craig Abaya*

"Day on the Green," Alameda County Stadium, Oakland, California. Saturday, October 9, 1976. *All photos by Craig Abaya*

"Day on the Green," Alameda County Stadium, Oakland, California. Saturday, October 9, 1976. *All photos by Craig Abaya*

Seattle Center Coliseum, Seattle, Washington. Thursday, October 14, 1976. *All photos by Craig Perry*

Seattle Center Coliseum, Seattle, Washington. Thursday, October 14, 1976. *Photo by Gary Yager*

CHAPTER 18

"Life on the Line"

by Irish Jack

On Friday, the first day of September 1978, I called the Who's management office, Trinifold, at Wardour Street in the heart of London's Soho. I had just completed three months working with Essex Music on a project called the Who Exhibition at the I.C.A. Gallery in the Mall near Buckingham Palace, and was now preparing research for the planned film *Quadrophenia*.

I had arranged to go along to a local private cinema with the Who's manager, Bill Curbishley, and his wife, Jackie, to take a look at the unknown actor who was being considered for the part of young Jimmy the Mod for the film.

Bill, Jackie, and I sat alone in a tiny little forty-seater and quietly watched a private rerun of a television play called *Hangin' Around*, which had been written by Barry Keefe.

The guy playing the lead role looked completely loose, speed-freak skinny, and, in my view, perfect for the part of Jimmy. Bill Curbishley, who was the executive producer of the film, agreed with me that this person was the very guy we'd been looking for.

"What's his name, Bill?" I inquired.

"Phil Daniels!" Curbishley replied, with a note of satisfaction in his voice.

When Bill, Jackie, and myself returned to the Trinifold office, we were surprised to see none other than Keith Moon sitting in reception. He was perched on the edge of a low coffee table with the inevitable glass of something in one hand, and the telephone cradled to his ear with the other. He wore a bright-red, sun-island T-shirt tucked inside white jeans, over which an unmistakable gut had begun to form. He looked like he could have done with some regular exercise—or a good blistering Who gig. I settled into one of the reception sofas as Keith waved me with a hand gesture to a glass bottle he'd just opened. He appeared to be listening intently to the person at the other end of the line. I helped myself to a generous measure of his cognac and eased back, watching Moon's facial expressions switch from one absurdity to another.

Bill and Jackie Curbishley had taken some messages from Yvonne, the receptionist, and gone to an upstairs office to make their calls. I was left in the company of the Who's publicist, Keith Altham, and Moon's bodyguard, Richard Dorse. The three of us lounged in comfort and swapped new bits on the progress of the casting for *Quadrophenia*. While we talked, our conversation was becoming a little sidetracked as, bit by bit, we became more and more aware of what Moon was saying on the telephone. Between the gaps in our conversation, it was becoming increasingly apparent that Moon was obviously talking to none other than Tony Prior, the newly appointed director of the Who's publicity company at Shepperton Studios. And judging by the way the conversation was going, it was obvious that the tough and uncompromising Prior was having difficulty in persuading Moon that some stunt the Who's drummer had dreamed up was far too expensive for even the Who's budget.

Keith Moon was now arguing back down the telephone line, having suddenly adopted the articulate tones of the classic Eton Old Boy. Richard Dorse, Keith Altham, and I looked at each other in amusement, since by now we could almost visualize the ever-patient Tony Prior closing his eyes at the daftness of Keith Moon's sudden change of voice—not to mention the proposed stunt the drummer was forcibly suggesting. From the other end of the line, it is not unreasonable to assume that at some stage Prior must have made the point that in any event, as far as the stunt was concerned, the danger far outweighed the risk. A condition of odds, by the way, which was usually the prerequisite for Keith Moon's involvement in any enterprise in the first place. As the conversation on the telephone began to heat up, all I could gather as to what it was all about was Moon's fanatic-like reference to "the jump, the jump."

Several images came to form in my mind as to what insane part Keith Moon intended to play in this mysterious "jump."

And when I think back, this is what was so incredible about Keith Moon and indeed separated him from the average party joker. Your everyday house-comedian will pick up the telephone and start off great with a totally outrageous, posh accent, but very soon he'll become aware of the fact he's got an audience, and that's the point where he'll completely dry up and run out of words. But Keith Moon was the ultimate loony; possessed of an utter conviction with foolproof delivery to keep the act going to the point where the person at the other end of the line temporarily forgot that Moon was just "putting on" this Eton Old Boy accent, and that person at the other end became completely engrossed in the bone of the argument point for point, as if Moon had always spoken in such absurd tones. I had a feeling that the uninitiated Tony Prior was now going through this very adjustment as he listened to the preposterous Keith Moon. At any rate, Prior must have finally seen the futility in trying to change the Who drummer's mind and, feeling pretty exasperated, must have said something like, "Look, Keith, it's just too much money to put on the line." Because Keith Moon came back with a retort that could only have come straight out of something like *Brideshead Revisited*: "Eddie Kidd's putting his bloody *life* on the line, dear boy!"

An air of quiet disbelief filled the reception room as Altham, Dorse, and I looked at each other in total amazement. And immediately upon hearing the name Eddie Kidd, I had a vivid picture of the celebrated stunt rider possibly accelerating off the roof of the Houses of Parliament—with the Who's Keith Moon naturally strapped on behind! I never did find out if Eddie Kidd made that jump.

About an hour later, a party of us walked out of the Trinifold office across the courtyard to the Ship Bar. There were Bill and Jackie Curbishley, Keith Moon and his bodyguard Richard Dorse, and Steve Gibbons with some members of his band. The Steve Gibbons Band was under the same management as the Who at the time.

The interior of the old Ship Bar in Wardour Street hasn't changed very much since those fashion-conscious days of the 1960s, when it would get packed out with Mods strutting cool reserve in desert boots and Carnaby Street seersucker and hands in their jacket pockets like the Duke of Edinburgh. It seems ironic in a way after all the years in the rock business that the Who's management office Trinifold should have been situated less than six or seven steps across a tiny little courtyard from the legendary Ship Bar. And not only close to the Ship was Trinifold, but a twenty-second walk down Wardour Street from the Marquee Club where the Who first cut their teeth on a sixteen-week residency back in 1964.

The best thing about the Ship Bar in the old days was its proximity to the Marquee Club. You could hang around in the Ship and wait for the Marquee crowd to arrive for their interval drink: that was when you found out whether it was worth your while or not to go down to the Marquee. I should point out to the uninitiated here that at that particular time in the 1960s, the Marquee Club did not have its own bar, so as soon as the interval arrived, the crowd would usually rush out of the Marquee and make a beeline up Wardour Street to the Ship. So if you got told that the band was useless, you just carried on drinking. But if the band was blowing a storm, you found out who they were and ventured down to the Marquee. When you got to the door, you could try to con the bouncer with the story that you had lost your pass out on the way up to the Ship. He then might become a little suspicious and ask you what band was playing. Well, of course, you would have found that out already. Still not entirely satisfied, the bouncer might ask what was the last number the band played before the interval, and of course if you hadn't found that out and you offered a guess like "Green Onions" and it turned out to be "Watermelon Man," you probably got your walking papers and were barred from the Marquee for the next six months.

During their sixteen-week residency at the Marquee Club in 1964, the Who drank in the Ship Bar every Tuesday night before going onstage and during the interval. In those days the main band had a first and second half, and each main band set was preceded by the support band. In the Who's case, it would have been the Boys, who later called themselves the Action. And they were also supported by a band called the Clique. Practically every band who played in the Marquee at the time found their way up to the now-famous Ship Bar. I remember one such night standing in that packed little Ship alongside a certain guitarist. He stood in a corner with his girlfriend, bass player, and drummer and smiled rather shyly while the entire bar toasted the electrifying performance he had just delivered down in the packed Marquee. Who was he? None other than Jimi Hendrix—his second gig in London.

Anyway, back in that same little Ship Bar on that particular Friday evening in September 1978, while the others found some seats, I remained talking at the bar with Steve Gibbons and Moon's bodyguard, Richard Dorse.

About half an hour later, Moon was preparing to leave. Earlier in the Trinifold office he had told me about a gymnasium he was planning to set up down at Shepperton Studios while filming on *Quadrophenia* was in progress. In fact, Dorse himself had already promised to take me through his own personal workout. Quite what that entailed is anyone's guess, but considering the physical appearance of Moon's bodyguard, Richard Dorse, I shuddered at the prospect. At any rate, considering my own skinny physique, I playfully reminded Keith as he left the Ship not to forget about my workout. Moon looked at me and laughed about it, and then he became a little serious, saying, "Well, behave yourself, Jack."

To be honest, I didn't pay too much attention to this particular imparting. But later that night, as I thought back on the events of the day, it occurred to me that in all the years I'd known him, Keith had never before used that particular phrase with me. It wasn't even part of the Keith Moon vocabulary. It was really a well-used Cockney term of friendly caution. In any event, my remembering it didn't imply any hidden messages. I just gave it a few moments thought and then dismissed it. I did find it a little amusing, to say the least, that of all people to offer me advice on behavior, it should be none other than Moon the Loon!

Two days later I flew back home to Cork for a short break before filming on *Quadrophenia* started in Brighton. In all, I'd been away nearly four months and hadn't realized just how much I had missed my wife and kids. A few nights later I was in the home of a good friend who lived nearby, Joe O'Herlihy, who is sound engineer with U2 and one guy who really enjoys a good story. We sat in his kitchen and I filled him in on the latest developments with *Quadrophenia*. I had decided to keep the best wine until last: I knew Joe would positively crack up once I had told him about Moon on the phone to Tony Prior.

At somewhere around 10:30, with the story just about to buzz in my head, there came a ring at the doorbell. Joe answered it to find my wife, Maura, standing there. She had been given the news by my brother Pat, who had driven to my house with his wife, Marion.

My wife, Maura, was in shock: "There was something on the radio about Keith Moon being found dead," she said.

At first, I didn't register. It was like a kind of a gibberish. I must have blanched, for she repeated it. Then I said something like, "That's impossible . . ." Of course I didn't believe it. Who would? Somehow I clung to the hope that there had to be a horrible mistake and probably a very simple explanation to follow. And then from out of the sky, someone threw me a life jacket:

"Of course"—I heard myself say—"It's that other guy Moon. Y'know, the sect leader, Sun Yat."

There was an uneasy air of relief. I was so sure. And there I was, wishing death on another man. Yet, I couldn't leave the kitchen, gratefully accepting a large brandy to steady me as we waited for the eleven o'clock news on Radio Luxembourg. I was unable to sit but preferred to stand against the kitchen sink, watching the minute hand on the clock crawl to eleven—as if that was the appointed time for my brother's execution. I was incapable of following the small talk as Joe's wife, Marion, handed me a second brandy that didn't even taste as it went down. And then, like a bad dream, came the Radio Luxembourg News with that flamboyant trumpet fanfare. And y'know, the most awful sound in the world is not the words you hear when you're jilted and it breaks your teenage heart. Or the kick in your brain when you're chased along the beach by forty Rockers. The most awful sound in the world, my friend, is the flat and unemotional voice of a news reader telling you the impossible has happened, and tearing your safe little rock and roll world apart.

Keith Moon was dead—and less than a week after I had guzzled his cognac.

The next morning, I realized there was only one place on earth I wanted to be, had to be: the Who's Trinifold office. I used up my return air ticket and caught a morning flight. I went straight to Trinifold, where I found Bill and Jackie Curbishley in tears. Bill's assistant, Chris Chappell, was unable to work at his desk and refused to go home, preferring instead to sit alone in his office, numbed and surrounded by Who paraphernalia. In fact, the only person who was capable of talking and telling me about what had happened was Mike Shaw, the Who's one-time lighting man. Indeed, Mike himself was no stranger to showing a brave face under such unbearable circumstances. He had lost the use of both legs as the result of a car crash while driving to Liverpool to promote a charity event to keep the Cavern Club open in the Who's early days, and after a long spell rehabilitating at Stoke Manderville Hospital, Mike had returned to work for the Who from behind a desk at Trinifold. An admirable and very brave paraplegic.

I looked around the office that day and saw it in a way I had never seen it before. It seemed like a million miles away from the comfortable, gold-album-decorated reception of just a week earlier. And as I watched the various Who personnel arrive and depart with whatever task they had been entrusted to perform, it occurred to me that we were all members of a family called WHO: except that usually we were all too taken up with something or other to stop and realize it.

It was Mike Shaw's calm that talked me through it that day, and it is to him that I shall be eternally grateful. Bill and Jackie told me they had been up all night manning the switchboard, trying to cope with hundreds of calls coming in from musicians, fans, and the press. One can only imagine the unbearable repetition they must have gone through. Painful but necessary.

Drummers of well-known and unknown bands were already phoning in offering their services to the Who. Each one without a hint of bandwagoning or even thought of their own careers, but merely showing their respect for Keith Moon, one of rock's greatest drummers.

Mike Shaw's office had a glass partition separating it from reception that allowed Mike to look out at passing activity from his wheelchair. As I sat with him, part of the day began to slowly drift by in a haze, and we two hadn't been closer in the fourteen years I had known him. Mike was telling me some of his own special memories of Keith; each one seemed so outrageously funny and typical of the born comic that Moon surely was.

While he spoke and took time to tell each little anecdote, I had a feeling that Mike was deliberately slowing me down, keeping me occupied, suspecting that if he didn't do something, I would soon be over in the Ship Bar on a one-way ticket. As I sat and listened to him, I had the sensation of settling into a kind of artificial calm. As if, without warning, the sheer effort of weeks and weeks of hard work on the exhibition had finally crept up on me, and now I felt emotionally drained. I was half slouched in my seat, listening to Mike, when after a while I realized I had spent the last five or maybe ten minutes staring, absentmindedly, out through the glass partition at the telephone resting dead on the coffee table in reception, where Keith Moon had sat some days before. My eyes focused on the telephone, and it was like seeing him again just for a brief flash, as Keith Moon's voice came back to me loud and clear with all the Etonian refinery he had mustered up a week earlier on the phone to Tony Prior.

"Eddie Kidd's putting his bloody life on the line, dear boy. Eddie Kidd!"

CHAPTER 19

Conclusion: The Song Is Over

Although *Who's Next* and *Quadrophenia* established newfound heights for the Who in the recording studio and sold really well, *Quadrophenia* failed to replace *Tommy* as the centerpiece of its live performances, its power on the world music stage being derived from that. And as much as Pete Townshend would over the years claim to dislike performing concerts and touring, it was his experiences (and the band's) live—as performer or observer—that fueled his creative spirit and his drive to move forward. Yet, the band seemed to be chased by an indelible past. The success of the *Tommy* film renewed public interest in the work, leading the Who to put tracks from the album back in its set lists and to renounce the idea of having left it behind.

Quadrophenia, the most ambitious, elaborate, and demanding work of the Who, intended as their ultimate bet, probably represented the symptom of imminent collapse. John, looking back to that time, admitted he was seriously considering leaving the group, and Pete himself recalled 1974–75 as the time he was nursing to split and start a solo career.

"That is true . . . ," said Jeremy Goodwin, stepson of Pete's friend and the band's hairstylist Dallas Amos. "He told me so when I had the audacity as a teenager to show him ways in which I thought the Who might update their music via a little funk and soul à la Little Feat. [That Californian band later played a supporting role in the Who's 1976 Charlton Football Ground concert, ranked soon afterward by *The Guinness Book of World Records* as the loudest ever recorded.] He also told me that one of his favorite recording artists was Stevie Wonder, but that Keith Moon would fall on the floor laughing, completely unable to play if he ever attempted anything like that in the studio. He then dropped the bomb. He was thinking about disbanding the Who. He was fed up with being the axman of a white-boy rock band. I hadn't expected that, and I was shocked into silence."

In his letter to lawyer Edward "Ted" Oldman in 1973, Pete wrote that *Quadrophenia* and the tour that would follow would be the last projects he wanted to be involved in with the Who as a group. His words were full of disenchantment and dissatisfaction. It came across in his work too. The studio albums following *Quadrophenia* reflected his artistic disorientation. Some even felt that their concerts after 1973 seemed far from the live experience the Who became famous for. Others would say that this wasn't really the case until 1979, when they first toured without Keith Moon less than a year after his death. Regardless, there was a feeling that something had changed onstage after *Quadrophenia*. However much the Who had grown onstage in recent years, having become tighter than ever, especially during their last North American tour with Keith Moon in 1976, their live act passed from being a cathartic, almost spiritual event to an exciting and highly entertaining if predictable performance of their greatest hits. They were becoming what they feared most, a parody of themselves, a criticism that Pete had already leveled at one of his favorite bands, the Rolling Stones. That memory goes back to a particular episode, when Pete had seemed to finally come to terms with the evidence that the times were changing, and not only for the Who. On June 10, 1974, during the first of four concerts at Madison Square Garden in New York, Pete struggled to stay focused while people in the first rows teased him for his usual restless presence onstage. He suddenly found himself witnessing with some embarrassment how his leaps, twirls, and windmills were no longer perceived as a serious, essential aesthetic trait of his multifaceted way of performing, but as an almost sterile gimmick, more like a reiterated circus act. This episode, according to Chris Charlesworth, "had a profound effect on his attitude towards his work."[1] It was not the only reaction from that sold-out crowd that disturbed him, however. Other, die-hard Who fans were ready to defend the band under any circumstance, ready to take in whatever new material was released, good or bad. "This blind faith," added Charlesworth, "depressed Pete yet further."[2]

In a particular interview with disk jockey Alan Freeman, back in 1966, Pete's words poured out torrid restlessness, the same inquietude that previously led the Who to turn frustration into such creative energy. Somehow, in retrospect, those words reported seem farther than ever:

We were playing rhythm and blues years before anyone here, even before the Stones. It's always been like that with us. Whatever we're doing at the moment, we change to something else as soon as others get in on it.[3]

The Rolling Stones–like title the Who gave their 1975 tour, "Greatest Rock 'n' Roll Band in the World," in all of its irony, can be read simultaneously as a finish line and an epitaph.[4]

But is this writing off the Who really fair? Such a thesis rests on the band's goal of freeing itself from the constraints of *Tommy*'s success; perhaps its excess. *Quadrophenia* might itself be viewed through the prism of its own success and excess, although also through the lens of a whole new generation of fans who saw themselves as the protagonist Jimmy, teenagers seeking a way to define themselves as individuals rather than merely as members of a group. This

makes it possible to consider *Tommy* and *Quadrophenia* as musical creations with their own historical and intrinsic merits rather than mere moments in time formed in opposition to one another. Taken this way, and viewing the Who's career as a whole, the two concept albums rise up like mountains, forming complementary twin peaks. It is no surprise that today, Townshend rates *Quadrophenia* as his mostly satisfying work, maybe for its ability to endure the hostile circumstances following its release. It undoubtedly embodied one of Pete's dearest ambitions, as he had once explained back in 1968 to film director Tony Palmer:

I'm very interested in getting complete control over my music. In other words, I would write a piece of music, arrange it, play every instrument myself, record it all myself, in my own studio, sing any part that needed singing, produce it myself and also distribute it myself. Complete control. The more control you've got over what you're involved in, the nearer the finished product is to what you intended. It will be good when every individual can make music in the same way that every individual can now paint a picture.[5]

After fifty-six years, we have a fuller picture of the Who's career. One way of viewing it suggests that the ever-present tension and restlessness of the band that produced art as music, with its momentary resolution of conflict and subsequent reemergence, were silently aiming toward *Quadrophenia*.

With that album, Pete managed to channel his instinct and give form to what took almost ten years to complete, using the Who as a vehicle for its production.

He could finally almost explain that feeling inside.

Quadrophenia was also the control that Pete had been longing for since that interview in 1968; it was the point where the creative process reached its peak and where the song subsequently ended. But with that end came tremendous release, just like at a Who concert when the final number comes to its close. It's at that point that the audience roars loudest. Pete smashed his guitar to symbolically neutralize every materialistic implication of music, searching low and high to find that Note, a vibration that had less to do with music than life itself, a consciousness close to what these pages have been trying to define. It was a process that produced a polyphony that became the trademark of the Who and, in a broader sense, one of the pillars of rock and roll. The Who was thus a manifestation of many lives and evolutionary unfoldings, a few of which are captured in this book.

There is something interesting Bob Dylan said to film director Martin Scorsese when he was asked what remained to this day from his experience of the Rolling Thunder Review tour in 1975 and 1976. His answer was almost shocking—as provocative as it was evocative:

"Nothing . . . not a single thing. Ashes."

It was of course but one man's opinion, even if it was, to him, truth. One might similarly argue that almost everything from those great days of the Who is now gone. But is it really that simple?

Those days and the music that helped shape them became indelibly imprinted on the lives of the people who experienced them. And as philosopher Andrea Emo said, "Favored memories become meaning," which is why those featured in this book recall their treasured moments so emotionally. Remember the guy crying, "It was the most wonderful thing that ever happened to me!" as he ran out of a Who concert at the Fillmore West in 1968? That feeling stayed with him!

Our past doesn't just cease to be. It adds shadows and shape to the present.

Regardless, when the last chord is played and silence follows, that Note will continue to resonate. After all, wasn't that what Pete was trying to say through *Lifehouse*?

No matter what, the Note is eternal.

Berkeley Community Theater, California. Tuesday, June 16, 1970. *Photo by Dennis McCoy, copyright of Brad Rodgers, www.whocollection.com*

Endnotes

Chapter 1

1. *The Who Sings My Generation*'s liner notes (DL 74664).

2. Keith Moon would answer, "To stay young forever." Various authors, "The Who—Article Archive: 1964–1979," 27.

3. Jann Wenner, "The Rolling Stone Interview: Peter Townshend," *Rolling Stone* 17–18 (September 18 and 24, 1968).

4. Tom Wright and Susan VanHecke, *Roadwork: Rock & Roll Turned Inside Out* (New York: Hal Leonard Books, 2007), 40.

5. Jann Wenner, "Rock and Roll Music," *Rolling Stone* 4 (January 20, 1968).

6. Tony Palmer, *Born Under a Bad Sign* (London: HarperCollins, 1970), 131.

7. Ray Tolliday, "Well, What Would You Have Done after Tommy?," *Cream*, October 1971.

8. Mitch Howard, "The Working Class Heroes," *Cream* 19 (December 1972).

9. Various authors, "The Who—Article Archive: 1964–1979," 269.

10. Palmer, *Born under a Bad Sign*, 123.

11. Ibid., 122.

12. Ibid.

13. Valerie Mabbs, "College Cheques Don't Bounce!," *Record Mirror*, March 29 1969.

14. Ben Marshall, Pete Townshend, and Roger Daltrey, *The Who: The Official History* (London: Virgin Books, 2015), 60.

15. Various authors, "The Who, Article Archive: 1964–1979," 22.

16. Maureen O'Grady, "The Who Did You Say?," *Rave*, unknown date.

17. Pete Townshend and Jeff Young, *Lifehouse: Adapted for Radio by Jeff Young* (London: Pocket Books, 1999).

18. Stephen Rodrick, "The Who by Fire," *Rolling Stone*, November 25, 2019.

19. Wright and VanHecke, *Roadwork: Rock & Roll Turned Inside Out*, 44.

20. Pete Townshend, "The Pete Townshend Page," *Melody Maker*, December 12, 1970.

21. Dialogue taken from a bootleg recording. Author's archive.

22. Tolliday, "Well, What Would You Have Done after Tommy?"

Chapter 3

1. Mark Plummer, "Producing Records . . . by Do-It-Yourself Kit," *Melody Maker*, October 31, 1970.

2. "Really Smashing," *Guitar Player*, October 1967.

3. Andrew Neill and Matt Kent, *Anyway Anyhow Anywhere: The Complete Chronicle of the Who, 1958–1978* (London: Virgin Books, 2007), p. 65.

4. John Lawless, "Who's Still Who," *The Observer*, March 19, 1972.

5. Tony Palmer, *Born under A Bad Sign*, 123.

6. Neill and Kent, *Anyway Anyhow Anywhere*, 108.

7. Pete mixed up the identities of actress Lillie Langtry with the English theatrical producer Lilian Bayliss: "The idea was inspired by a picture my girlfriend had on her wall of an old Vaudeville star—Lily Bayliss" (Rikky Rooksby, *Lyrics: Writing Better Words for Your Songs* [Milwaukee, WI: Backbeat Books, 2006]).

8. Nick Logan, "We Talk All the Time about Politics, Religion, Spiritual Desperation, Abstract Concepts . . . ," *NME*, December 16, 1972. Townshend calls them "cameo."

9. Pete Townshend, *Who I Am* (London: HarperCollins, 2012), 111.

10. Alan Freeman, "The Truth about Our Generation," *Rave*, unknown issue.

11. Lawless, "Who's Still Who."

12. Ibid.

13. Howard, "The Working Class Heroes."

14. Neill and Kent, *Anyway Anyhow Anywhere*, 166.

15. Ngā Taonga Sound & Vision, *Peter Townshend*, RNZ collection, ID25183.

16. Wenner, "Rock and Roll Music."

17. Wright and VanHecke, *Roadwork: Rock & Roll Turned Inside Out*.

18. Derek Boltwood, "America: They Just Don't Know Who We Are, Says Who Keith Moon," *Record Mirror*, May 11, 1968.

19. Various authors, "The Who—Article Archive: 1964–1979," 150.

20. Howard, "The Working Class Heroes."

21. "Frustration of the Who," *NME*, April 8, 1972.

22. Lawless, "Who's Still Who."

23. Palmer, *Born under A Bad Sign*, 124.

24. Tolliday, "Well, What Would You Have Done after Tommy?"

25. Stage banter taken from a recording from the Fillmore Auditorium, San Francisco, California, on February 22, 1968. Author's archive.

26. Wenner, "Rock and Roll Music."

27. Neill and Kent, *Anyway Anyhow Anywhere*, 149.

28. Ibid.

29. Jann Wenner, "B.O., Baked Beans, Buns and the Who," *Rolling Stone* 3 (December 14, 1967).

30. Ibid.

31. Jann Wenner, "Who Album Banned in New York," *Rolling Stone* 5 (February 10, 1968).

32. Jann Wenner, "Who Take New Album on Faith," *Rolling Stone* 6 (February 24, 1968).

Chapter 5

1. Jean-Luc Godard initially involved independent filmmakers D. A. Pennebaker and Richard Leacock in the making of a film to be named *One A.M.: One American Movie*, but eventually regretted having done so. According to Godard, the footage they filmed was stylistically far from his conception of what he felt the film should have been. Godard finally got himself out of the project, and Pennebaker and Leacock later used the footage they had filmed for another project, *One P.M.: One Parallel Movie*, named sarcastically in opposition to the first *One A.M.*

2. Tolliday, "Well, What Would You Have Done after Tommy?"

3. Townshend, *Who I Am*, 137.

4. Pete Townshend, *Odds & Sods*' liner notes (Track Super 2406 116).

5. John Entwistle tells Derek Boltwood: "I wrote 'Silas Stingy' for that record, but we used it on our last album instead. 'Silas Stingy' is really the story of myself. It's about an old miser who's frightened of getting his money stolen, so he buys a safe to put it in, and then he buys a house to put the safe in, and then a dog to guard the house. And by the time he's done, all that he discovers he doesn't have any money left. Which is more or less exactly what's happening to me!" (Derek Boltwood, "Triumphant Return for the Who . . . Operatics in View," *Record Mirror*, October 12, 1968).

6. Neill and Kent, *Anyway Anyhow Anywhere*, 192, 204.

7. Various authors, "The Who—Article Archive: 1964–1979," 330.

8. Ian Middleton, "Keith Moon: Pop Has Now Turned a Full Circle," *Record Mirror*, November 16, 1968.

9. Wright and VanHecke, *Roadwork: Rock & Roll Turned Inside Out*, 93.

10. Thom Lukas's story in the "1968" chapter, in Neill and Kent, *Anyway Anyhow Anywhere*.

11. Michael Brooks, "Peter Townshend," *Guitar Player*, June 1972.

12. Walter Benjamin, *The Work of Art in the Age of Technological Reproducibility* (Cambridge, MA: Belknap Press of Harvard University Press, 2008).

13. Wenner, "The Rolling Stone Interview: Peter Townshend," 12.

14. Ibid. *Now I Am a Farmer* was recorded in 1968 but eventually put aside. It would appear for the first time in 1974 in *Odds & Sods*, along with other rarities.

15. Wenner, "The Rolling Stone Interview: Peter Townshend," 17. Pete Townshend considers rock and roll not simply as a genre, but rather as a "category of the spirit": Pete would say to *Eye Magazine* in September 1968 that he would like to "take things right back to the glamour, power, and insanity of the Elvis Presley age" (Various authors, "The Who—Article Archive: 1964–1979," 200).

16. Tolliday, "Well, What Would You Have Done after Tommy?"

Chapter 7

1. Stage banter from a bootleg recording. Author's archive.

2. "Frustration of the Who."

3. Tony Palmer, phone interview with the author, April 21, 2019.

4. Chet Flippo, "Entwistle: Not So Silent after All." *Rolling Stone*, December 5, 1974.

5. Radio interview with Pete Townshend and Roger Daltrey aired on May 16, 1969, to promote the two shows of the Who at the Fillmore East that night and the following night.

6. Tolliday, "Well, What Would You Have Done after Tommy?"

7. Pete refers to the Quads project, planned in 1966 but never realized (Jann Wenner, "Who Does Full-Length Rock Opera," *Rolling Stone* 15 [August 10, 1968]).

8. Various authors, "The Who—Article Archive: 1964–1979," 28.

9. "Glow Girl" would be released only in 1974, on *Odds & Sods* (Pete Townshend, *Odds & Sods* liner notes [Track Super 2406 116]).

10. Various authors, "The Who—Article Archive: 1964–1979," 218.

11. Radio interview with Pete Townshend and Roger Daltrey aired on May 16, 1969, to promote the two shows of the Who at the Fillmore East that night and the following night.

12. Kit Lambert interviewed by Tony Palmer in the film *All My Loving* (1968).

13. The Who, *The Who: Tommy*, Elite Standard Gift Books (Miami, FL: Charles Hansen, 1969).

14. Pete Townshend, "In Love with Meher Baba," *Rolling Stone* 71 (November 26, 1970).

15. Radio Bremen, *Beat Club*, recorded on August 26 and 28, 1969, broadcast on September 27, 1969.

16. Ibid.

17. Martin R. Smith, dir., *The Who Sensation: The Story of Tommy*, DVD (New York: Eagle Vision, 2013).

18. Townshend, "In Love with Meher Baba."

19. Radio Bremen, *Beat Club*.

20. Townshend, "In Love with Meher Baba."

21. Ibid.

22. Ibid.

23. Townshend, *Who I Am*, 144.

24. Wenner, "The Rolling Stone Interview: Peter Townshend," 13.

25. Wright and VanHecke, *Roadwork: Rock & Roll Turned Inside Out*, 129.

26. Boltwood, "Triumphant Return For the Who . . . Operatics in View."

27. Ibid.

28. Various authors, "The Who—Article Archive: 1964–1979," 218.

29. Ibid. "Auntie" was the nickname for BBC Radio 1.

30. Lon Goddard, "And They Preview LP at Ronnie's . . . ," *Record Mirror*, May 1969.

31. Various authors, "The Who—Article Archive: 1964–1979," 218.

32. Ibid.

33. Radio Bremen, *Beat Club*.

34. Pete Townshend, book essay inside the *Quadrophenia: Director's Cut* "super-deluxe" limited-edition box set (Santa Monica, CA: Universal Music, 2011), 20.

35. Jann Wenner interviewed in the film *Rolling Stone: Stories from the Edge*, directed by Blair Foster and Alex Gibney, 2017.

36. Nigel Cawthorne, *The Who and the Making of Tommy* (London: Unanimous, 2005), 106.

Chapter 8

1. Joe McMichael and Jack Lyons, *The Who: Concert File* (London: Omnibus, 2004), 121.

2. This Ferris wheel can be seen on the Super 8 film taken by Derek Redmond and Paul Campbell on the following website: http://cj3b.info/woodstock/who.html, at minute 1:00.

Chapter 9

1. Nik Cohn, "Finally, the Full Force of the Who," *New York Times*, March 8, 1970.

2. Roy Carr, "The Who," *Classic Rock*, January 2011, 75.

3. Chris Charlesworth, "Whole Lotta Who Gear," *Melody Maker*, November 7, 1970.

4. Excerpt taken from the video "Manager Bill Graham talks about the Fillmore and booking rock bands at the Metropolitan Opera House in NYC," courtesy of Historic Films Archive.

5. McMichael and Lyons, *The Who: Concert File*, 146–147.

6. Tolliday, "Well, What Would You Have Done after Tommy?"

Chapter 11

1. Bill Graham and Robert Greenfield, *Bill Graham Presents: My Life inside Rock and Out* (Boston: Da Capo, 2004), 200.

2. A Bill Graham interview by *Eyewitness News* for a special about Fillmore West in January 1969.

3. Graham and Greenfield, *Bill Graham Presents: My Life inside Rock and Out*, 119.

4. Elizabeth Pepin and Lewis Watts, *Harlem of the West: The San Francisco Fillmore Jazz Era* (San Francisco: Chronicle Books, 2005).

5. Graham and Greenfield, *Bill Graham Presents: My Life inside Rock and Out*, 142.

6. Ibid., 132.

7. Ibid.

8. Ibid., 221.

9. Ibid., 207.

10. "Fillmore Scene Moves to New Carousel Hall," *Rolling Stone*, 15 (August 10, 1968).

11. Jann Wenner interviewed for the film *Rolling Stone: Stories from the Edge*, directed by Blair Foster and Alex Gibney, 2017.

12. Graham and Greenfield, *Bill Graham Presents: My Life inside Rock and Out*, 202–203.

Chapter 12

1. "I blamed the frustration it caused me on its innate simplicity and my innate verbosity; one cancelled the other." (Townshend and Young, *Lifehouse: Adapted for Radio by Jeff Young*, 1).

2. "Pete Townshend: Rock Music in the Future," *Sounds*, July 24, 1971.

3. Ibid.

4. Ibid.

5. Max Horkheimer and Theodor W. Adorno, *Dialectic of Enlightenment* (New York: Herder and Herder, 1972).

6. "Pete Townshend: Rock Music in the Future."

7. Ibid.

8. When Pete started his "Pete Townshend Page" on *Melody Maker*, he was living in a cottage on the Osea Island with his wife, Karen, and his little child, Emma. It was after the third Isle of Wight Festival and after the minitour around England with the James Gang (Townshend, *Who I Am*, 201).

9. Townshend, *Who I Am*, 205.

10. "Who's Future in a World of Science Fantasy!," *Disc & Music Echo*, October 24 1970.

11. Townshend, *Who I Am*, 203.

12. "Pete Townshend: Rock Music in the Future."

13. "400 People In Who Rock Film," *Melody Maker*, January 23, 1971.

14. Bill McAllister, "Pete's Plan for the 'New' Who," *Record Mirror*, January 23, 1971.

15. Neill and Kent, *Anyway Anyhow Anywhere: The Complete Chronicle of the Who, 1958–1978*, 273.

16. Ibid., 277.

17. "Pete Townshend: Rock Music in the Future."

18. Townshend, *Who I Am*, 211.

19. Ibid.

20. Pete pointed out in his autobiography *Who I Am*: "The first workshop was held during the day, so attended only by truants. Also, frightened we would be overrun, we made no announcements at all. So in fact no one knew what we were doing" (Townshend, *Who I Am*, 212).

21. Townshend and Young, *Lifehouse: Adapted for Radio by Jeff Young*, 1.

22. "Pete Townshend: Rock Music in the Future."

23. Townshend and Young, *Lifehouse: Adapted for Radio by Jeff Young*, 1.

Chapter 14

1. Chris Charlesworth, private message to author, August 3, 2017.

2. Brooks, "Peter Townshend."

3. Neill and Kent, *Anyway Anyhow Anywhere: The Complete Chronicle of the Who, 1958–1978*, 286.

4. "Frustration of the Who."

5. Townshend, book essay inside the *Quadrophenia: Director's Cut* "super-deluxe" limited-edition box set, 19.

6. Roy Carr, "There's Nothing Worse, When You're Trying to Be Serious, Than to Have a Human Wasp Flying All over the Studio!," *NME*, July 8, 1972.

7. Townshend, *Who I Am*, 229.

8. Chris Welch, "Quadrophenia," *Melody Maker*, October 27, 1973.

9. Townshend, book essay inside the *Quadrophenia: Director's Cut* "super-deluxe" limited-edition box set, 10.

10. Tony Palmer, phone interview with the author, April 21, 2019.

Chapter 15

1. Brian Southall, "Pete Townshend Interview," *Disc & Music Echo*, October 21, 1972.

Chapter 16

1. Logan, "We Talk All The Time About Politics, Religion, Spiritual Desperation, Abstract Concepts...," *NME*, December 16, 1972.

2. Nick Logan, "We Talk All the Time about Politics, Religion, Spiritual Desperation, Abstract Concepts . . ."

3. Robin Denselow, "Townshend Prays, Writes New Opera," *Rolling Stone*, October 26, 1972.

4. Townshend, *Who I Am*, 238.

5. Jeremy Goodwin, from a conversation with the author.

6. Welch, "Quadrophenia."

7. Jeremy Goodwin, conversation with the author.

8. Denselow, "Townshend Prays, Writes New Opera." Pete called himself "unsettled, introspective, spiritual seeker."

9. Townshend, book essay inside the *Quadrophenia: Director's Cut* "super-deluxe" limited-edition box set, 20.

10. Ibid., 25.

11. Logan, "We Talk All the Time about Politics, Religion, Spiritual Desperation, Abstract Concepts . . ."

12. Welch, "Quadrophenia."

13. Charles Shaar Murray, "Quadrophenia," *NME*, October 27, 1973.

14. Tony Palmer, phone interview with the author, April 21, 2019. The band would finally side against their two historical managers, favoring the entrance of Bill Curbishley, who worked for Track Records, to the management and the foundation of Trinifold.

15. Tony Stewart, "Roger Daltrey," *NME*, October 6, 1973.

16. Welch, "Quadrophenia."

17. Ibid.

Chapter 18

1. McMichael and Lyons, *The Who: Concert File*, 220.

2. Ibid.

3. Freeman, "The Truth about Our Generation."

4. On November 27, 1969, during the Rolling Stones concert at Madison Square Garden, as shown in Albert and David Maysles's documentary *Gimme Shelter*, Sam Cutler introduces the band as "the greatest rock and roll band in the world."

5. Palmer, *Born under A Bad Sign*, 132.

Bibliography

"400 People in Who Rock Film." *Melody Maker*, January 23, 1971.

Benjamin, Walter. *The Work of Art in the Age of Technological Reproducibility*. Cambridge, MA: Belknap Press of Harvard University Press, 2008.

Boltwood, Derek. "America: They Just Don't Know Who We Are, Says Who Keith Moon." *Record Mirror*, May 11, 1968.

Boltwood, Derek. "Triumphant Return for the Who . . . Operatics in View." *Record Mirror*, October 12, 1968.

Brooks, Michael. "Peter Townshend." *Guitar Player*, June 1972.

Carr, Roy. "The Who." *Classic Rock*, January 2011.

Carr, Roy. "There's Nothing Worse, When You're Trying to Be Serious, Than to Have a Human Wasp Flying All over the Studio!" *NME*, July 8 1972.

Cawthorne, Nigel. *The Who and the Making of Tommy*. London: Unanimous, 2005.

Charlesworth, Chris. "Whole Lotta Who Gear." *Melody Maker*, November 7, 1970.

Cohn, Nik. "Finally, the Full Force of the Who." *New York Times*, March 8, 1970.

Denselow, Robin. "Townshend Prays, Writes New Opera." *Rolling Stone*, October 26, 1972.

Emo, Andrea. *Aforismi per vivere: Tutte le parole non dette si ricordano di noi*. Milan: Mimesis, 2007.

Fillmore East. *Fillmore East Program*. New York: Fillmore East, June 5, 1969.

"Fillmore Scene Moves to New Carousel Hall." *Rolling Stone* 15 (August 10, 1968).

Flippo, Chet. "Entwistle: Not So Silent after All." *Rolling Stone*, December 5, 1974.

Freeman, Alan. "The Truth about Our Generation." *Rave*, unknown issue.

"Frustration of the Who." *NME*, April 8, 1972.

Goddard, Lon. "And They Preview LP At Ronnie's . . ." *Record Mirror*, May 1 1969.

Graham, Bill, and Robert Greenfield. *Bill Graham Presents: My Life inside Rock and Out*. Boston: Da Capo, 2004.

Horkheimer, Max, and Theodor Adorno. *Dialectic of Enlightenment*. New York: Herder and Herder, 1972.

Howard, Mitch. "The Working Class Heroes." *Cream* 19 (December 1972).

Khan, Hazrat Inayat. *The Mysticism of Sound and Music*. Banff, AB: Ekstasis Editions, 2003.

Jahn, Mike. *Mike Jahn* (blog). https://mikejahn.moxietype.com/.

Lang, Michael. *Woodstock: 3 Days of Peace & Music*. London: Reel Art, 2019.

Lawless, John. "Who's Still Who." *The Observer*, March 19, 1972.

Logan, Nick. "We Talk All the Time about Politics, Religion, Spiritual Desperation, Abstract Concepts . . ." *NME*, December 16, 1972.

Lux, Brian. *One in the Crowd: My Life as a Music Fan*. Centralia, PA: Gorham, 2018.

Mabbs, Valerie. "College Cheques Don't Bounce!" *Record Mirror*, March 29, 1969.

Marshall, Ben, Pete Townshend, and Roger Daltrey. *The Who: The Official History*. London: Virgin Books, 2015.

McAllister, Bill. "Pete's Plan for the 'New' Who." *Record Mirror*, January 23, 1971.

McMichael, Joe, and Jack Lyons. *The Who: Concert File*. London: Omnibus, 2004.

Meher Baba: My Companion & True Friend. On the teachings of Meher Baba, 1894–1969, a Hindu spiritual leader; articles. Pune, India: Meher Era, 1974.

Middleton, Ian. "Keith Moon: 'Pop Has Now Turned a Full Circle.'" *Record Mirror*, November 16, 1968.

Neill, Andrew. *A Fortnight of Furore: The Who and the Small Faces Down Under*. London: Mutley, 1998.

Neill, Andrew, and Matt Kent. *Anyway Anyhow Anywhere: The Complete Chronicle of the Who, 1958–1978*. London: Virgin Books, 2007.

Ngā Taonga Sound & Vision. *Peter Townshend*. RNZ collection, ID25183.

O'Grady, Maureen. "The Who Did You Say?" *Rave*, unknown date.

Palmer, Tony. *Born under a Bad Sign*. London: HarperCollins, 1970.

Pepin, Elizabeth, and Lewis Watts. *Harlem of the West: The San Francisco Fillmore Jazz Era*. San Francisco: Chronicle Books, 2005.

"Pete Townshend: Rock Music in the Future." *Sounds*, July 24, 1971.

Plummer, Mark. "Producing Records . . . by Do-It-Yourself Kit." *Melody Maker*, October 31, 1970.

Radio Bremen. *Beat Club*. Recorded on August 26 and 28, 1969; broadcast on September 27, 1969.

Redmond, Derek, and Paul Campbell. "Woodstock 1969: How It Looked to Us." https://cj3b.info/woodstock/index.html.

Rodrick, Stephen. "The Who by Fire." *Rolling Stone*, November 25, 2019.

Rooksby, Rikky. *Lyrics: Writing Better Words for Your Songs*. Milwaukee, WI: Backbeat Books, 2006.

Selvin, Joel. *Altamont: The Rolling Stones, the Hells Angels, and the Inside Story of Rock's Darkest Day*. New York: Dey Street Books–HarperCollins, 2016.

Selvin, Joel. *The Haight: Love, Rock and Revolution; The Photography of Jim Marshall*. San Francisco: Insight Editions, 2014.

Selvin, Joel. *Summer of Love: The Inside Story of LSD, Rock & Roll, Free Love, and High Times in the Wild West*. New York: E. P. Dutton, 1994.

Shaar Murray, Charles. "Quadrophenia." *NME*, October 27, 1973.

Smith, Martin R., dir. *The Who Sensation: The Story of Tommy*. DVD. New York: Eagle Vision, 2013.

Southall, Brian. "Pete Townshend Interview." *Disc & Music Echo*, October 21, 1972.

Stewart, Tony. "Roger Daltrey." *NME*, October 6, 1973.

Tolliday, Ray. "Well, What Would You Have Done after Tommy?" *Cream*, October 1971.

Townshend, Pete. "In Love with Meher Baba." *Rolling Stone* 71 (November 26, 1970).

Townshend, Pete. "The Pete Townshend Page." *Melody Maker*, December 12, 1970.

Townshend, Pete. Book essay inside the *Quadrophenia: Director's Cut* "super-deluxe" limited-edition box set. Santa Monica, CA: Universal Music, 2011.

Townshend, Pete. *Who I Am*. London: HarperCollins, 2012.

Townshend, Pete, and Jeff Young. *Lifehouse: Adapted for Radio by Jeff Young*. London: Pocket Books, 1999.

Welch, Chris. "Quadrophenia." *Melody Maker*, October 27, 1973.

Wenner, Jann. "B.O., Baked Beans, Buns and the Who." *Rolling Stone* 3 (December 14, 1967).

Wenner, Jann. "Rock and Roll Music." *Rolling Stone* 4 (January 20, 1968).

Wenner, Jann. "The Rolling Stone Interview: Peter Townshend." *Rolling Stone*, 17–18 (September 18 and 24, 1968).

Wenner, Jann. "Who Album Banned in New York." *Rolling Stone* 5 (February 10, 1968).

Wenner, Jann. "Who Does Full-Length Rock Opera." *Rolling Stone* 15 (August 10, 1968).

Wenner, Jann. "Who Take New Album on Faith." *Rolling Stone* 6 (February 24, 1968).

The Who. *The Who: Tommy*. Elite Standard Gift Books. Miami, FL: Charles Hansen, 1969.

"Who's Future in a World of Science Fantasy!" *Disc & Music Echo*, October 24, 1970.

Wright, Tom, and Susan VanHecke. *Roadwork: Rock & Roll Turned Inside Out*. New York: Hal Leonard Books, 2007.

Index